THE MODERN MAKER VOL. 1
MEN'S DOUBLETS

MATHEW GNAGY

by Mathew Gnagy

The Modern Maker Vol. 1: Men's Doublets

Edited by Drea Leed

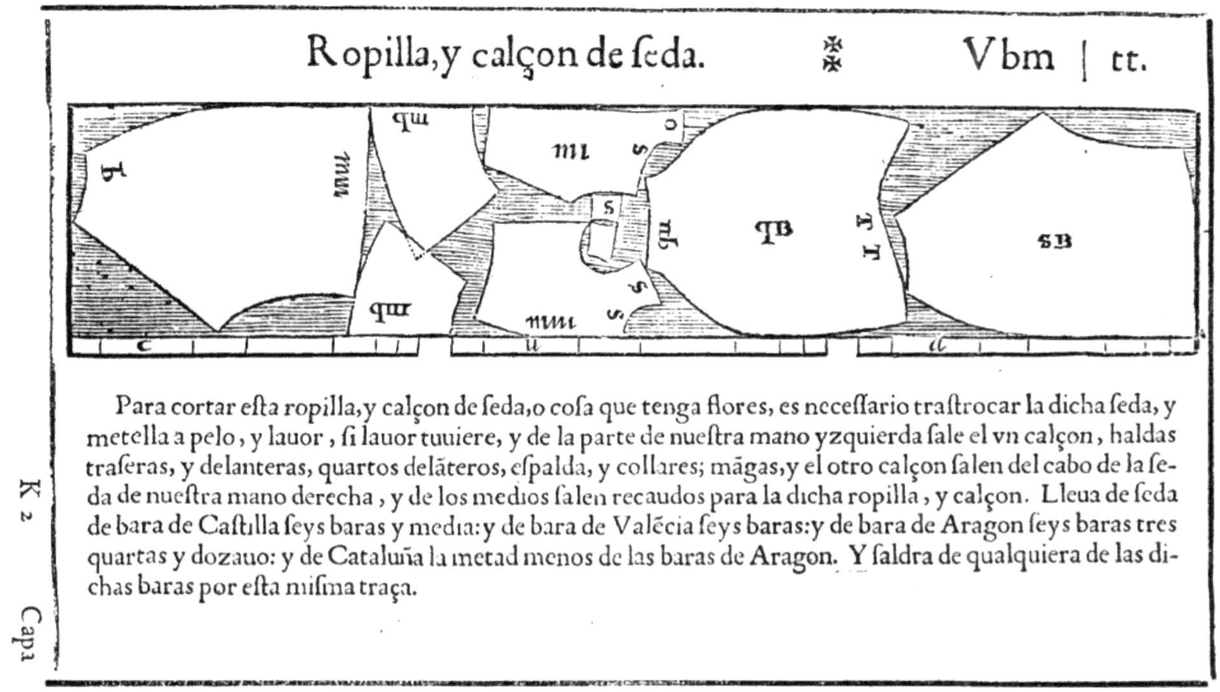
Ropilla,y calçon de ſeda. ⁂ Vbm | tt.

Para cortar eſta ropilla,y calçon de ſeda,o coſa que tenga flores, es neceſſario traſtrocar la dicha ſeda, y metella a pelo, y lauor, ſi lauor tuuiere, y de la parte de nueſtra mano yzquierda ſale el vn calçon, haldas traſeras, y delanteras, quartos delãteros, eſpalda, y collares; mãgas,y el otro calçon ſalen del cabo de la ſeda de nueſtra mano derecha, y de los medios ſalen recaudos para la dicha ropilla, y calçon. Lleua de ſeda de bara de Caſtilla ſeys baras y media:y de bara de Valẽcia ſeys baras:y de bara de Aragon ſeys baras tres quartas y dozauo: y de Cataluña la metad menos de las baras de Aragon. Y ſaldra de qualquiera de las dichas baras por eſta miſma traça.

K 2 Capa

From Geometria y Traça, 1618, Burguen. Photograph courtesy of the Victoria and Albert Museum, London

First published 2014

ISBN-13: 9780692264843

Printed in the USA by createspace.com Charleston SC

Design by Mathew Gnagy
Edited by Drea Leed
Photography by Mathew Gnagy; Drea Leed; Mark Goodman

Contents

Foreword   1

Introduction   2

1. The Principles of Tailoring   5
2. Fabrics   11
3. Making the Pattern   15
4. Cutting the Pieces   37
5. Hand Sewing Techniques   45

      Basting stitch   48
      Running stitch   49
      Whip stitch/Diagonal baste/Pad stitch   50
      Back stitch   54
      Pick stitch   55
      Felling stitch   56
      Cross stitch   57
      Catch stitch   58
      Buttonholes   59
      Eyelets   72
      Buttons   74

6. Making Up   83
7. Surviving Garments   123
8. Construction Details   128

Acknowledgments   138

Suggested Reading   139

Suppliers   140

About the Author   141

Foreword

When I first began studying historic dress, more than 22 years ago now, the number of reliable, high-quality publications on 16th and 17th-century costume construction could be counted on the fingers. Luckily for all of us, this number has increased over the years. All of these new works have approached the topic from familiar and well-recognized perspectives: we have practical how-to manuals on 16th century costume construction, examinations of the patterns and construction of extant garments, books that tease tidbits of costume knowledge from various types of documentary evidence, and works focusing on more abstract aspects of historic dress: the social meaning of clothing, the economics of its creation, and the material culture that underlay it.

At first glance, *The Modern Maker Vol. 1: Men's Doublets* may seem to fall squarely into the first category: a how-to manual on making an authentically cut and constructed doublet. It is, however, much more than that.

Unlike most costume historians, who either entered the field through the avenue of theatrical costume design, museum conservation, or the academic realm, Gnagy's introduction to costume was via the venerable art of the bespoke men's suit tailoring industry. He is a professional tailor in every sense of the word.

Therefore, when he first began to look at historic dress and patterns, he did so with a tailor's eye. In his examination of extant garments and the patterns used to construct them, he discovered heretofore-unnoticed echoes of techniques and traditions still found in today's world of high-end tailoring.

And when he began making reproductions of doublets, kirtles and gowns, he approached the cutting and construction of a historical garment from the perspective of a traditional tailor, using the skills and techniques gained through his experience in that industry.

This book is not merely a how-to manual for those interested in simply making an authentically-cut and constructed 17th century doublet. It is also an informative, hands-on guide for those interested in recreating not only the garments of the time, but also the techniques used to produce those garments. Gnagy's tailoring knowledge, combined with his deep understanding of historic dress from both a theoretical and practical point of view, allow him to illuminate details of historic pattern development and clothing construction that have been previously overlooked.

This book, and its revelations about doublet patterning and construction, will raise the bar for historic doublet reconstruction. I look forward to seeing its effect upon historic costumers, and look forward to adding it to my shelf of well-thumbed "go-to" books on 16th and 17th century dress.

—Drea Leed

1

Introduction

Recreating a garment of the past is, at best, an educated guessing game. Something frequently overlooked when recreating such a garment is that, in order to recreate it accurately, one also needs to recreate the process of making the garment. You can make a doublet using the same materials and pattern as the original, but it is only by applying the same techniques used by the actual tailor—or as close an approximation to them as you can—that you can come close to reaching true authenticity.

Making a doublet with the methods we learn as costumers is a relatively simple affair. We cut out the different layers of fabric, stack them up, and sew them together. Often we apply some surface decoration as well. The lining is then cut and installed. All the layers are generally cut to the same shape. The interlining and the shell of the garment are "flat-lined" (the two layers are stitched together and treated as a one) and then sewn. The lining is made up separately and then generally "bagged." This means putting the right sides of outer fabric and lining together and sewing them together around the outside edge, then turning it right side out and giving it a good press.

While many surviving garments appear to be made in this manner when examined in a photograph or on display, this is usually an illusion based on our modern understanding of clothing construction. The process of "bagging" became commonplace only with the advent of the sewing machine, as a quick way of putting in a lining.

In reality, however, linings in many extant garments were sewn to the outer layer at the seams. Incorporating this seemingly small change, and many other lesser-known historic tailoring techniques, can raise the level of accuracy and wearability when producing historic clothing. When creating a garment by hand, you will see that the order of operations is not the same as when machine-sewing one, nor quite so simple.

In contrast to modern costuming methods, where all the layers are cut to the same shape, the layers of a tailored garment are rarely cut identically. In the case of garments that are slashed, the underlining and the shell are often cut to the same shape. The canvas, however, is not cut exactly the same size or shape. It is cut slightly larger than the shell of the garment, and then small cuts are made in the canvas pieces in strategic areas and small gussets are inserted to spread these cuts open. In other locations, the edges are drawn in slightly and shrunk by using stay tapes and careful stitching, though these areas of shrinking are more common in women's clothing than the man's doublet we will make in this book.

All of these seemingly minor changes cause the flat plane of the fabric to become "warped," more sculpted and three dimensional. The human body has neither flat planes nor straight edges, and the practice of tailoring recognizes this fact in all stages of the construction process. The manipulation of the surface greatly affects the fit of the garment and its overall beauty and wearability. What makes these techniques hard to understand for the novice costumer or tailor is that they are nearly invisible in the finished garment and to the untrained eye. When all we see are the main construction seams, we lose sight of the crucial steps that make a flat piece of fabric conform to our lumpy, curvy, organic bodies.

When I first began studying historic dress and examining extant items—men's doublets in particular—I discovered that my training as a professional tailor of modern men's suits let me see and understand the subtleties of the tailoring techniques used in creating these older garments. Some of these techniques are still in use today by the modern bespoke tailor.

As a tailor and researcher, I have studied jackets and waistcoats back through time, century by century, and have observed how these techniques have evolved. From this I have extrapolated a logical and plausible set of classic tailoring manipulations that regularly appear in doublets of the late 16th and early 17th centuries. Although the shaping techniques used in the creation of the lapels of modern coats are irrelevant to garments of the era we are studying in this book (as the main body garments rarely have what we know as lapels, or revers), modern manipulations used for shaping the armhole, the shoulder, and the neckline appear time and again in extant garments housed in museums around the world.

In the early 17th century padded garments began to fall out of favor and were replaced by garments with less padding and fewer, stiffer layers.

Introduction

It is interesting to note that different tailors created different solutions to problems surrounding fit and manipulation of the fabric. The doublet that we will create with this book is neither stiffened nor padded, but is tailored with a softer line. Remember though, just as today, some tailors chose not to use the stretching or shrinking techniques we will use. The tailoring trade wasn't like today's mass-produced, ready-to-wear clothing industry. Each tailor was known for his or her unique approach. Clients would select a tailor whose work met their budgetary and aesthetic preferences. Additionally, as fashion changed, the requirements of tailoring shifted according to the needs of newer styles. The nature of certain fabrics may have also led a tailor to adjust his approach to tailoring a garment. It is important to always remember that no single method was used across all styles and all centuries.

As I mentioned before, it takes a trained eye to recognize a tailor's manipulations in extant garments. As you work through the process laid out in this book, however, you will begin to see the subtle changes in fit caused by these shaping techniques and gain a new appreciation of the level of skill attained by tailors of the past.

—Mathew Gnagy

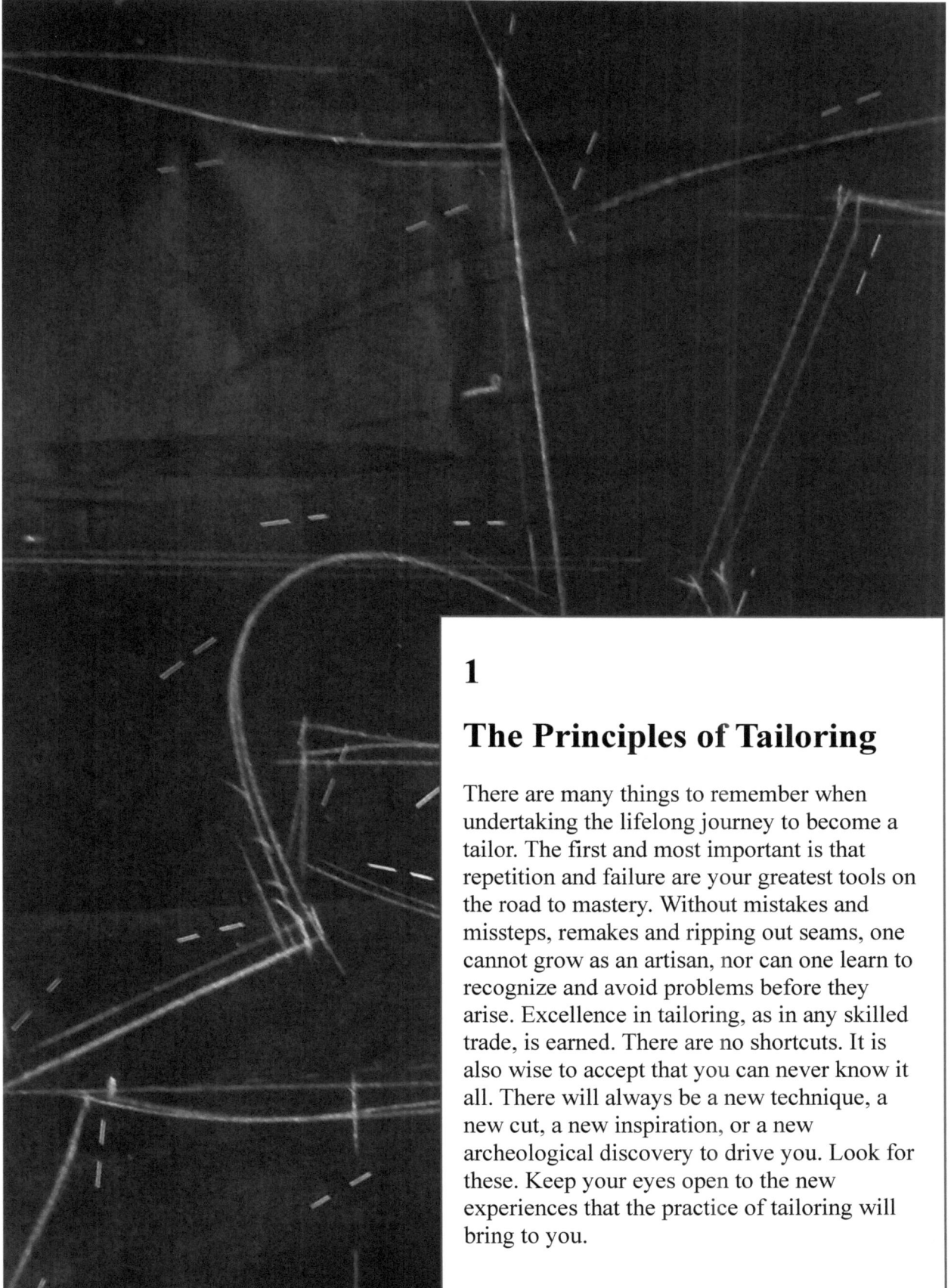

1

The Principles of Tailoring

There are many things to remember when undertaking the lifelong journey to become a tailor. The first and most important is that repetition and failure are your greatest tools on the road to mastery. Without mistakes and missteps, remakes and ripping out seams, one cannot grow as an artisan, nor can one learn to recognize and avoid problems before they arise. Excellence in tailoring, as in any skilled trade, is earned. There are no shortcuts. It is also wise to accept that you can never know it all. There will always be a new technique, a new cut, a new inspiration, or a new archeological discovery to drive you. Look for these. Keep your eyes open to the new experiences that the practice of tailoring will bring to you.

THE GARMENT

There are some basic principles that govern the choices a tailor makes when creating a new piece of clothing.

1. Cut and fit are exceptionally important. The right cut for the particular body and a flawless fit are essential.

2. Minimal decoration reveals the art and mastery of the tailor; endless layers of trim are a distraction.

3. Linings should be smooth and comfortable.

4. A well-made garment will move easily with the wearer and return to its resting position without effort or adjustment.

5. Exterior edges should incline gracefully toward the body, except where the cut or style demands otherwise.

6. A well-set sleeve is a mark of excellence in craftsmanship.

7. Each layer of clothing should be cut and constructed to rest comfortably on top of the layer over which it is intended to be worn.

8. If possible, it is the tailor's mission to create a garment that can visually "correct" any physical flaws of the wearer, such as balance, symmetry, or proportion. This could mean adding a layer of padding to one side of the garment to balance a low shoulder, or carefully shortening a sleeve to accommodate a discrepancy in arm length.

9. Better that the lining be too big rather than the slightest bit too small.

10. The garment should be fitted to skim the figure and hold its shape. It should not be pulled tight to the body.

11. The canvas should "lead" the shape of the garment.

Understanding these basic principles can aid in decisions of fit and choice of cut. These principles underlie the ideals of quality construction.

In the course of this book, we will explore these principles as they pertain to a doublet in the style of 1618. The pattern for this doublet comes from a book entitled *Geometria y traça pertenecientes al oficio de los sastres,* by Francisco de la Rocha Burguen.

Here are front and back photos of the doublet that we will be making with this book. It is a close fit, but easy through the armscye and just slightly long through the back to allow for vertical ease when bending or working. The sleeves are ample in width and longer than our modern styles. The fullness in the fabric at the underarm is a result of the shallow sleeve cap height of the period. This type of sleeve cap allows for great ease of movement. There are other styles in this era which have no sleeve cap curvature at all and are simply straight across. While a sleeve of this type may bunch under the arm when the wearer is at rest, it allows tremendous freedom of movement when it is in action. The collar shown here is of a medium height, and the skirts are left rather small so that other garments may be layered over it. The shoulder wings are narrow and small. Again, this allows for another garment to be easily worn over it.

THE TAILOR'S TRADE

The word "tailoring", when used in a modern context, often describes the work of one who *alters* clothing so that it fits better. Actually, a tailor is one who makes suits from scratch rather than one who merely performs alterations, in the same way that a shoemaker makes shoes while a cobbler only repairs them. Although the method presented in this book uses paper patterns for the ease of the novice drafter, in an era when paper patterns were rare and expensive, a 17th century tailor had to learn the draft of the garment so well that he could use a piece of chalk and a ruler to lay the garment out directly on the cloth, leaving strategically placed margins in certain areas to allow for fitting. The skill of these traditional tailors cannot be overstated. Each tailor had to spend years, first as an apprentice and then as a journeyman, learning about all the relevant garments, proportions, and construction techniques. The doublet we are creating will be sewn entirely by hand, without the use of a sewing machine, as tailors of the time would have sewn it.

BODY POSITION

If you look at images of tailors through the centuries, you will find that they are shown sitting in a specific way: cross-legged, sometimes on the floor or on top of a table, but usually on a chair or bench. The reason this posture is so efficient is that it is generally comfortable. In a chair, it keeps the spine straighter, thus reducing body stress and tension over time. When the legs are crossed one knee is raised up closer to the eyes, putting it at an ideal and comfortable distance for detail work. Crossed legs also provide the tailor with a ready surface upon which to place the work. It is important to analyze and understand your posture to make certain that you are comfortable and can maintain a working position for hours at a time. It is also important to take regular breaks as you work, to prevent stiffness and pain; creating a comfortable working posture can speed up your execution of a garment and make long hours of handwork more enjoyable.

PRINCIPLES OF MOVEMENT

In today's busy world, many people hand sew for fun and leisure. When chosen for relaxation, the movements of hand sewing are often performed slowly and are in many cases unnecessarily precise. While there is nothing wrong with this approach, a professional tailor must work quickly. As we work, we expend energy. By reducing expended energy, we can speed up our movements and reduce the amount of time it takes to create a garment. Here are some simple time and energy saving concepts:

Rhythm

Find the rhythm. The human body is made for repeated motions. As you begin a line of stitches, concentrate on the quiet rhythm of your motions as the needle is inserted, pushed, exits, and is gripped and drawn. Once your body has established the rhythm, you can speed it up or slow it down as you choose by simply changing the tempo.

A Larger Needle

Use a larger gauge needle. A larger needle temporarily stretches a slightly bigger hole than the average, finer gauge needle. This larger hole allows the thread to pass through it with less pressure, thus reducing the amount of twist that gets pushed down the thread. As a result, the tendency for the thread to snarl and kink is also reduced. Match the size of the needle to your fabric. Finely-woven silks, for instance, require a finer gauge needle, reducing the amount of energy spent pushing it through the fabric. I choose the shortest, fattest needle that I can push comfortably through the fabrics of the area that I'm working. Different sizes can be used for different construction steps. Attention to the proper choice of needle greatly reduces many potential problems and can save you the time and aggravation of untangling thread over the course of making the garment.

Shorter Thread

Use shorter lengths of thread. The best thread length for most people is about 20-30" (50-75 cm). In most instances, thread should be a single strand, not doubled. Keeping the thread short reduces your draw length and saves time and energy by reducing the distance the arm must travel to complete a stitch. Stitches can be worked surprisingly quickly with a shorter thread. Additionally, it preserves the life of the thread that holds your garment together. As each draw pulls the thread through the fabric, it is abraded. This slowly weakens the working thread, thus weakening the seam you are creating. Keep your thread short to work quickly and give the seams, and the garment, a long life.

Batching Your Tasks

Always batch your tasks. This simple concept yields big results. Group like tasks together. For example, when chalking your lines, chalk out everything on the fabric at one time. When you lay out and cut, do all of the cutting in one session. Baste all pieces at the same time. Stitch as many seams as possible before stopping to press them or moving on to the next step. Prepare and press multiple pieces of sewing thread at the same time so that you spend less time moving between your workstation and the iron. Seconds captured here and there add up to minutes, which add up to hours of time and labor saved.

Prepare Your Environment

Proper preparation of your working environment is essential for working efficiently. Spend a little time analyzing and understanding your natural tendencies in a work environment, and set up your workspace and tools accordingly. Taking just a moment to assess the surroundings in which you work will save you a lot of time in the long run.

Use a small table, a stool, or even a spare chair as a place to lay the pieces with which you are working, keeping the area where you place tools free from clutter.

Everything In Its Proper Place

Place the tools you need where you can reach them and work with them efficiently. Place all the things you don't need or are not using at the moment to one side. Remove the scissors used for cutting when you are done with that step. Clean as you go. When you've finished drafting, put away the rulers. Put aside all but the few pins and needles you'll need to hold your work together and make your stitches. Putting away the things you don't need and setting up the things you do need with thoughtfulness and intention will serve you very well in this and many other crafts.

2
Fabrics

The selection of fabrics is an important step in the process. Our modern-day fabric stores are full of astounding possibilities, but only a few of the available textiles are appropriate for a project such as this doublet. In the next few pages, we will explore the textiles that I have chosen for this garment and how they relate to actual materials that were used in the 17th century. For information on ordering fabrics, please see the list of suppliers at the back of the book.

HANDKERCHIEF LINEN (far left)

This is a lightweight, 3-4 oz./yard linen used to line the doublet. It is an even weave fabric, meaning that it has the same number of vertical and horizontal threads per inch. Linen linings in surviving 16th and 17th-century garments were usually white and undyed; white is also frequently the only color of handkerchief linen available in many fabric stores. The linen in the photo is approximately 3.7 oz./yard.

LINEN CANVAS (lower center)

This product is a heavy woven linen in a canvas weave, lighter in weight than upholstery-weight linen but heavier than the garment-weight linen used for men's summer sport coats. Linen canvas is sometimes used for trousers. This product is not always available in fabric stores. If you cannot find canvas-weight linen, you may substitute one layer of washed and pressed cotton duck cloth, which is available at almost any local fabric store. The linen canvas shown is 11 oz./yard.

WOOL FLANNEL (lower right)

Men's fall sport coats and trousers are often made of this weight of wool, which is commonly found in fabric stores during the fall and winter months. Wool is an ideal fabric for tailoring; it steams well, molds beautifully to any shape, and is durable and warm for fall and winter whilst also offering superior breathability and coolness for the warmer months. Wool fibers, being porous and protein-based, do not retain moisture well. When combined with a linen lining, the resulting attire's wicking and evaporation effect can make even a hot summer's day quite comfortable. As long as you keep to wool and linen for your main body textiles, you should be comfortable in most temperatures.

SILK (top)

Silk is a remarkable material: it is quite strong, yet scissors cut it with merely a whisper of the blades. As it is not very breathable, it is useful as interior insulating layer of a garment or as a lining for garments meant to be worn during the cold months. Silk can also be used for a garment's exterior. It handles stretching and manipulation well, though not as well as wool. The vast majority of surviving doublets with cuts and slashes in the surface are made of silk, combined with heavily padded linings to achieve the proper look.

For this doublet, we will be using the silk for facings and edgings rather than as a full lining. If you live in a colder climate, I do recommend using silk for the entire lining. Drapery weight silk taffeta and drapery weight low-slub shantung are the best modern silks for approximating the average period textile. For satins, bridal satin is best, though you may want to double check that it is 100% silk. Most versions of bridal satin are partially or completely synthetic.

Silk dupioni can be used as a last resort, although the quality of this textile is well below even the cheapest silks of the early 17th century. If you use dupioni for the exterior fabric, I recommend that you use a second layer of handkerchief linen together with the silk, treating them as though they are one layer. This will approximate the correct body and movement of an early 17th century silk more accurately than using dupioni alone.

MELTON

Melton (shown on the following page) is a heavily fulled wool, 20-30 oz./yard, most commonly used in modern winter coats. In this doublet, it is carefully stitched into position as padding over the shoulder and upper chest area, to add structure and support to the garment.

The best varieties of this fabric are, of course, 100% wool. Melton also comes in a variety of blends depending on the price. As you buy fabrics for your doublet, look for the highest percentage of wool possible. Too much synthetic fiber can lead to a garment that doesn't move well, as well as one that is inconsistent in its insulating capabilities and durability.

The doublet presented here is made with three main layers.

1. The canvas: The canvas is the layer which receives all the major manipulation and modification with gussets and shaping. This is the heavier of the two linens. The term "canvas" refers to the weave structure rather than the fiber content, and in this case is the linen canvas described above. The wool melton is applied to it with sculpting and pad stitching to shape the doublet.
2. The exterior, or shell: This is the wool flannel. It can also be referred to as the "fashion fabric" or "self fabric". Once the canvas is assembled, the flannel is basted to the canvas in a specific way that gently stretches the flannel as it is attached. These basting stitches are removed when the garment is complete.
3. The lining: This is the handkerchief linen. As the garment is assembled, the lining is laid into place one panel at a time.

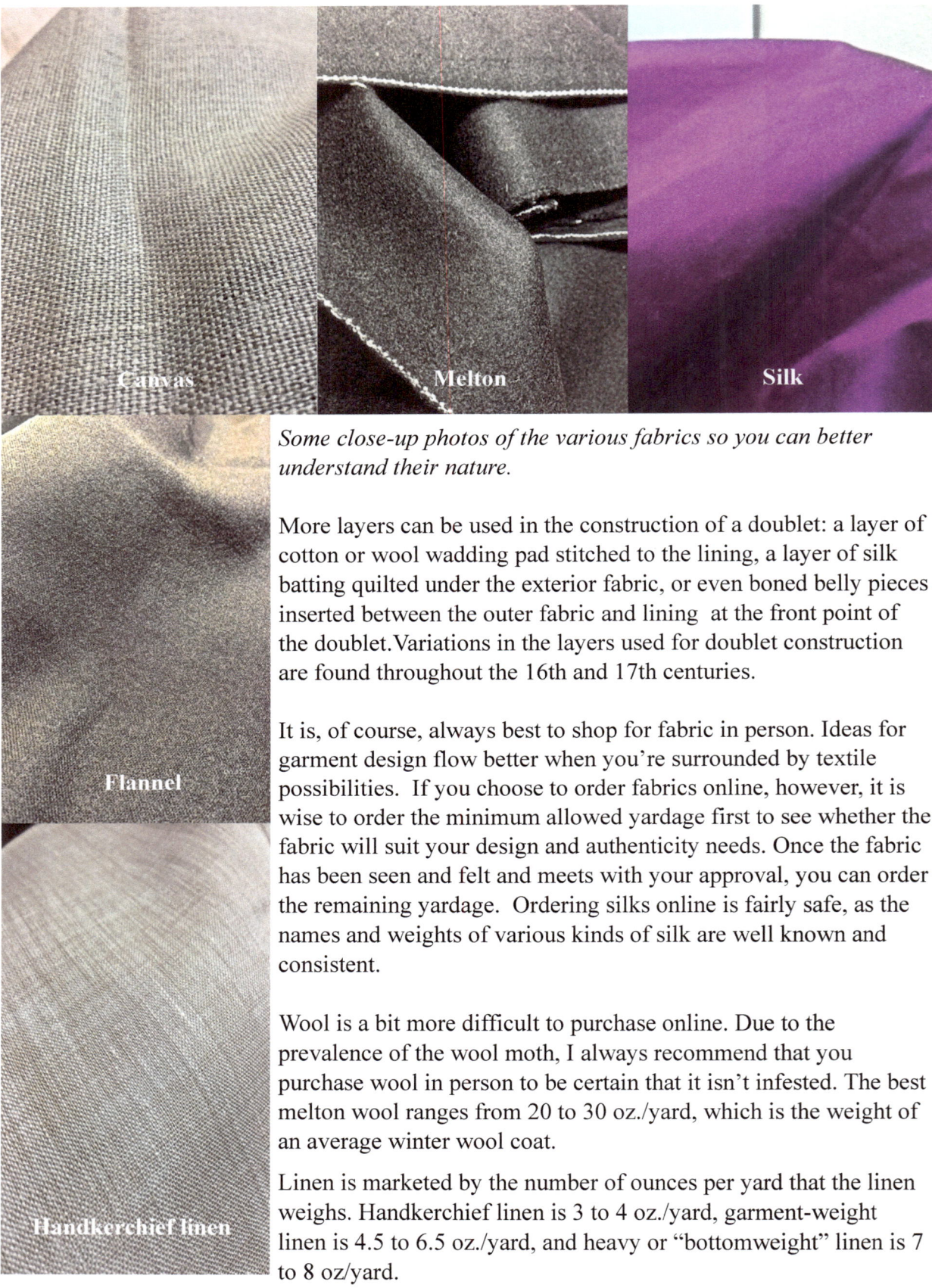

Canvas

Melton

Silk

Flannel

Handkerchief linen

Some close-up photos of the various fabrics so you can better understand their nature.

More layers can be used in the construction of a doublet: a layer of cotton or wool wadding pad stitched to the lining, a layer of silk batting quilted under the exterior fabric, or even boned belly pieces inserted between the outer fabric and lining at the front point of the doublet. Variations in the layers used for doublet construction are found throughout the 16th and 17th centuries.

It is, of course, always best to shop for fabric in person. Ideas for garment design flow better when you're surrounded by textile possibilities. If you choose to order fabrics online, however, it is wise to order the minimum allowed yardage first to see whether the fabric will suit your design and authenticity needs. Once the fabric has been seen and felt and meets with your approval, you can order the remaining yardage. Ordering silks online is fairly safe, as the names and weights of various kinds of silk are well known and consistent.

Wool is a bit more difficult to purchase online. Due to the prevalence of the wool moth, I always recommend that you purchase wool in person to be certain that it isn't infested. The best melton wool ranges from 20 to 30 oz./yard, which is the weight of an average winter wool coat.

Linen is marketed by the number of ounces per yard that the linen weighs. Handkerchief linen is 3 to 4 oz./yard, garment-weight linen is 4.5 to 6.5 oz./yard, and heavy or "bottomweight" linen is 7 to 8 oz/yard.

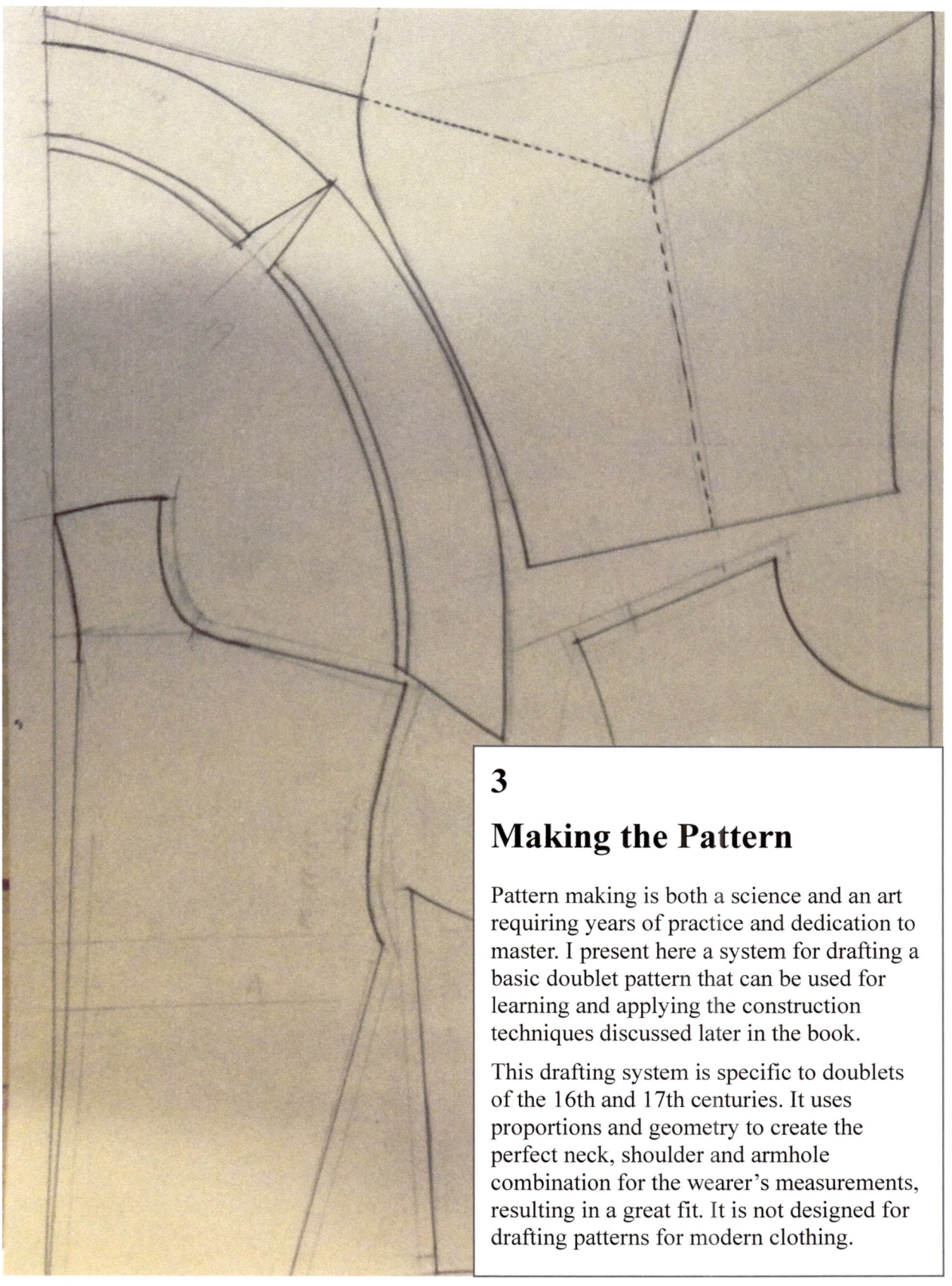

3

Making the Pattern

Pattern making is both a science and an art requiring years of practice and dedication to master. I present here a system for drafting a basic doublet pattern that can be used for learning and applying the construction techniques discussed later in the book.

This drafting system is specific to doublets of the 16th and 17th centuries. It uses proportions and geometry to create the perfect neck, shoulder and armhole combination for the wearer's measurements, resulting in a great fit. It is not designed for drafting patterns for modern clothing.

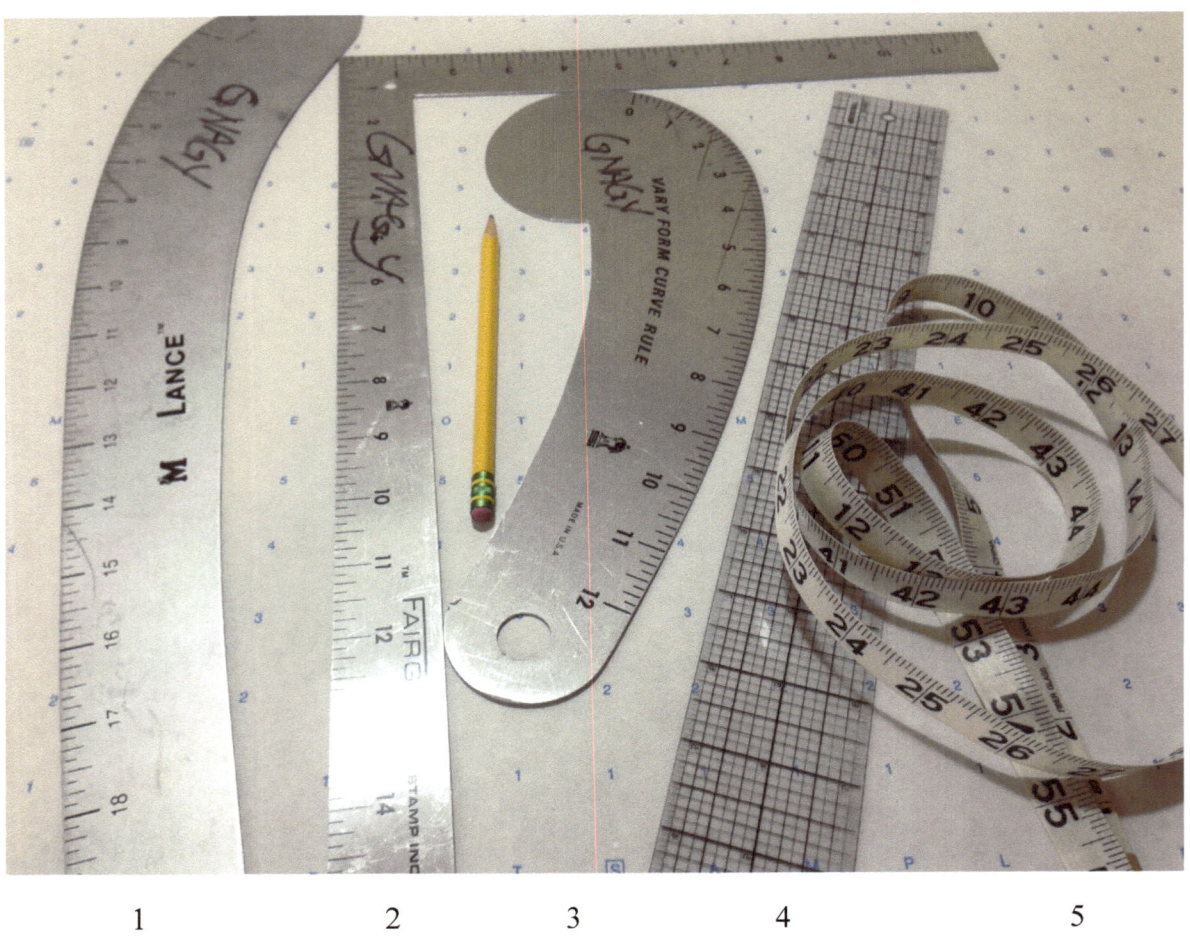

| 1 | 2 | 3 | 4 | 5 |

DRAFTING

The supplies needed for drafting are few. Curved rulers are available at any craft, hardware, or art supply store. You will need:

1. A long French Curve, also known as a hip curve.
2. A right angle square. It should ideally be thin and lightweight.
3. An armhole curve, available in most fabric stores.
4. A see-through plastic ruler, available at any craft store. These rulers are clear, flexible and incredibly useful for drafting.
5. A tape measure is available at any craft store.

You will need a good pencil and large sheets of paper. Any paper will do, as long as it's relatively strong: brown paper bags, heavy wrapping paper, butcher paper, and large format printer paper are but a few of the possibilities. The type of paper shown in the photograph above is called sample dot paper.

Most of these items are sold by general fabric stores. If you want the exact items in the photograph, however, you will need visit an online notions supply company like Atlanta Thread Supply. Please see the supplier list at the back of this book for details.

Making the Pattern

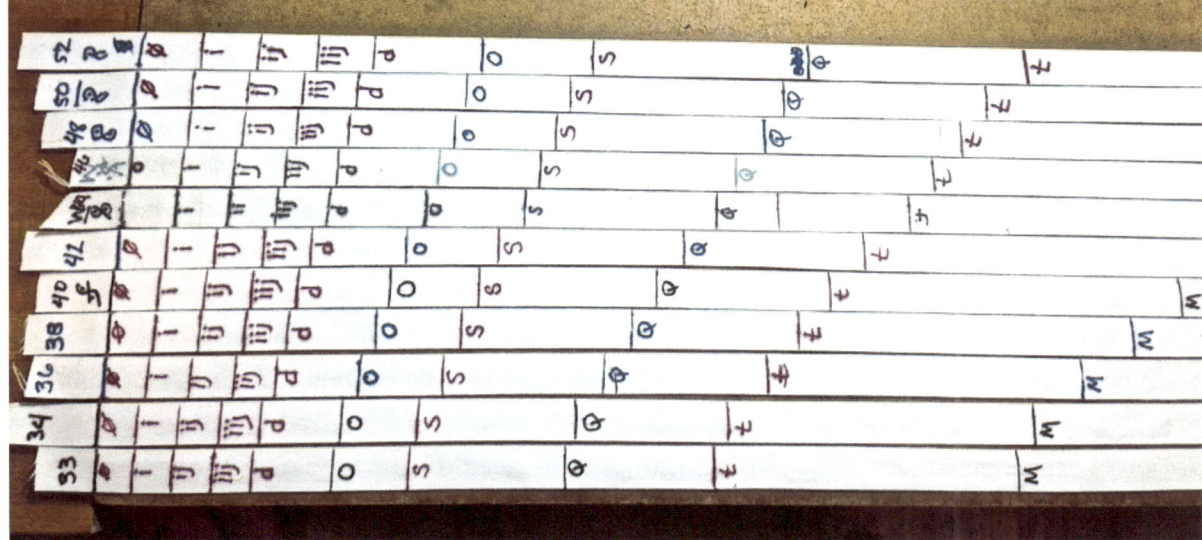

In surviving Spanish tailor's manuals, several pages are always devoted to the description of the measuring system used in the manual. This measurement system was based on the *bara,* an Old Spanish word analogous to "yard". It is not, however, one yard long. In fact, the Spanish *bara* was not even consistent between the various regions of Spain.

The Castilian bara used by Juan de Alçega in his tailor's manual *Libro de Geometria y Traça* was 84 cm or just over 33 inches in length. In the book there is a small line given that describes the *dedo,* the smallest increment of measure in the *bara* and the historical equivalent to an inch. It is 11/16 of an inch in length, or approximately 1.75 cm.

What follows is a modern translation of Alcega's description of the bara. The full text is quite lengthy, and much of it is in prose form rather than concise bullet points. Here I will simply describe each division of the *bara* with its accompanying symbols.

i	one *dedo,* the smallest increment of measure in the *bara.* There are 48 *dedos* per *bara.*
ii	two *dedos.*
iii	three *dedos.*
d	one twelfth of a *bara,* or four *dedos.* An abbreviation of the Old Spanish word *dozavo.*
o	one eighth of a *bara,* an abbreviation of the Old Spanish word *ochavo.*
s	one sixth of a *bara,* an abbreviation of the Old Spanish word *sesma.*
Q	one quarter of a *bara,* an abbreviation of the Old Spanish word *quarto.*
t	one third of a *bara,* an abbreviation of the Old Spanish word *tercia.*
M	one half of a *bara,* an abbreviation of the Old Spanish word *media.*
tt	two thirds of a *bara.*
QQQ	three quarters of a *bara.*
B	one *bara.*

It is very important to note that when using this method, combinations of the numbers follow the same rules as those in Roman numerals: When a smaller number precedes a larger number, the smaller is subtracted from the larger. When a smaller number follows a larger number, the smaller number is added to the larger. For example, BB stands for two *baras*, while qBB stands for 1 and 3/4 *baras* and BBq represents 2 and 1/4 *baras*.

After many years of research and experimentation, I've concluded that 17th century tailors used a drafting system that incorporated scaled measuring tapes. In a 1618 Spanish tailor's manual, *Geometria y traça perteneciente al oficio de sastres,* the author Francisco de la Rocha Burguen describes in some detail the process of making and using tapes that are scaled to the client's height and chest in the pattern drafting process.

Using this method, a client was brought to the tailor and a tape wrapped around his or her chest. This tape was then divided into quarters, eighths, thirds, twelfths, etc.—the same divisions used for the standard *bara*. With this custom tape measure, and another tape scaled for the height of the individual that was marked and divided in exactly the same way, the tailor could lay out the pattern directly onto the cloth, trusting that the fit would be quite close to correct for the client.

Use of such a proportion-based system eliminates the need for the time-consuming mathematics and calculation involved in modern pattern drafting. A tailor needed to learn only one set of proportions for drafting each garment style and apply them using the custom scaled tape measures of the client, automatically creating a garment of the correct size. The seam allowances are included in these proportionate drafts, thus eliminating the time required for the additional step of drawing them in.

Of course, the process of fitting and perfecting the initial garment draft is essential to a properly finished piece. Even today, it is customary that a client receive a minimum of two fittings. Fitting and perfecting a pattern is essential to the process. Always make an inexpensive sample before using high quality fabrics. My suggestion is to make a complete garment by machine to test the pattern. It will familiarize you with the techniques and fitting needs of the garment and the client.

In the following pages, you will be shown the method of folding and marking the measuring tape that will be used to draft your doublet. The step-by-step process of making the tape measure is shown for a 33" (82.5 cm) tape. The same folding, divisions and markings are used for any size of tape that you wish to make. To save time in my own shop, I chose to make a full set of tapes in 2" (5cm) increments that range from 32" (80 cm) to 54" (137 cm). These are shown on the previous page. With this range of tapes, I am able to work with most chest sizes and heights without the need to make new tapes.

We will use two different colors of marker to create the tape. In the photos, blue is used for quarters and halves and eighths, and red is used for thirds, sixths and twelfths.

SCALED MEASURING TAPE SUPPLIES:

1. A long ruler or tape measure, for marking off the initial length on the tape.
2. Two colors of marker or pencil. One color is for divisions of halves, quarters and eighths; the other is for divisions of thirds, sixths, twelfths and *dedos.*
3. A piece of ribbon, straight fabric selvedge, strong parchment, or other firm, non stretchy material with which to make the tape measure.
4. Scissors to cut the tape to size.

NOTE: The surviving manuals were often printed with the final *i* written as *j*. Thus, *iii* becomes *iij*. There is no difference in meaning. For clarity in the writing of this book, I have standardized the notation without this affectation. However, the tape measure in the following photos is made with the archaic writing convention of the final *i* written as *j*.

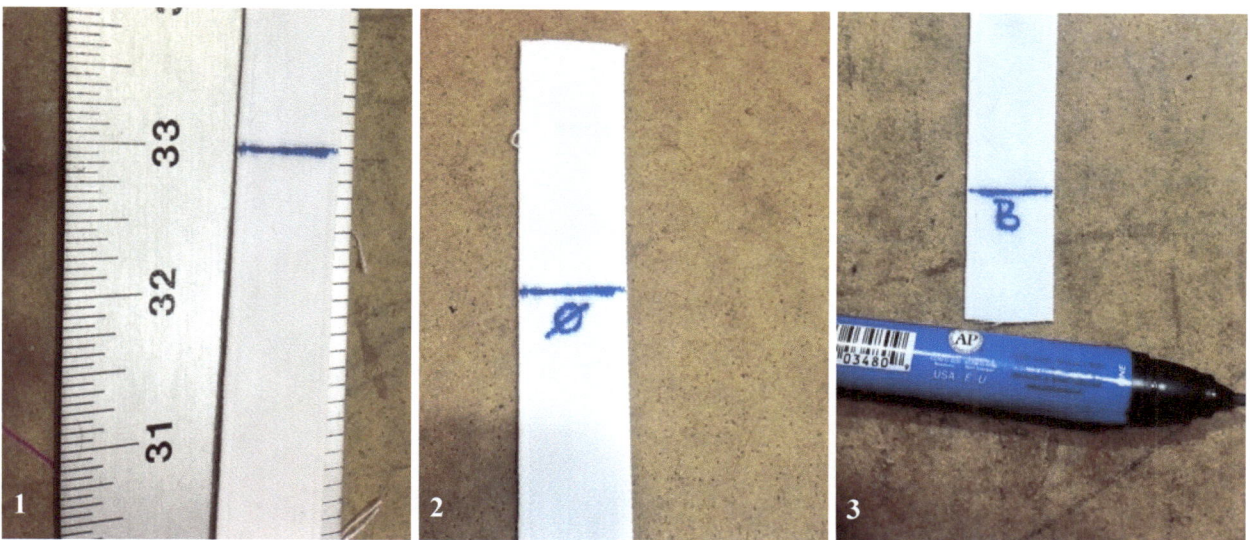

1. Using the blue marker (or color of your choice) make a mark near the end of the tape, and measure out the length you intend to use from this point. If you're making a standard tape, measure off 33" (82.5 cm). If you're making a scaled tape for an individual, wrap the tape around the widest part of the person's chest as viewed from the front. Once wrapped around their chest, make a second mark for other end of the tape at the point that it meets the first mark.
2. Mark one end 0.
3. Mark the other end with the letter *B*.

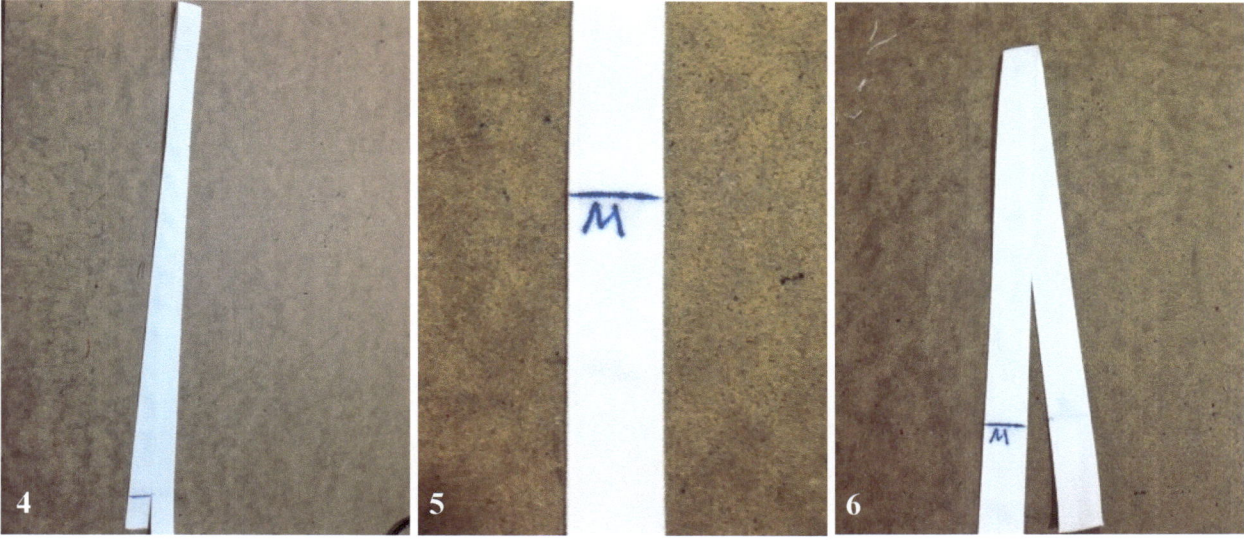

4. Fold the tape in half, matching the end marks.
5. Mark the midway point with an *M*.
6. Fold the tape so that the 0 meets the *M*.

Making the Pattern

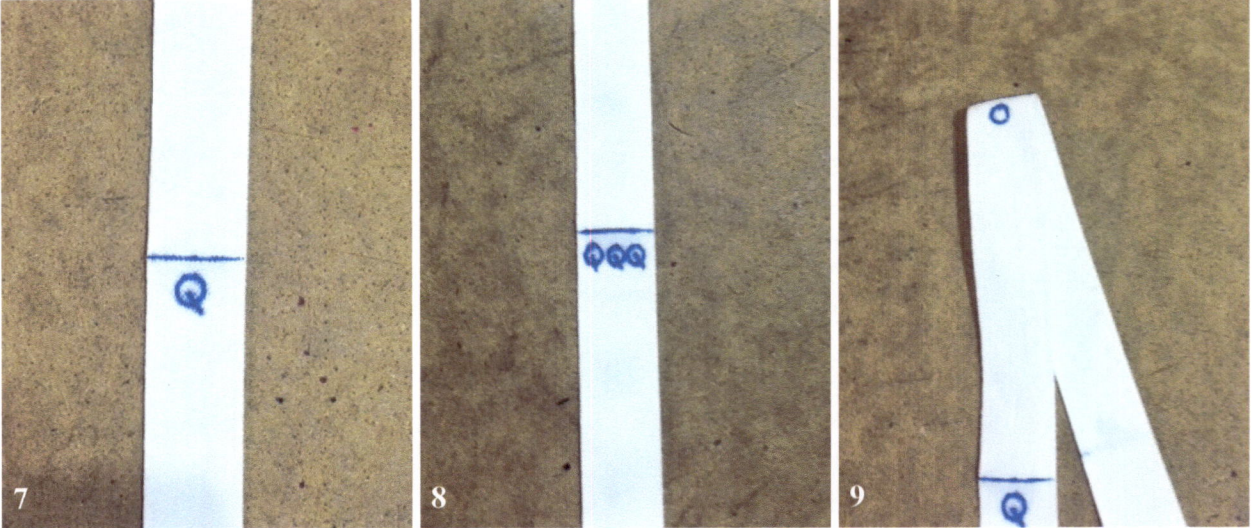

7. Mark the halfway point from 0 to *M* with the letter *Q*.
8. Fold the tape so that the *M* point meets the *B* point, and mark this *QQQ*.
9. Fold the tape so that the 0 point meets the *Q*, and mark it with the letter *o*.

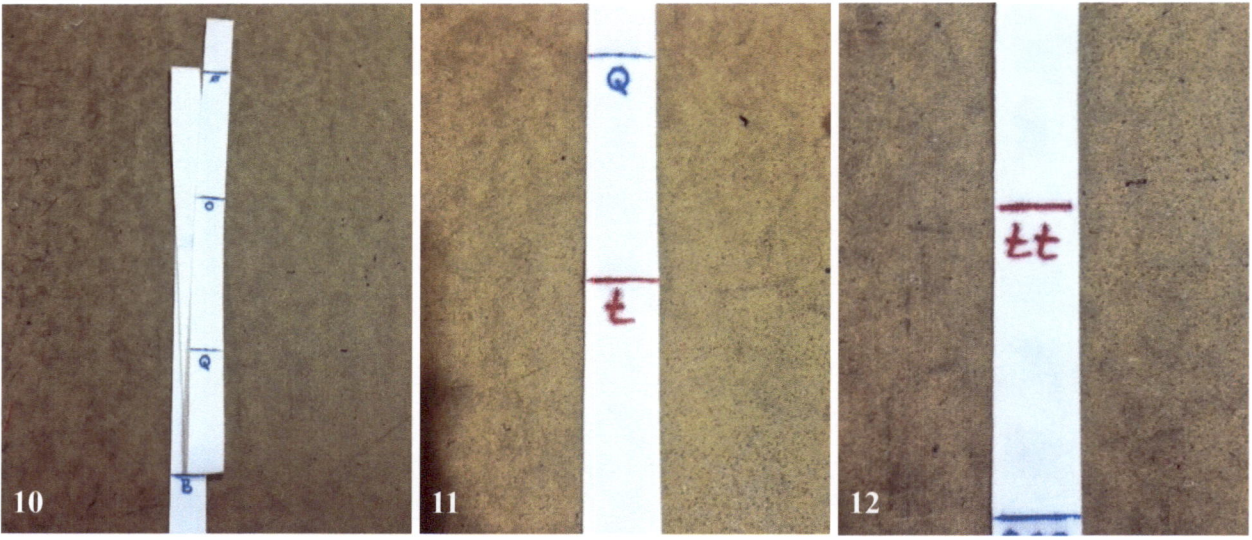

10. Next, carefully fold the tape into the thirds as shown, with the *B* and 0 points each meeting a fold.
11. Using the red marker, mark the fold between the *Q* and the *M* as *t*.
12. Mark the fold between the *M* and the *QQQ* as *tt*.

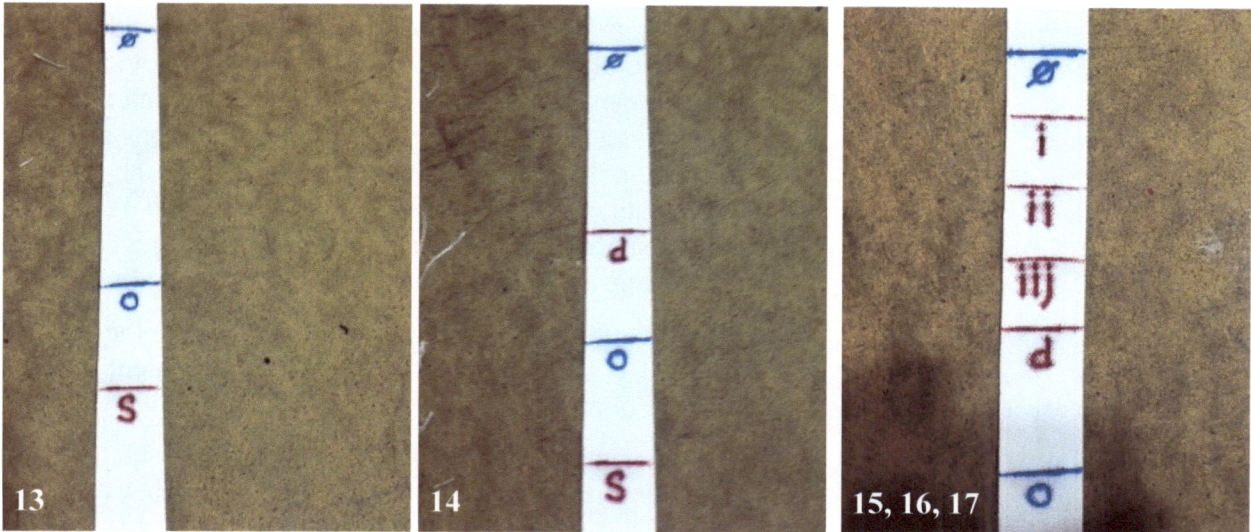

13. Fold the tape so that 0 meets T, and mark *s*.
14. Fold the tape so that 0 meets *s*, and mark *d*.
15. Fold the tape so that 0 meets *d*, and mark *ii*.
16. Fold the tape so that 0 meets *ii*, and mark *i*.
17. Fold the tape so that *ii* meets *d*, and mark *iii*.

This completes the creation of the graded tape measure. All graded tape measures are made with this method regardless of size.

The process of calculating which length of tape to use for height is a little bit complicated, so I present here a simple table (to the right) for making the correct tape based on height.

If, however, you would like to work it out for yourself, here are the calculations (metric version in parentheses):

1. Height in inches (cm) - 9in (17.7 cm) = cape length [CL]

2. CL ÷ 60.5 (153.7) = Graded Increment [GI]

3. GI x 36 (91.5) = Length of Height tape (referred to in the text as the **length** tape).

Height in./cm.	Tape length in inches	Tape length in cm.
6'4"/193cm	39	96
6'3"/191cm	39	96
6'2"/188cm	38	94
6'1"/186cm	38	94
6'0"/183cm	37	91.5
5'11"/180cm	37	91.5
5'10"/178cm	36	89
5'9"/175cm	36	89
5'8"/173cm	35	86.5
5'7"/170cm	35	86.5
5'6"/168cm	34	84
5'5"/165cm	34	84
5'4"/163cm	33	81.5
5'3"/160cm	33	81.5
5'2"/157cm	32	78.5
5'1"/155cm	32	78.5
5'0"/152cm	31	76

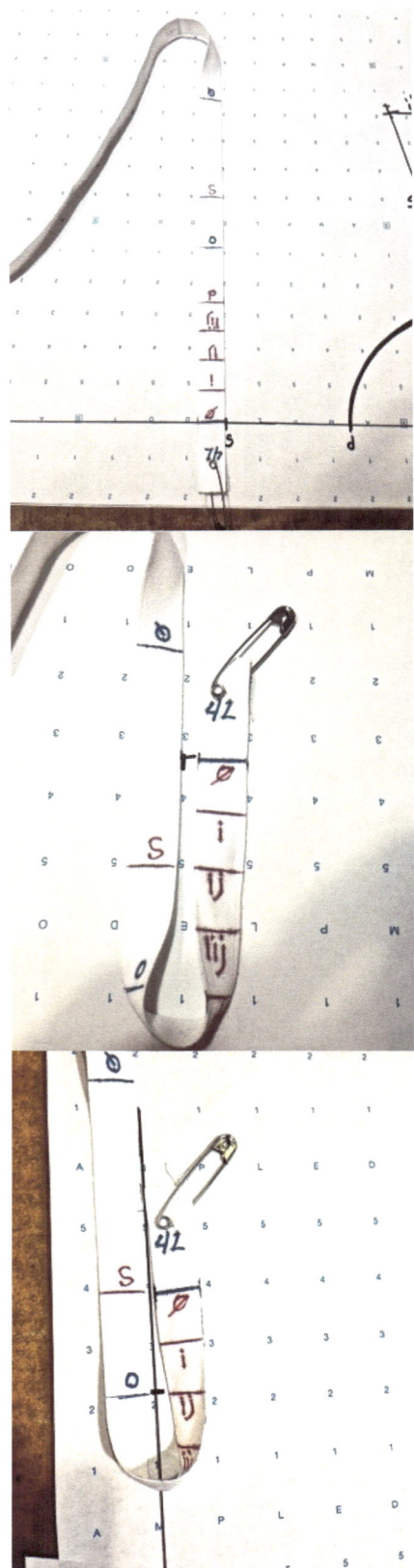

When developing a pattern, you will use this custom bara tape measure in much the same way as you would an ordinary tape measure. You will lay out a measurement and make a mark. Many measurements are combinations of increments on the tape. The method of notation is the same as Roman numerals. Smaller increments preceding a larger indicates a subtraction of the smaller from the larger. When a smaller increment follows a larger they are added together.

An example of this measuring method is shown in the photos to the left. The top two photos show the measurement *sii*. The bottom photo shows *iis*.

Lay the tape out perpendicular to the mark from which you are measuring, as shown in the top left photograph.

Hold the tape down at point s (or whatever measurement you're using) with one hand, and bring the 0 end of the tape around. Align the mark you wish to add to the distance with the original point measured.

In this case, we are adding *s* and *ii* for a total of *sii*. The mark for *ii* is aligned with s, and then a mark made at 0. You can see this mark drawn in black just next to the 0 in the center photograph to the left.

In the case where you are subtracting a smaller increment from a larger, you will align the 0 with the larger increment and make the mark next to the smaller increment that's being subtracted from the larger. This is demonstrated in the lower left photograph, which incidentally shows that *iis* (one sixth of a *bara* minus two *dedos*) is the same as o (one eighth of a *bara*).

You can also create a subtracted distance by reversing the tape and placing the larger increment's mark on the point that you are measuring from and stopping short of the 0 end of the tape measure, making your mark next to the smaller of the two combined increments.

This system may feel somewhat awkward at first, as you become accustomed to reading the order of the increments. Soon, however, you will find working without the typical mathematics associated with pattern making to be quite liberating.

With enough practice, you will be able to dispense with paper patterns entirely and draft your garment patterns directly onto cloth. However, I do not recommend this until you've had several years of practice with the system.

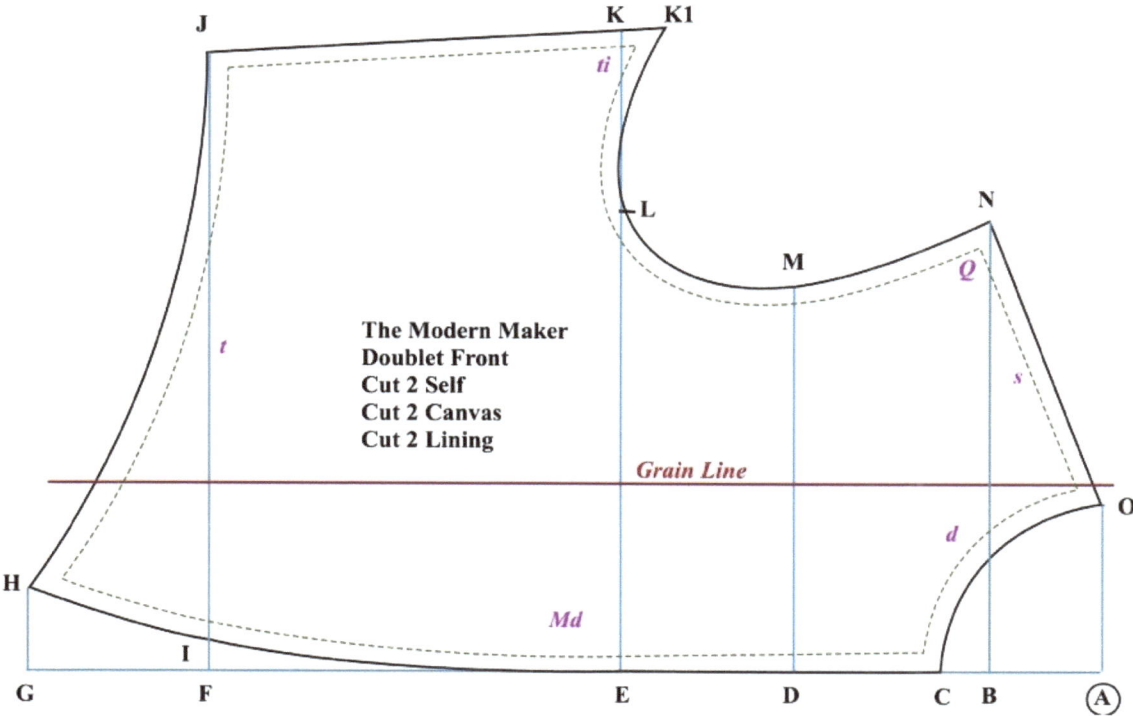

The Modern Maker
Doublet Front
Cut 2 Self
Cut 2 Canvas
Cut 2 Lining

Grain Line

DRAFTING THE DOUBLET FRONT

The process of drafting begins with a horizontal line and the placement of various points along that line. This is followed by a series of vertical measurements that plot the specific points of the draft. Connecting the dots of these plotted points creates a pattern which is automatically adjusted to the size of the tapes that have been used.

This draft is for a height/weight proportionate figure with a waist that is 4 to 6 inches (10-15.2 cm) smaller than the chest. If the waist of the client is more than six inches (15 cm) smaller than the chest, or less than four inches (10 cm) smaller than the chest, *including waists equal to or larger than the chest measurement,* please follow the alternative drafting instructions on page 31. Only the front, back and skirts are affected by this change. The letters indicated in purple represent the way pattern dimensions are labeled in surviving tailor's manuals.

NOTE: The proportionate doublet front is made almost entirely with the chest tape.

There is one measurement that requires the length tape. Measurements made with the length tape are underlined.

1. Beginning at A, draw a horizontal base line to the left. Using the **chest** tape, place the 0 end at A, and make marks at the following measurements.
    B = *iii*
    C = *d*
    D = *sii*
    E = *Qi*
    F = *M*
    G = *Md*

2. Using the **chest** tape, measure vertically from each of the points along the base line.
    G to H = *ii*
    F to I = *i*
    F to J = *t* (please note that J will be moved in a later step)
    E to K = *ti*
    E to L = *Qi*
    D to M = *sii*
    B to N = *Q*
    A to O = *d*

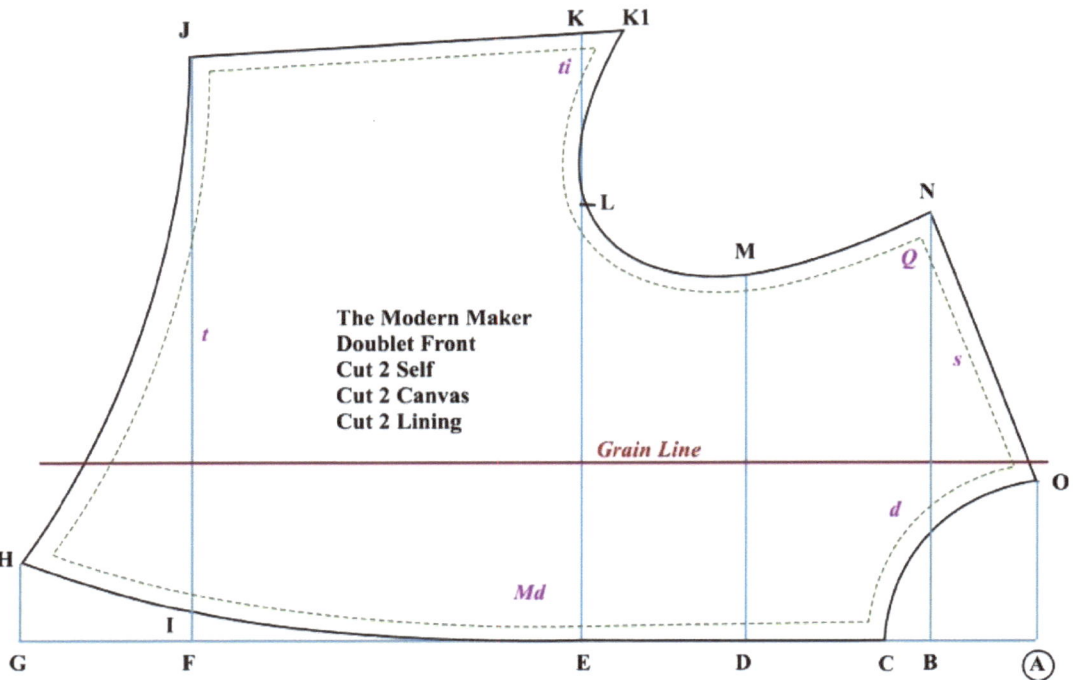

The Modern Maker
Doublet Front
Cut 2 Self
Cut 2 Canvas
Cut 2 Lining

Grain Line

3. Beginning at C, connect the points as follows:

- Connect C to E with a straight line.
- From E, draw a slightly curved line through I to H.
- Connect H to J with a shallow curved line.
- Draw a straight line from J through K. and a bit beyond. Place the 0 end of the **chest** tape at K and measure to the right *ii*. Mark K1.
- Using the **length** tape, place the 0 end at K and measure to the left along the line toward J. Make a mark at *Q*. Label this mark as J and cross out the old J.
- Using an armhole curve, or drawing freehand, connect K1 to L to M to N. When drawing freehand, be certain to place your hand in the armhole area, not in the body of the pattern. Graceful curves are best drawn from the interior of the curve.
- Connect N to O with a straight line. Measure this line with the chest tape. It should equal *s*. If it does not, remove the excess at N and blend the line smoothly to M.

- Connect C to O with a 1/4 circle line.

4. Mark the seam allowances as shown. They are 3/8" (7 mm) around all edges. At the shoulder and side back seam, you may use 1/2" (12 mm) allowances for a slightly closer fit if you desire. Please note that you are not ADDING allowances to the pattern; they are already included in the draft. This step is simply marking them for clarity. It is always wise to mark these allowances as it a quick reference for anyone using this pattern. Additionally, many costume professionals prefer to work without allowances on their patterns. After marking they can be easily trimmed off if it is preferred to have a pattern with no allowances included.

5. Label the pattern as shown and mark the grain line.

6. Cut out the pattern along the black line.

7. Make a small matching notch at L. This mark will align with a notch that we will place on the under-sleeve.

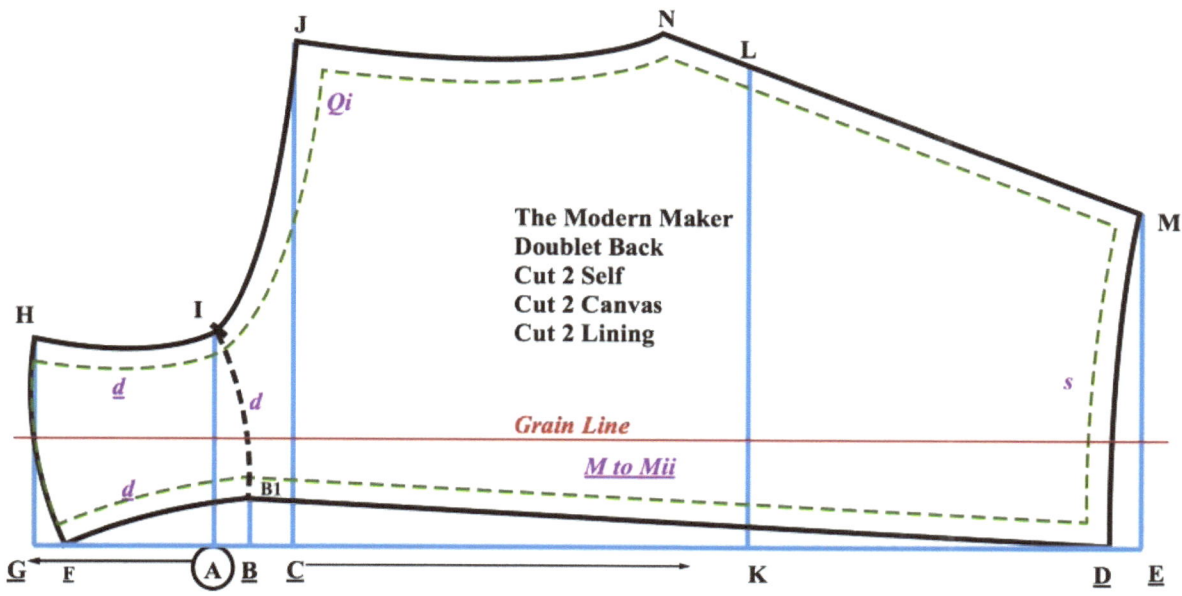

The Modern Maker
Doublet Back
Cut 2 Self
Cut 2 Canvas
Cut 2 Lining

Grain Line
M to Mii

DRAFTING THE DOUBLET BACK
(Length and chest tapes are used)

Again, this simple method uses horizontal points along a baseline with vertical points measured up from the line. This draft is for a proportionate figure with a chest 4 to 6 inches (10-15.2 cm) larger than the waist. For atypical figures, please use the alternate drafting method on page 33. **Please note that all measurements made with the length tape are underlined.**

1. Beginning at A, draw a straight line to the right and left with a ruler. Place the 0 end of the **length** tape at A. Measure to the RIGHT and make marks as follows:
   $\underline{B} = i$
   $\underline{C} = ii$
   (K is measured with a different tape, skip it for now)
   $\underline{D} = iM$
   $\underline{E} = M$ (or desired length)
2. Place the 0 end of **length** tape at A. Measure to the LEFT as follows:
   $\underline{F} = iii$
   $\underline{G} = d$
3. Place the 0 end of the **chest** tape at A and measure to the RIGHT Qi for point K
4. Using the **chest** tape only, mark the vertical measurements as follows:

$\underline{G}$ to $H = di$
A to $\underline{I} = di$
$\underline{B}$ to $B1 = i$
$\underline{C}$ to $J = Qi$
K to $L = sd$
$\underline{E}$ to $M = s$

5. Connect the points in the following order.

- Connect B1 to $\underline{D}$ with a straight line.
- Connect $\underline{D}$ to M with a shallow inward curved line.
- Connect M to L to N which is equal to J to K to K1 from the front draft.
- Connect N to J with a shallow inward curved line. Keep right angles at J.
- Connect J to I with a shallow inward curved line.
- Connect I to H with a shallow inward curved line.
- Connect H to $\underline{F}$ with a shallow outward curved line.
- Connect $\underline{F}$ to B1 with a shallow inward curved line.

6. Label the pattern, mark 3/8" (7 mm) seam allowances as shown in green. Mark the grain line. Cut out on the black line. Clip a small matching notch at I. This is where the front collar seam will align when the shoulder is sewn.

Two-piece front collar

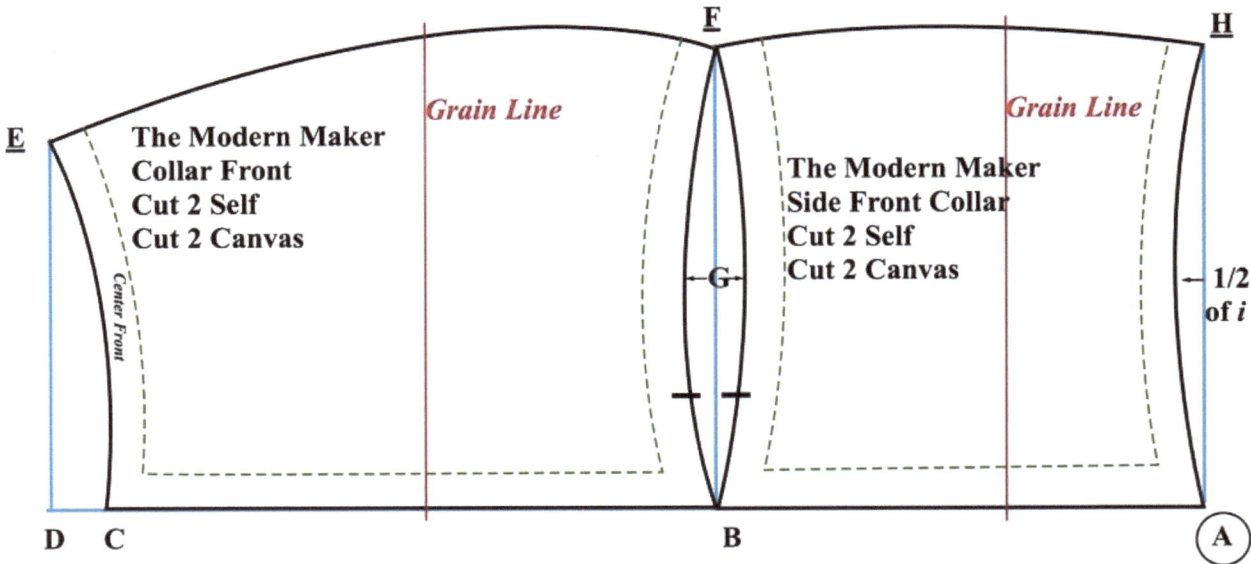

DRAFTING THE FRONT COLLARS

The front collars are drafted using both the **chest** and **length** tapes.

1. Using a ruler, draw a horizontal base line from A to the LEFT. Place the 0 end of the **chest** tape at A. Measure to the left and mark as follows:

   B = d
   C = si
   D = sii

2. The vertical measurements are made with the **length** tape as follows:

   D to E = iii
   B to F = d
   B to G = 1/2 of B to F
   A to H = d

3. At G, center i over line B-F to mark the width of the curvature for the side front collar seam. Follow the same curvature on line A to H as indicated.

4. Close the collar shapes as follows:

- Connect A to H with an inward curve following the guide mark.
- Connect H to F with an outward, barely curved line.
- Connect F to B With an inward curved following the mark at G. Mirror this curve for the other edge of the side front collar seam.
- Connect F to E with an outward curve, slightly more curved at F and more flat at E.
- Connect E to C with an inward curve.

5. Mark seam allowance guides. 3/8" (7 mm) seam allowances are included in the draft. Mark the grain line

6. Cut out the pattern pieces.

7. Make small matching notches where indicated between G and B. These marks will help you sew the correct edges together for the side front collar seam. They will also help you identify the correct edge that should be sewn into the front neckline.

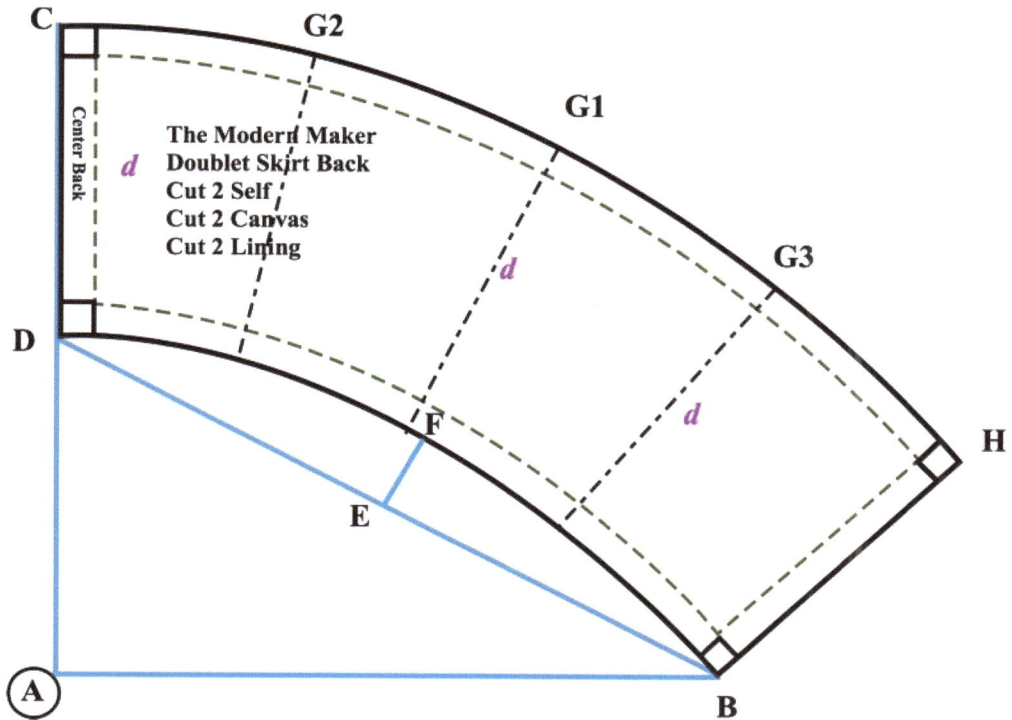

DRAFTING THE BACK SKIRT

The front and back skirts are drafted separately. While the existing manuals from the 16th and 17th centuries are somewhat vague on the dimensions of the doublet skirts, garments in museums share some common features in their skirtings: The shapes and grain lines were inconsistent, they were often cut from several pieces of leftover scraps, and frequently contained many joining seams in order to achieve the correct shape. Although all indications are that the skirts were cut as an afterthought, in this book I give a precise pattern for ease of use.

This draft is is drafted entirely with the **chest tape** for a proportionate figure with a chest 4 to 6 inches (10-15.2 cm) larger than the waist. For atypical figures, please see the alternate drafting method on page 34.

1. Draw right angle lines with a square at A. Place the 0 end of the **chest** tape at A and measure as follows:

A to C = s
A to D = d
D to B = s
E = 1/2 of D to B
E to F = i
Make a right angle at B
B to H = d

2. Connect D to F to B with an even, curved line. After drawing this curve, place the 0 end of the **chest** tape at D and measure along the curve. Adjust the length so it is exactly s, which matches the back doublet body.

3. Close the shape as follows:

- Measure d from Curve D-F-B in several places to G1,G2, and G3.

- Connect C through G1, G2, and G3 to H.

- Please note that all 4 corners should be 90° angles.

4. Mark seam allowance guides. 3/8" (7mm) seam allowances are included in the draft.

5. Cut out the pattern piece.

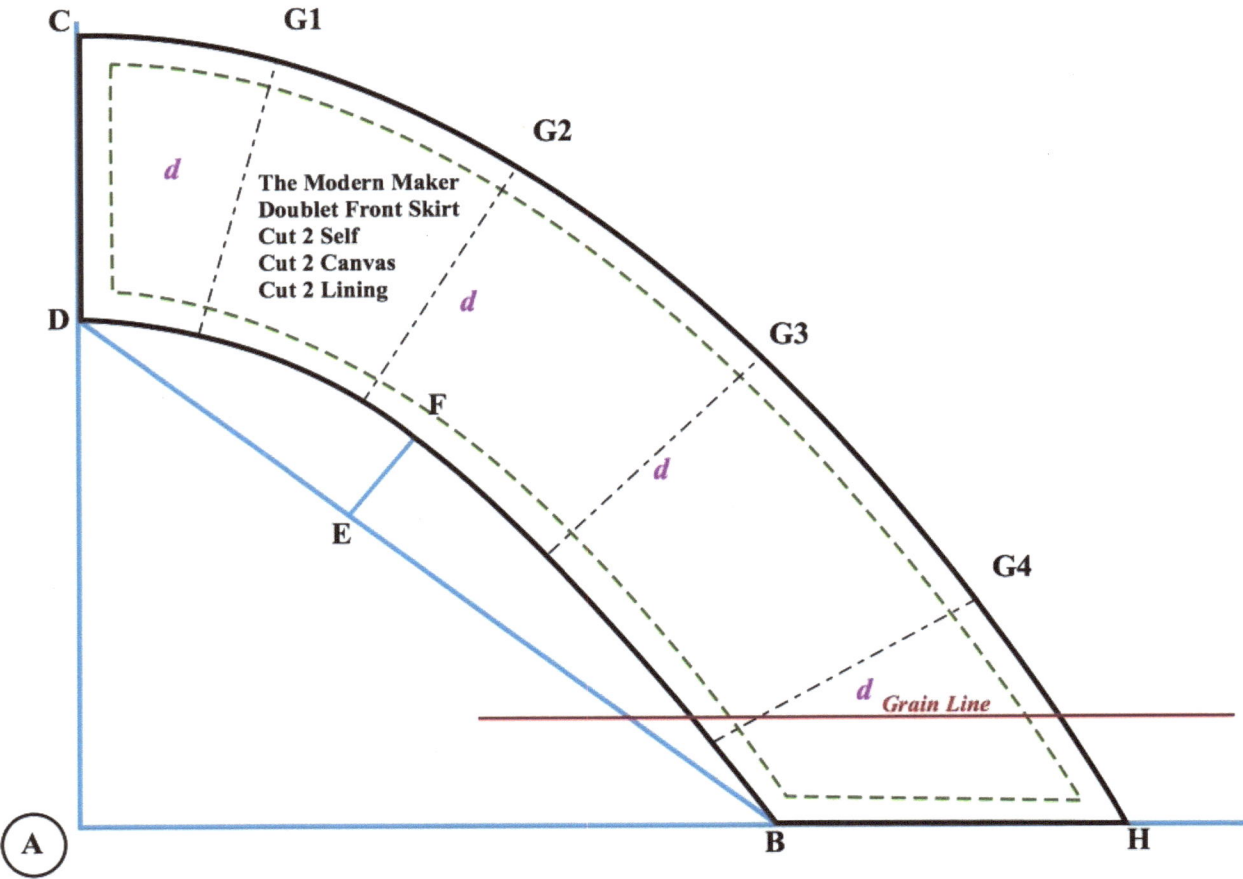

The Modern Maker
Doublet Front Skirt
Cut 2 Self
Cut 2 Canvas
Cut 2 Lining

Grain Line

DRAFTING THE FRONT SKIRT

The same principle of drafting the back skirt is applied to the front skirt, with some minor changes due to the difference in curvature of the pattern piece. For a proportionate figure with a chest 4 to 6 inches (10-15.2 cm) larger than the waist, the entire front skirt is drafted with the **chest tape**. For atypical figures, please see the alternate drafting method on page 35.

1. Draw square lines from A. Using the **chest** tape, measure and mark as follows:
   A to B = iQ
   A to D = Qi
   D to C = d
   D to E = o
   E to F = ii

2. Draw the waist curve from D through F to B keeping the curve a bit stronger from D to F and more flat from F to B. After Drawing this curve, place the 0 end of the **chest** tape at D and measure along the curve. Adjust the length so it matches the waist edge of the front body pattern exactly.

3. Close the shape as follows:

• Measure d from Curve D-F-B in several places to G1,G2, G3 and G4.

• Connect C through G1, G2, and G3 to H.

• Please note that corners C and D should be 90° angles.

4. Mark seam allowance guides. 3/8" (7mm) seam allowances are included in the draft. Mark the grain line if desired. Keep in mind that grain lines on skirts for this era tend to be quite fliexible

5. Cut out the pattern piece.

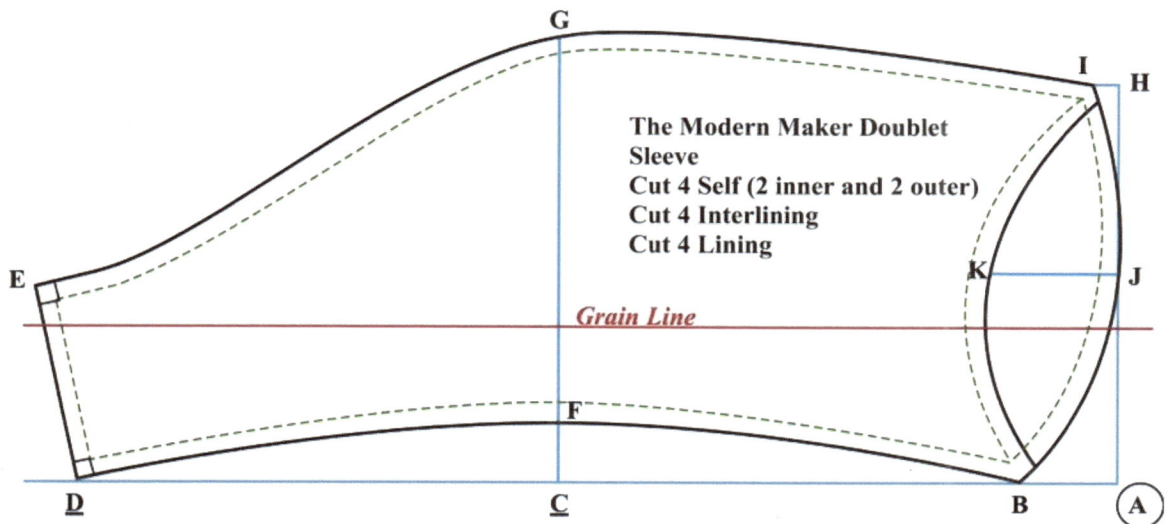

The Modern Maker Doublet
Sleeve
Cut 4 Self (2 inner and 2 outer)
Cut 4 Interlining
Cut 4 Lining

Grain Line

DRAFTING THE SLEEVE

The sleeve is drafted using both the **length** and the **chest** tapes. The base line is drawn and the curve of the front seam is defined, followed by the sleeve cap and the widths of both elbow and wrist. I find it easiest to plot all the points and then connect them at the end of the process.

The outer and inner halves of the sleeve are drafted as though they were lying on top of each other. This helps keep the draft correct, as well as helping one visualize the completed sleeve. Once drafted, you may choose to copy off the outer sleeve to have two pattern pieces. The sleeve drafting method does not change for atypical sizes.

1. Draw a horizontal base line. Label A at the right-hand end of the line.
2. Placing the 0 end of the **length** tape at A Make the following marks along the line to the left:

   A to $\underline{C}$ = t
   A to $\underline{D}$ = QQQ
3. Place the 0 end of the **chest** tape at A and make the following mark:

   A to B = iii
4. The remainder of the sleeve is drafted using the **chest** tape.

$\underline{C}$ to F = ii
$\underline{C}$ to G = Q
A to J = o
A to H = Qi
H to I = i
$\underline{D}$ to E = o
J to K = d

5. Complete the pattern shape as follows: Beginning at B, draw a smooth curved line through F to $\underline{D}$. Connect $\underline{D}$ to E with a straight line keeping a 90° angle at $\underline{D}$. Connect E to G with a compound curve as shown, keeping 90° at E. Connect G to I with a very slightly curved line.

6. To draw the underarm curve, make marks along the sleeve cap curve above B and below I that are 3/8" (9 mm) to mark the width of the seam allowances. Connect these marks with a curved line through K as shown.

7. Label the pattern, mark 3/8" (7 mm) seam allowances as shown in green. Mark the grain line. Cut out on the black line. Clip a small matching notch at K. This is where the front collar seam will align when the shoulder is sewn.

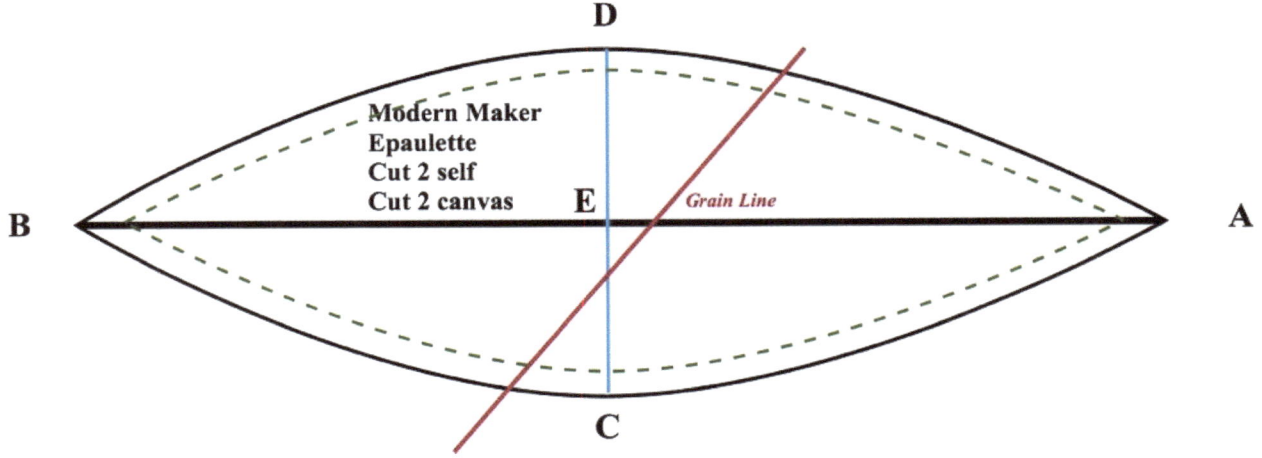

DRAFTING THE EPAULETTE

The entire epaulette is drafted using the **chest tape.** The method of drafting the epaulette does not change for atypical sizes.

1. Beginning at A, draw a straight line to the left.
2. Place the 0 end of the **chest** tape at A and make the following marks:

    A to B = *t*
    A to E = *s*
    E to C and E to D = *iii*

3. Close the shape by drawing curved lines as shown in the diagram.

4. Label the pattern and draw the grain line (this is optional)

The grain line for an epaulette of this type can vary considerably as it is made from the scraps of the material after the rest of the garment has been cut. Epaulettes come in many shapes and sizes; the shape shown is merely the simplest form. When I cut an epaulette, I usually cut from a section of scrap that is on the bias. This helps it hang more attractively and form into the armhole more easily. The majority of epaulettes in surviving garments are cut more frequently on straight grains than on bias. The choice is yours.

This piece is also optional, as not all doublets had epaulettes so you may skip this piece if you choose.

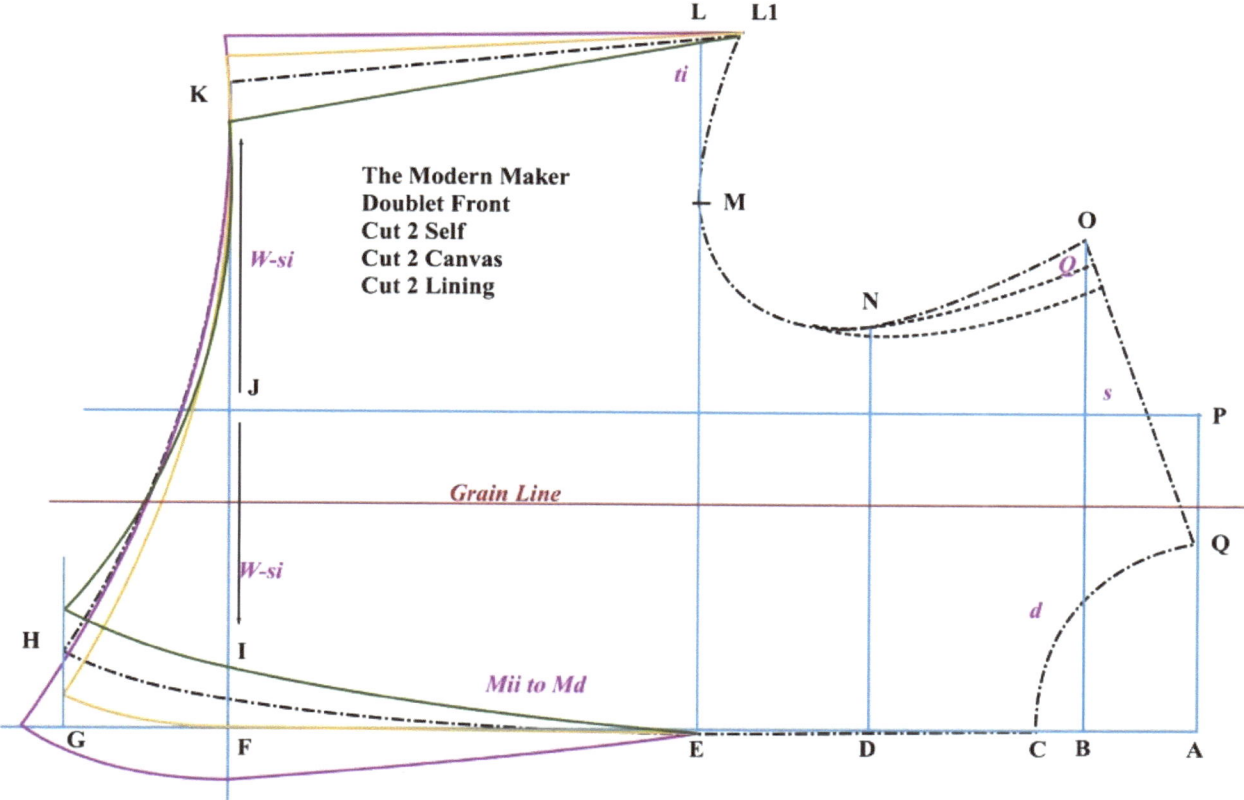

The Modern Maker
Doublet Front
Cut 2 Self
Cut 2 Canvas
Cut 2 Lining

Grain Line

Mii to Md

DRAFTING THE DOUBLET FRONT FOR AN ATYPICAL FIGURE

This draft is for a waist that is more than six inches (15 cm) smaller than the chest [large chest, very tapered to the waist], or less than four inches (10 cm) smaller than the chest [a waist which is marginally smaller than the chest, or waist which is larger than the chest]. For these atypical figures you must use a tape made from the **waist** measurement when drafting the waist line. This tape is made in exactly the same method as the **chest** and **length** tapes.

GREEN lines indicate a waist that is 8-10 inches (20.3 - 25 cm) *smaller* than the chest.
BLACK dot/dash lines indicate the proportionate draft.
YELLOW lines indicate a waist which is the *same* measurement as the chest.
PURPLE lines indicate a waist which is 2 inches (5 cm) *larger* than the chest.

NOTE: All three tapes are used to draft the front pattern.

1. Beginning at A, draw a horizontal base line to the left. Using the **chest** tape, place the 0 end at A, and make marks at the following measurements:
   B = *iii*
   C = *d*
   D = *sii*
   E = *Qi*
   F = *M* (Or desired length to waist level)
   G = *Md* (Or desired length to point)

2. Using the **chest** tape, measure vertically from each of the points along the base line:
   E to L = *ti*
   E to M = *Qi*
   D to N = *sii*
   B to O = *Q*
   A to Q = *d*
   A to P = *s*

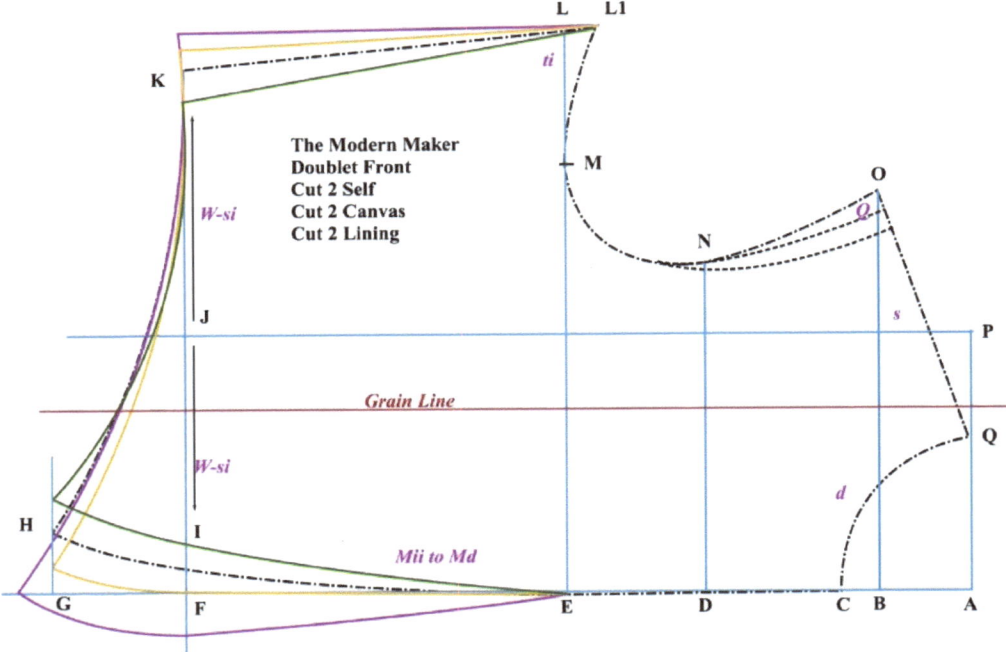

3. Draw a vertical line up from F. Beginning at P draw a horizontal line to the left intersecting with the vertical line from F. Mark point J at this intersection.

Using the **waist** tape, place the 0 at J and measure up *si*. Mark point K. Reverse the tape, place the 0 end at J and measure down *si*. Mark point I. **Please note that point K will be moved in a later step.**

As you can see from the diagram, the various waist sizes produce different results. When the waist is **smaller** than the chest, or the same as the chest, point H of the doublet is marked along the vertical line at G. When the waist is larger than the chest, this point is marked along the horizontal base line to the left of G.

Beginning at I, draw a straight line to the left. Where this line crosses the line at G, measure up *i* (with the **chest** tape) and mark point H.

4. To close the shape, begin at C and connect the points as follows:
- Connect C to E with a straight line.

- From E, draw a slightly curved line through I to H.
- Draw a straight line from K through L. and a bit beyond. Place the 0 end of the **chest** tape at L and measure to the right *ii*. Mark L1.
- Using the **length** tape, place the 0 end at L and measure to the left along the line toward K. Make a mark at *Q*. Label this mark as K and cross out the old K.
- Connect H to K with a shallow curved line.
- Using an armhole curve, or drawing free-hand, connect L1 to M to N to O. When drawing freehand, be certain to place your hand in the armhole area, not in the body of the pattern. Graceful curves are best drawn from the interior of the curve.
- Connect O to Q with a straight line. Measure this line with the chest tape. It should equal *s*. If it does not, remove the excess at O or use a direct shoulder measurement.
- Connect C to Q with a 1/4 circle line.

Return to step 4 of the proportionate draft to complete the pattern with markings and labels.

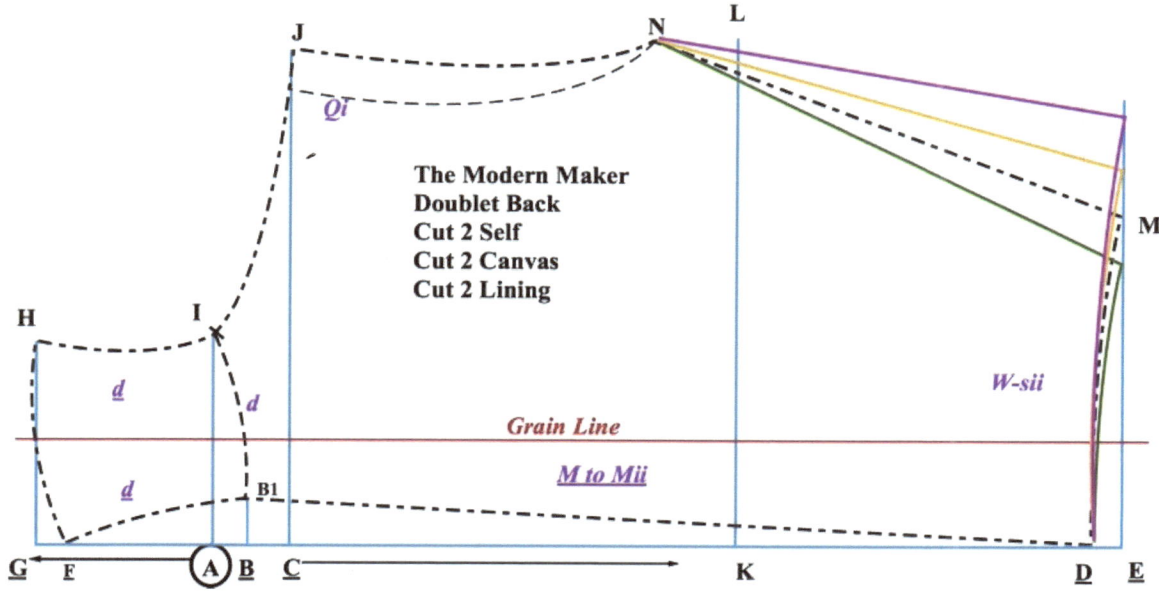

The Modern Maker
Doublet Back
Cut 2 Self
Cut 2 Canvas
Cut 2 Lining

Grain Line

M to Mii

DRAFTING THE DOUBLET BACK FOR AN ATYPICAL FIGURE

The draft is made in the same manner as the proportionate draft. The exception is that the waist is drafted using the **waist** tape rather than the chest tape. **Note that all measurements made with the *length* tape will be underlined.**

1. Beginning at A, draw a straight line to the right and left with a ruler. Place the 0 end of the **length** tape at A. Measure to the RIGHT and make marks as follows:
   $\underline{B} = i$
   $\underline{C} = ii$
   (K is measured with a different tape, skip it for now)
   $\underline{D} = iM$
   $\underline{E} = M$ *(or desired length)*
2. Place the 0 end of **length** tape at A. Measure to the LEFT as follows:
   $\underline{F} = iii$
   $\underline{G} = d$
3. Place the 0 end of the **chest** tape at A and measure to the RIGHT Qi for point K
4. Using the **chest** tape only, mark the vertical measurements as follows:
   $\underline{G}$ to H = di
   A to I = di
   $\underline{B}$ to B1 = i

C to J = Qi
K to L = sii
$\underline{E}$ to M = sii **measured with the waist tape**

5. Connect the points in the following order:

- Connect B1 to $\underline{D}$ with a straight line.
- Connect $\underline{D}$ to M with a shallow inward curved line.
- Connect M to N is equal to J to K1 from the front draft.
- Connect N to J with a shallow inward curved line. Keep right angles at J. I to J should be equal to *s*. If it does not equal *s*, make the correction at J as shown.
- Connect J to I with a shallow inward curved line.
- Connect I to H with a shallow inward curved line.
- Connect H to $\underline{F}$ with a shallow outward curved line.
- Connect $\underline{F}$ to B1 with a shallow inward curved line.

6. Label the pattern, mark 3/8" (7 mm) seam allowances as shown in green. Mark the grain line. Cut out on the black line. Clip a small matching notch at I. This is where the front collar seam will align when the shoulder is sewn.

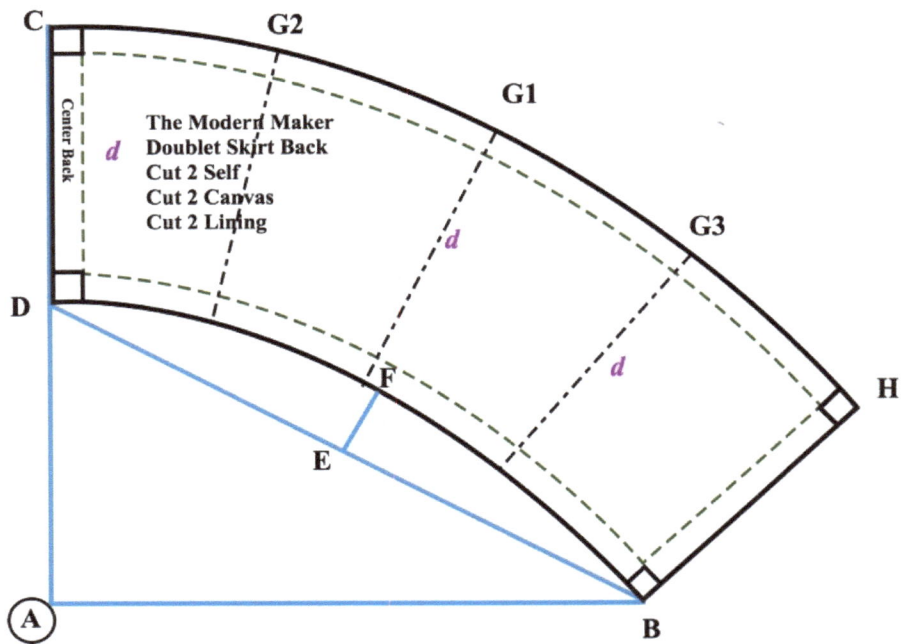

The Modern Maker
Doublet Skirt Back
Cut 2 Self
Cut 2 Canvas
Cut 2 Lining

DRAFTING THE BACK SKIRT FOR AN ATYPICAL FIGURE

The skirt draft is made in exactly the same manner as the proportionate draft with the exception that it is drafted entirely with the **waist** tape.

1. Draw right angle lines with a square at A. Place the 0 end of the **waist** tape at A and measure as follows:

   A to C = *s*
   A to D = *d*
   D to B = *sii*
   E = 1/2 of D to B
   E to F = *i*
   Make a right angle at B
   B to H = *d*

2. Connect D to F to B with an even, curved line. After Drawing this curve, place the 0 end of the **waist** tape at D and measure along the curve. Adjust the length so it is exactly *sii*, which matches the back doublet body.

3. Close the shape as follows:

- Measure d from Curve D-F-B in several places to G1,G2, and G3.

- Connect C through G1, G2, and G3 to H.

- Please note that all 4 corners should be 90° angles.

4. Mark seam allowances as shown. 3/8" (7mm) allowances are included in the draft.

5. Cut out the pattern piece.

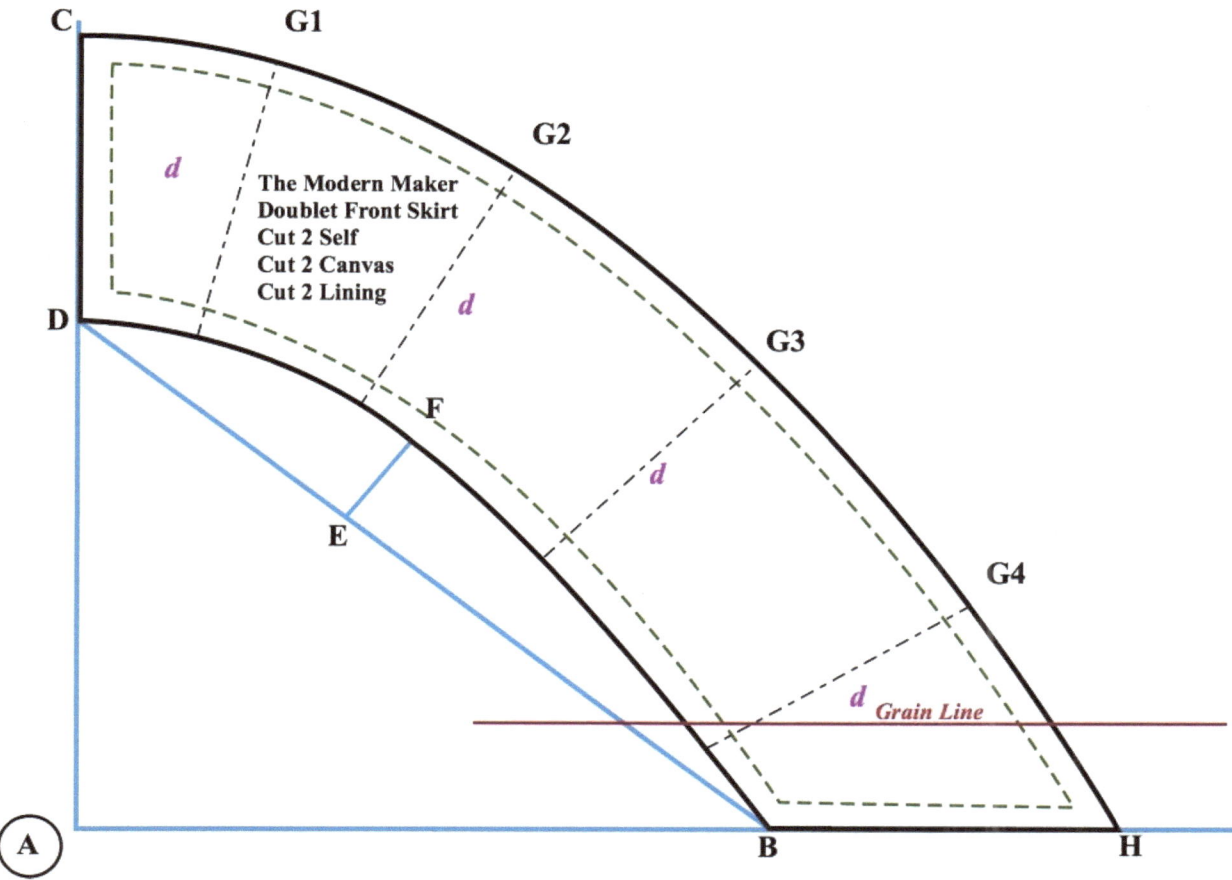

The Modern Maker
Doublet Front Skirt
Cut 2 Self
Cut 2 Canvas
Cut 2 Lining

Grain Line

DRAFTING THE FRONT SKIRT FOR AN ATYPICAL FIGURE

The same principle of drafting the back skirt is applied to the front skirt with some minor changes due to the difference in curvature of the pattern piece. The draft for an atypical figure is made entirely with the **waist** tape.

1. Draw square lines from A. Using the **waist** tape, measure and mark as follows:

   A to B = iQ
   A to D = Qi
   D to C = d
   D to E = o
   E to F = ii

2. Draw the waist curve from D through F to B keeping the curve a bit stronger from D to F and more flat from F to B. After drawing this curve, place the 0 end of the **waist** tape at D and measure along the curve. Adjust the length so it matches the waist edge of the front body pattern exactly.

3. Close the shape as follows:
- Measure d from Curve D-F-B in several places to G1, G2, G3 and G4.

- Connect C through G1, G2, and G3 to H.

- Please note that corners C and D should be 90° angles.

4. Mark seam allowance guides.
3/8" (7mm) seam allowances are included in the draft. Mark the grain line.

5. Cut out the pattern piece.

Making the pattern

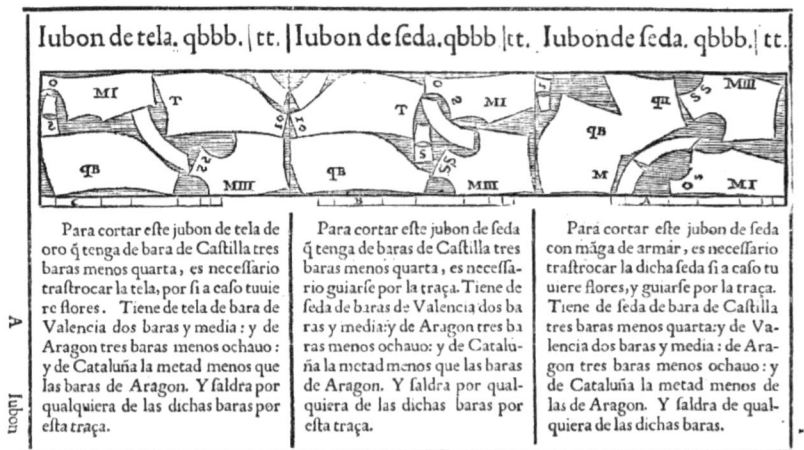

Iubon de tela. qbbb. | tt. | Iubon de feda.qbbb |tt. Iubonde feda. qbbb.| tt.

Para cortar efte jubon de tela de oro q̃ tenga de bara de Caftilla tres baras menos quarta, es neceffario traftrocar la tela, por fi a cafo tuuie re flores. Tiene de tela de bara de Valencia dos baras y media : y de Aragon tres baras menos ochauo : y de Cataluña la metad menos que las baras de Aragon. Y faldra por qualquiera de las dichas baras por efta traça.

Para cortar efte jubon de feda q̃ tenga de baras de Caftilla tres baras menos quarta, es neceffario guiarfe por la traça. Tiene de feda de baras de Valencia dos baras y media: y de Aragon tres baras menos ochauo: y de Cataluña la metad menos que las baras de Aragon. Y faldra por qualquiera de las dichas baras por efta traça.

Para cortar efte jubon de feda con mãga de armar, es neceffario traftrocar la dicha feda fi a cafo tuuiere flores, y guiarfe por la traça. Tiene de feda de bara de Caftilla tres baras menos quarta: y de Valencia dos baras y media : de Aragon tres baras menos ochauo: y de Cataluña la metad menos de las de Aragon. Y faldra de qualquiera de las dichas baras.

The image you see above is the first page in the pattern layout section of *Geometria y traça perteneciente al oficio de sastres,* a tailor's manual written by Francisco de la Rocha Burguen in 1618. The proportions and shapes that we have just created are taken directly from these layouts. As you can see, there are relatively few measurements shown on each pattern shape. The author presumed that the tailor would understand the remaining measurements needed, and would not need them identified in these diagrams. Utilizing standard and consistent measurements taken from this and three other manuals of the era (two earlier manuals and one later), the remaining proportions were extrapolated for the draft given in this book.

During the period when this book was in use, paper was not used for patterns in the way it is now. Rather, the master cutter would lay out the garment by chalking directly onto the fabric. This method is still in use today in some of the older bespoke tailoring houses, where it is considered one of the primary ways for a tailor to retain control over his unique cut and artistic style. When the paper pattern is removed from the drafting process, one begins to understand just how excellent these artisans had to be at their trade. One false swipe of the hand, and an expensive piece of cloth might be ruined by a misplaced chalk line.

In a trade where efficient use of time was necessary for success, tailor's layouts such as those in the above image were invaluable time-saving tools. They allowed tailors to use each width of fabric as economically as possible without chalking lines multiple times. For this reason, patterns shown in historic tailor's books of the 16th and 17th centuries have the seam allowances included in the pattern draft.

When a tailor of the era became proficient enough to be trained to cut, they were given a large piece of cheap felt and plain chalk with which to practice drafting. The novice would learn the proportions for a garment and chalk out the garment pieces. Once the master tailor checked the pattern draft, the felt would be beaten, the chalk marks erased, and another draft begun. This process was repeated dozens of times for each garment type, until the tailor perfected his technique through repetition and was eventually allowed to draft and cut a garment for their first client.

It is my recommendation that you practice the pattern draft at least 5 times before attempting to cut a garment. With each successive draft, you will train and perfect your ability to recognize the correct lines, curves and angles of that garment.

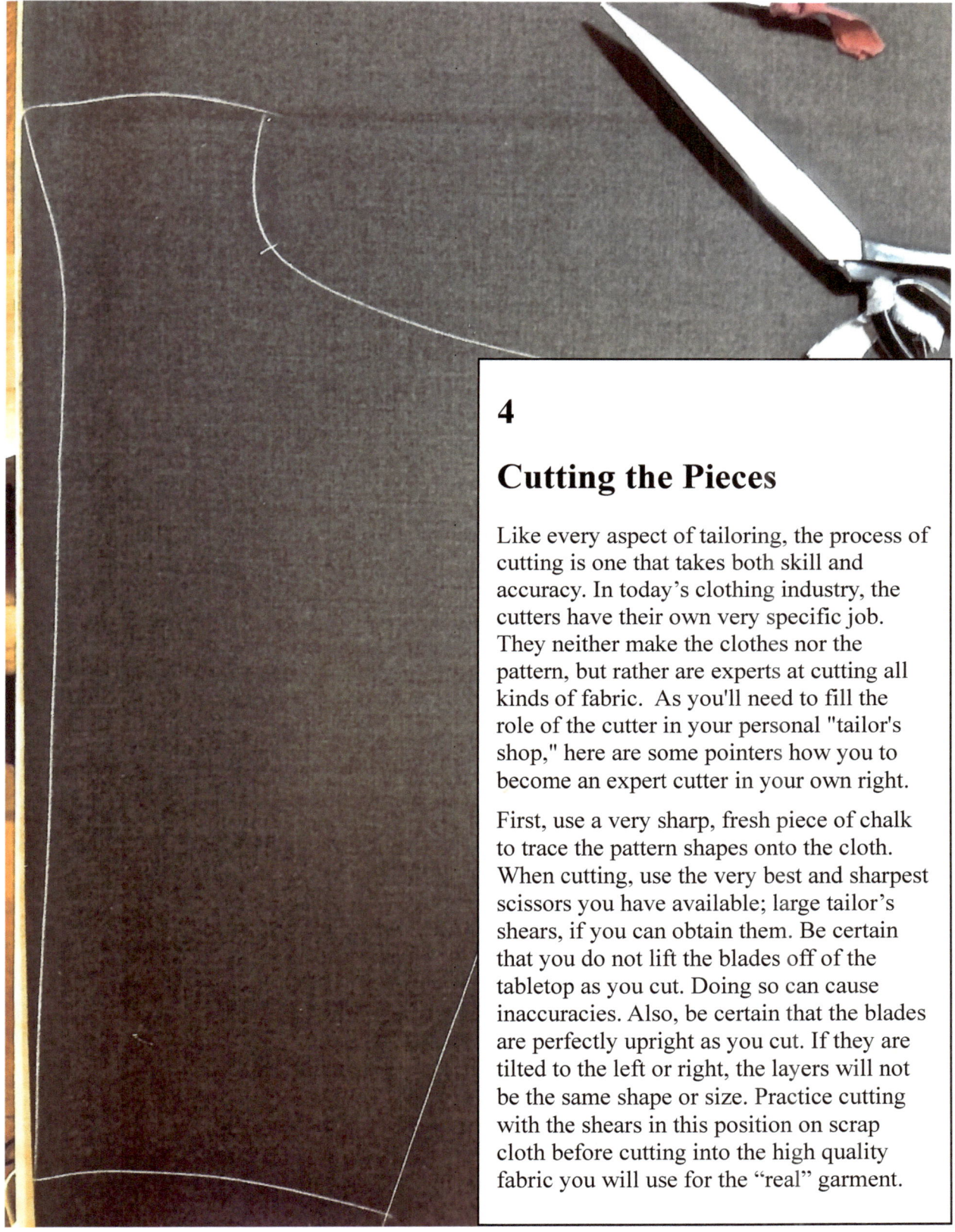

4

Cutting the Pieces

Like every aspect of tailoring, the process of cutting is one that takes both skill and accuracy. In today's clothing industry, the cutters have their own very specific job. They neither make the clothes nor the pattern, but rather are experts at cutting all kinds of fabric. As you'll need to fill the role of the cutter in your personal "tailor's shop," here are some pointers how you to become an expert cutter in your own right.

First, use a very sharp, fresh piece of chalk to trace the pattern shapes onto the cloth. When cutting, use the very best and sharpest scissors you have available; large tailor's shears, if you can obtain them. Be certain that you do not lift the blades off of the tabletop as you cut. Doing so can cause inaccuracies. Also, be certain that the blades are perfectly upright as you cut. If they are tilted to the left or right, the layers will not be the same shape or size. Practice cutting with the shears in this position on scrap cloth before cutting into the high quality fabric you will use for the "real" garment.

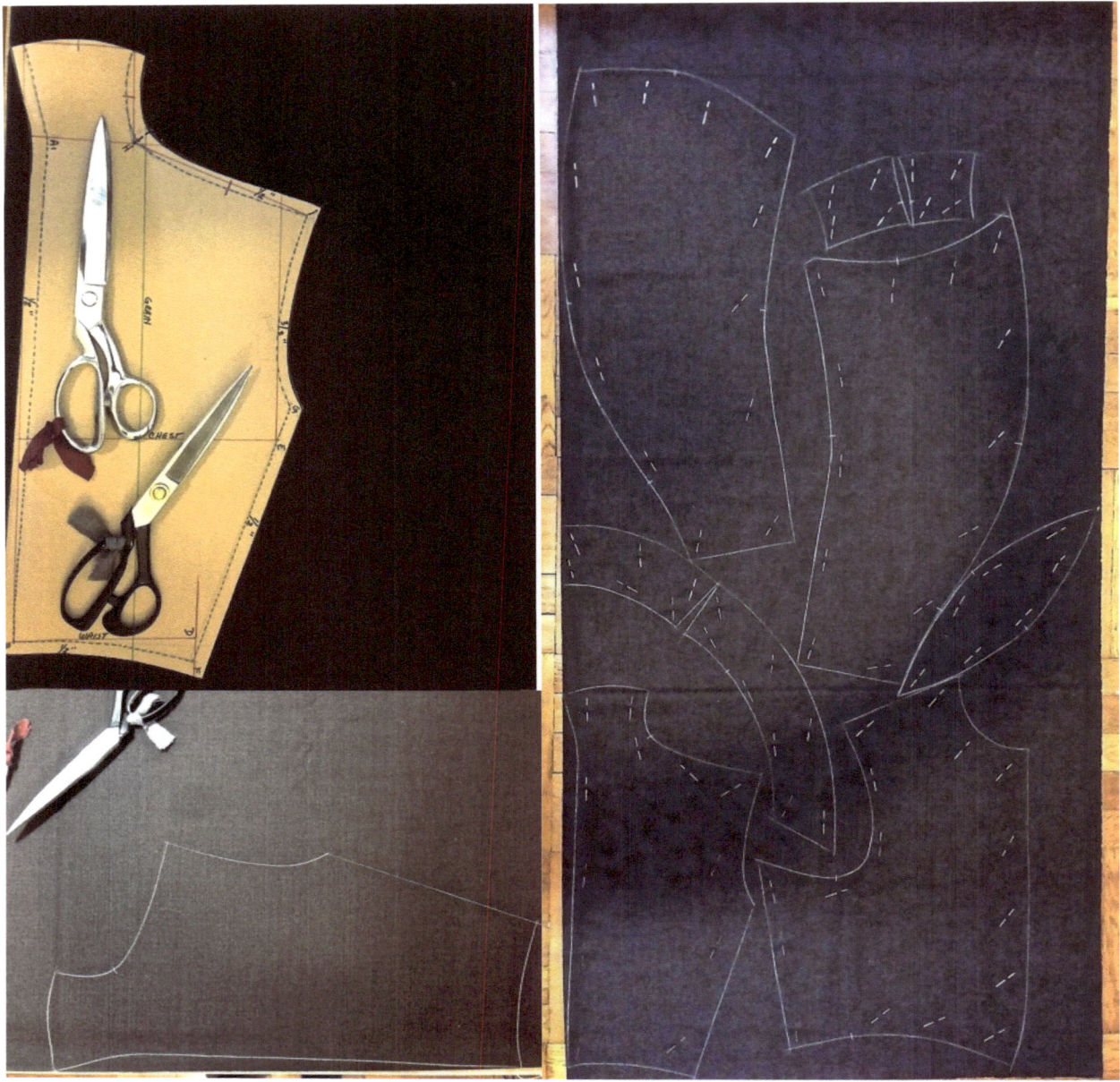

CUTTING THE EXTERIOR PIECES

1. Lay out the exterior fabric, folded, with right sides together.

2. Place each pattern piece on the cloth, right side up, so you can see all the markings clearly. Pay special attention to the grain line marked on the pattern piece. It is helpful to use a ruler and measure from the selvedge of the fabric to the ends of the grain line on the pattern to be certain that the piece is aligned with the grain of the cloth.

Make sure that there is no wasted space. *Efficient layouts will vary depending on the size of the pattern and the width of the cloth.* Use your best judgment to conserve your fabric.

3. Rather than pinning the pattern to the fabric, which distorts the surface and causes subtle changes in the pattern shape, place a weight on each pattern piece and trace around it carefully. Be certain that you mark every notch. Remove the pattern pieces as you finish tracing, and put them away once you finish using them. I recommend setting them aside neatly or folding them up and placing them in an envelope for storage.

4. Pin the two layers of folded fabric together inside the perimeter of the outline to secure the layers for cutting. Pins should be inserted at as slight an angle as possible. (See photo above, top left.) Inserting a pin straight up and down and then turning it shifts the layers and distorts the shape.

5. Begin cutting, using the scissors and cutting technique described above. As you cut each piece out, don't remove the pins. Leave them in the place, as you will need them when we cut the next layer. Also, do not forget to snip all the notches about 1/4" (7 mm) deep. Do not clip them too deeply, or they will weaken the seam. **Do not skip this step.**

6. Place the cut out pieces in piles according to the garment part to which they belong (collars, fronts, backs, etc.) As we cut the different layers, keeping the piles organized like this will assist us later in working efficiently.

CUTTING THE CANVAS/INTERLINING (EXCEPT THE FRONT)

1. Lay out the interlining/canvas fabric in the same manner as the exterior fabric. If the interlining fabric is the same width as the exterior fabric, use the same layout.

2. Lay the cut out pieces of the exterior fabric on the interlining in the most conservative way possible. Re-pin them to the canvas. It is permissible, when cutting the canvas, to shift a piece to a slightly different grain to conserve the material; though this should not be done unless necessary.

Do not lay out the body front panels. We will be adjusting their shape slightly when we cut the front canvas pieces.

3. Cut out the pieces and clip all notches.

Take extra care to avoid cutting the exterior fabric as you cut carefully around each piece. You will notice as you are cutting around the exterior pieces that the canvas pieces will end up just a tiny bit larger than the exterior fabric pieces. Don't worry about this; this is desirable and should be intentional. You want to be able to lightly stretch the exterior pieces onto the canvas to hold them taut during wear.

In addition, it is common for interlinings to shrink slightly over years of use in a garment. Cutting the interlinings slightly larger will offset this tendency, and guarantees that the shape of the garment will not be distorted over time.

Again, lay the pieces in piles according to the part of the garment. This process will also help you to familiarize yourself with the shapes of the various parts of the garment. Do not un-pin the layers.

CUTTING THE FRONT CANVAS

1.   To cut the front canvas, lay the fronts cut from the exterior fabric onto the canvas, paying special attention to the grain lines. Pin the front pieces to the canvas. Cut around the shape, leaving approximately 1/2" (1.2 cm) extra around all edges.

2.   Cut two small pieces of canvas that are 2"x5" (5 cm x 12.7 cm), and keep them with the front canvas pieces. These extra pieces will become wedge inserts for the armhole.

3.   Cut a bias strip of canvas that is 30" x 2" (75 cm x 5cm). This strip will become the stiffening that goes under the buttonholes. If you are using a very heavy canvas, this piece is not necessary.

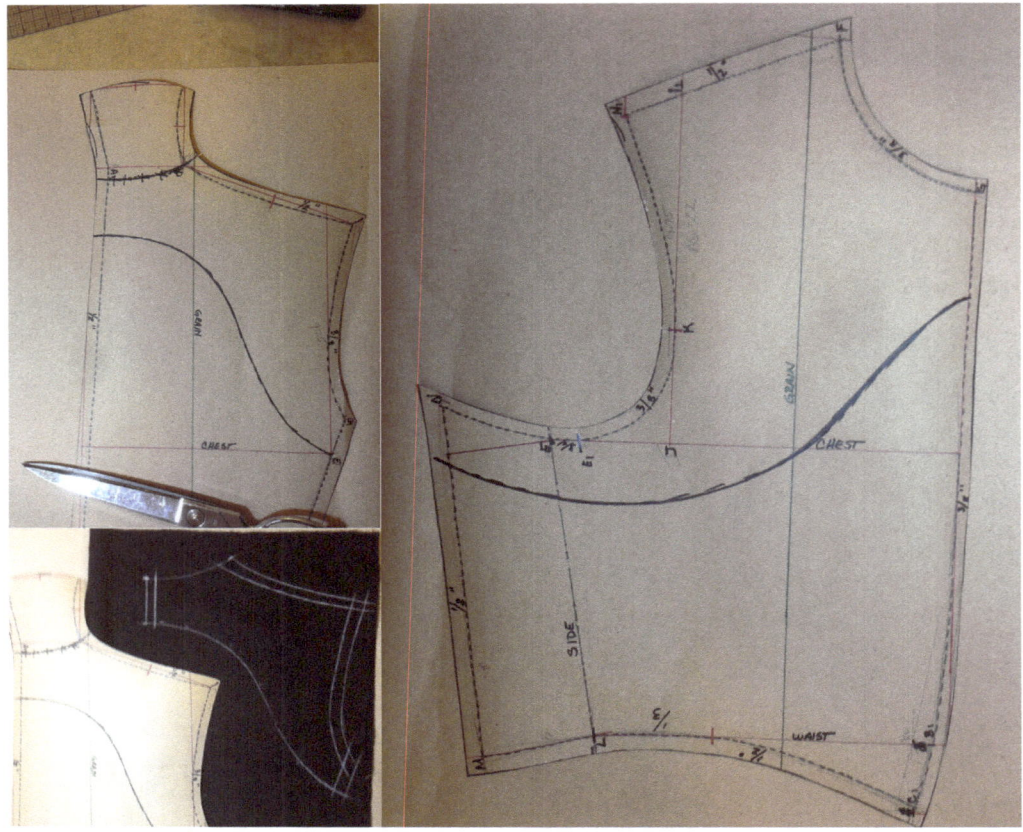

CUTTING THE UPPER BODY PADDING

1. Trace off a copy of the front and back body patterns onto a piece of paper. You only need to copy off a short portion of the center front/back, the shoulder, neckline and armhole areas as shown. Follow the graceful curved lines in the middle of the pattern pieces as shown with the heavy black lines drawn on the pattern pieces. With practice, you can skip this step and just use the full body pattern and freehand the lower cutting line with chalk directly on the fabric.

2. Use these patterns to cut out the wool padding for the body. The padding goes over the shoulder area, around the armhole, and into the front upper chest area. On the padding for the left front, trim away 1 1/2" (3.7 cm) along the front edge. This will eliminate excessive bulk in the buttonhole area.

CUTTING THE SLEEVE AND SKIRT LININGS

1. Fold the fabric in half along its length with wrong sides out.

2. Place the cut pieces of the skirts and sleeves onto the lining fabric, arranging them to produce the most efficient cut. In the previous steps, we used the exterior fabric pieces to cut the canvas, but did not unpin the outer fabric from the canvas. We now use the combined canvas/exterior pieces to cut the lining. Do not cut the front and back linings yet, as they have their own steps. However, it is advantageous to place the front and back pieces onto the lining fabric to plan out the locations where they can be most efficiently cut.

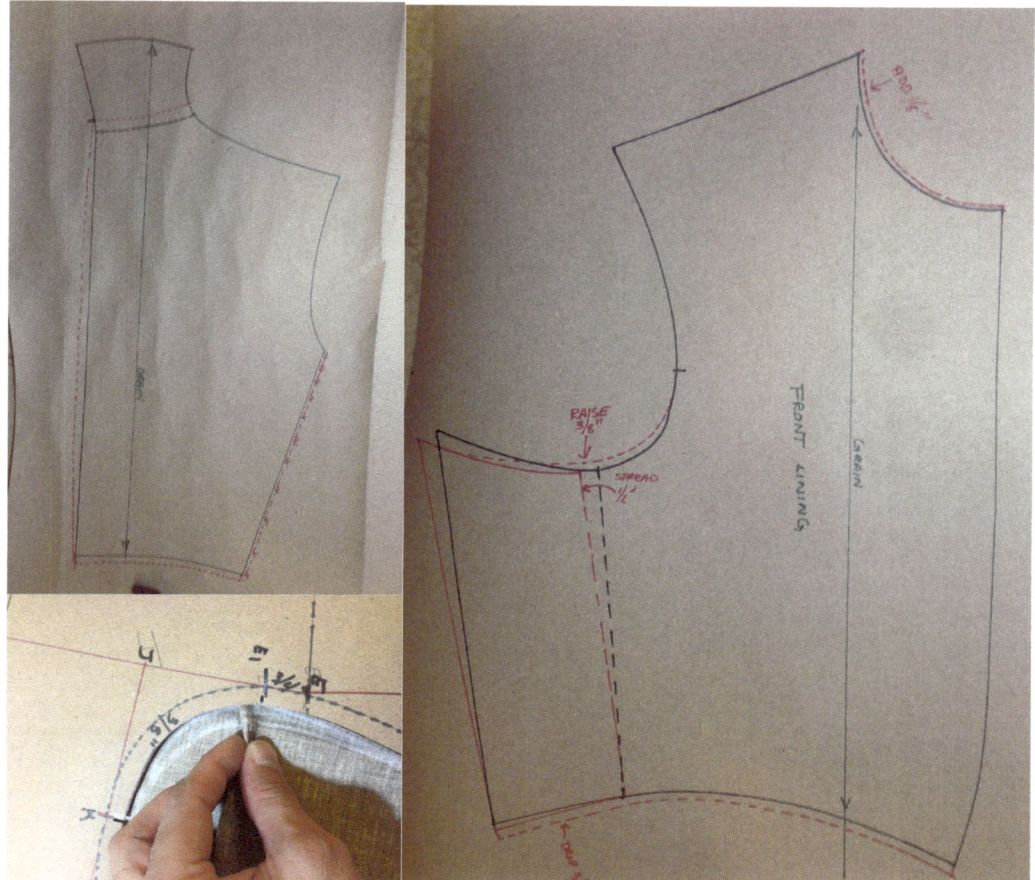

MAKING THE BACK LINING PATTERN
Trace off a copy of the back body pattern and mark the following small modifications to the shape before you cut.

- Drop the waist 3/8" (9 mm).

- Bow out the side and center back seams about 1/4" at the center blending to nothing at the top and bottom. Remove the collar leaving 3/8" (9 mm) seam allowance. The collar will be lined near the end of the construction process with a single separate piece of lining material.

MAKING THE FRONT LINING PATTERN
Trace of a copy of the front pattern onto paper and make the following adjustments:

- Open the underarm 1/2" (1.2 cm) at the bottom of the armhole.
- Raise the bottom of the armhole 3/8" (9 mm), blending to nothing at the front and back of the armhole as shown.
- Lower the waist 3/8" (9 mm).

Place the front and back lining patterns onto the lining fabric. Trace around the patterns, pin the layers together and cut them out.

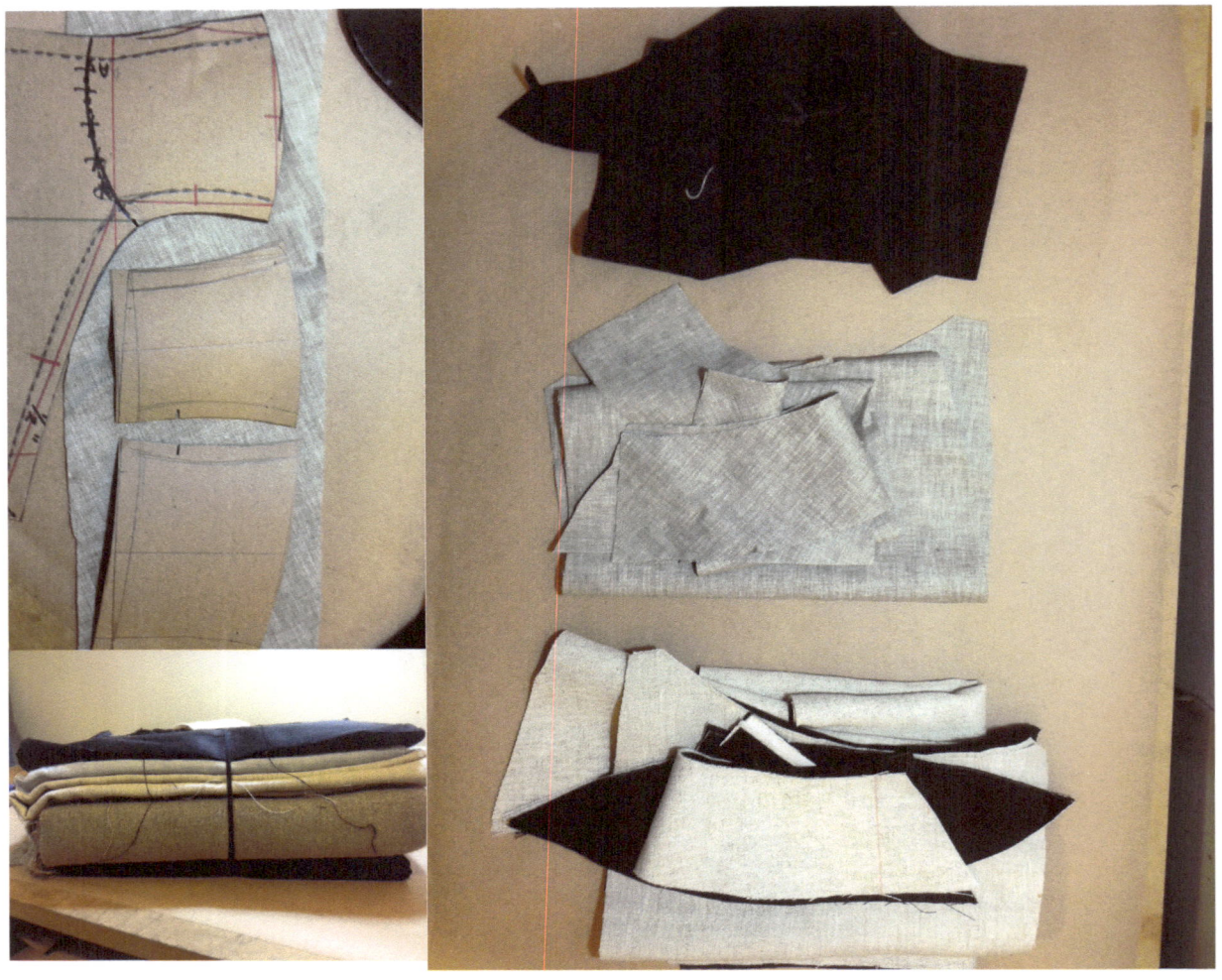

Once you are accustomed to making these pattern modifications, you can create them without a separate pattern piece by using the front pattern as you drafted it, tracing around the pattern, pinching up a little pleat in the fabric at the bottom of the armhole, and drawing the chalk line 3/8" (9 mm) higher in the armhole and lower at the waist while tracing or during cutting. (See photo on pg. 43, bottom left)

CUTTING THE COLLAR LINING

1. Place the collar pattern pieces next to each other on the lining, above the shoulder edge of the back doublet pattern piece, as shown in the photograph. Lay these pieces on the bias upon a doubled layer of fabric. Each pattern piece should be touching the one next to it.

2. Chalk around these pieces, leaving 1/4" (7 mm) of additional seam allowance along the top and bottom edges. Cut out the collar lining.

Now that all the pieces are cut, you can bundle the project for efficient storage until such time as you can begin to make it. Alternately, you can sort the pieces into their piles and get ready to stitch it all together!

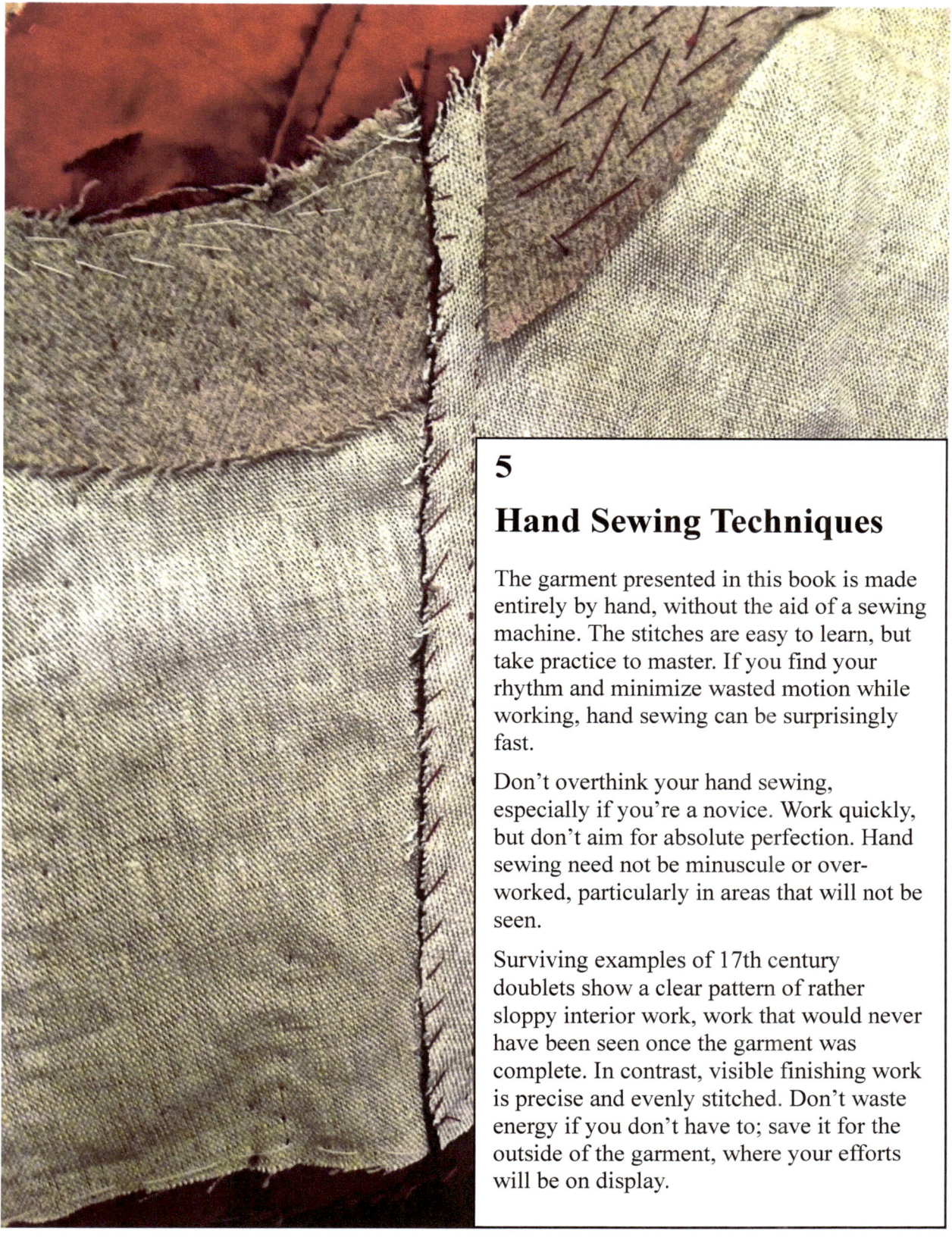

5

Hand Sewing Techniques

The garment presented in this book is made entirely by hand, without the aid of a sewing machine. The stitches are easy to learn, but take practice to master. If you find your rhythm and minimize wasted motion while working, hand sewing can be surprisingly fast.

Don't overthink your hand sewing, especially if you're a novice. Work quickly, but don't aim for absolute perfection. Hand sewing need not be minuscule or over-worked, particularly in areas that will not be seen.

Surviving examples of 17th century doublets show a clear pattern of rather sloppy interior work, work that would never have been seen once the garment was complete. In contrast, visible finishing work is precise and evenly stitched. Don't waste energy if you don't have to; save it for the outside of the garment, where your efforts will be on display.

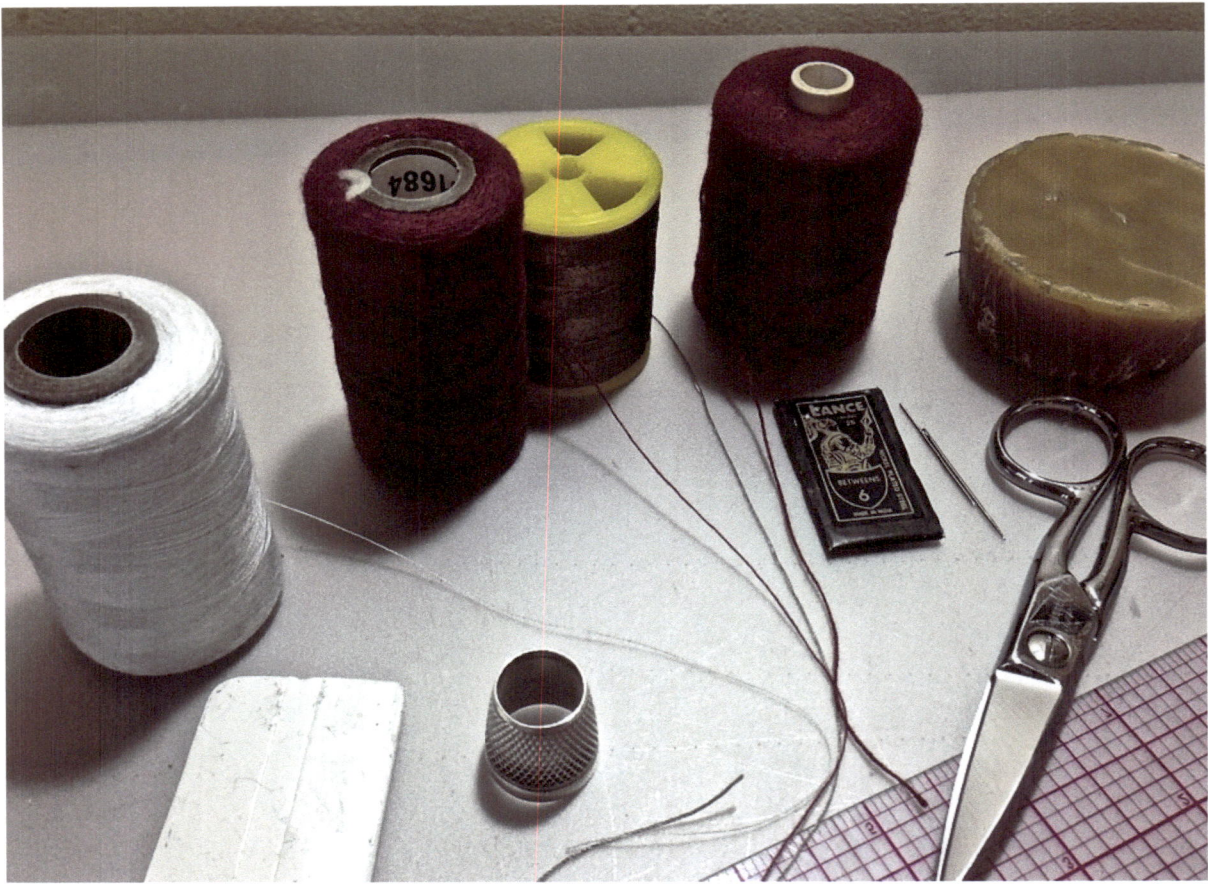

The supplies for hand sewing are simple and few.

Threads: These are manufactured by size. The "T" number is the thread size. Clockwise from the left in the photo above:

White Basting Thread: Size T-21. This is the same size as cheap serger thread. Basting thread is almost always a white, somewhat weak thread, that is seldom, if ever waxed. Although used for modern basting, non-silk threads in surviving garments do not appear in such a fine size; most are coarser, approximately .4 to .6 mm in diameter.

Topstitching Thread: Size T-60. Usually sold as topstitching thread. It is stronger and slightly thicker than regular machine sewing thread (usually size T-40). This is the standard thread that I use for all hand sewn main seams, and is similar in size and weight to the linen thread used to sew the main seams in surviving clothing from the 16th and 17th centuries.

Silk Buttonhole Twist: Size T-112 silk buttonhole twist is similar in size to T-80 non-silk thread. It is strong, heavy and excellent for pick stitching, as its sheen adds to the beauty of decorative stitching.

Heavy cotton cord thread: This is quite thick, about T-100. It is similar to lightweight Perle cotton thread that can be found in the embroidery section of most craft stores.

Beeswax: Beeswax is used to smooth thread before sewing. After you wax the thread, press it with an iron between two layers of paper, muslin, or scrap fabric. The wax will melt into the thread and make it much easier to work with. Ironing also eliminates any excess wax adhering to the thread which might flake off and stain your work.

Thread Snips: These should be pointed and sharp.

Sewing Needles: My preferred needles are quilter's "betweens," sizes 5 and 6. The shorter size of the betweens allows a much quicker push and draw of the needle with each stitch. Learning to use a shorter, thicker needle will save both time and energy. The larger hole it makes causes less friction on the thread, and also lessens the tendency for the twist of the thread to be pushed toward the end and snarl into knots. I prefer betweens as I find longs/sharps are tiring for the hand and are slower to work with.

Tailor's Thimble: Traditionally, tailor's thimbles are open-topped and are worn on the middle finger. Properly positioned on the middle finger, the tailor uses the thimble to push with the side of the finger, not the top. There is no need for a thimble with a top; in fact, a closed thimble can actually interfere with the finger sensitivity needed for tailoring.

Tailor's Chalk: A specially compounded tailor's chalk is traditionally used to mark the fabric prior to cutting. This is not ordinary blackboard chalk; check your local craft store for what's available. You can also use a thin sliver of plain bar soap, if you have no chalk at hand.

Ruler: A ruler is used to draw the lines for your seams, if you need a mark. With regular hand sewing practice, you will gradually learn to gauge your seam allowance by sight instead of following a chalked line. However, beginning tailors have enough to worry about without worrying about getting the right-size seam allowance. If you need a guideline, by all means chalk one using a ruler.

THE STITCHES

Practice makes perfect. It's an old saying, but it holds true in any skilled trade. In a traditional tailor's workshop, an apprentice was given the same task to execute repeatedly until he had mastered it. Next, he would practice a variety of applications in which that stitch was used. The apprentice would essentially become a little human "machine," churning out that one single stitch before moving on to master the next one. It was a stitch-by-stitch education.

Give yourself a similar experience by grouping your stitching tasks in such a way that you repeat the same type of stitch many times in succession. This repetition will help you master each stitch until its execution become second nature.

Proper motions and body mechanics are essential to efficiency. Learn your personal rhythms and limit your body movement to speed up your stitching. Small, quick motions are more efficient than large, slow ones.

With many stitches, such as basting, running, or felling stitches, you can take several short draws of thread between each stitch and then, after two or three stitches, take a long draw to pull the entirety of the thread through the fabric. Working in this manner makes for faster sewing, and also minimizes abrasion to the thread. Less abrasion means longer lasting thread, longer lasting seams, and a longer lasting garment.

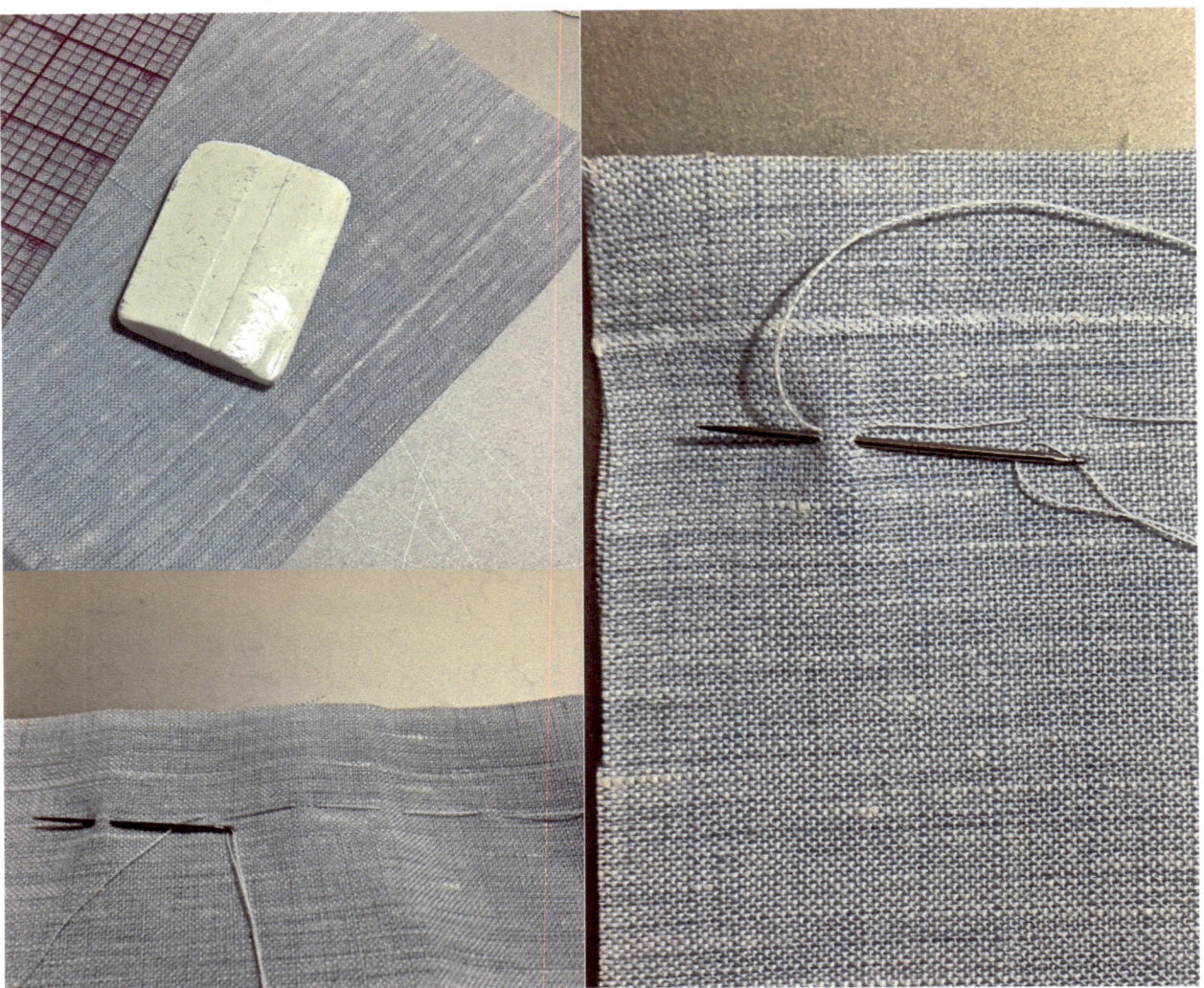

BASTING STITCH: Basting stitches are short or long depending on the needs of the task. Basting is primarily used to secure two or more layers of fabric together, either temporarily or permanently: stitches that are temporary rarely need to be small and delicate. In many ways, basting serves the same function as pinning.

a. (Top left photo) Draw the stitching line with the ruler and chalk. This line is for the stitching that will happen after the basting is applied. Generally, you should not put temporary stitches through lines that will have permanent stitching on them. As you can see in the photo, the basting is stitched below the actual line.

b. Cut off a length of basting thread. Don't cut it too long. Fighting the knots that will inevitably occur when using an overlong thread is both frustrating and a waste of time. Avoid knots by choosing shorter lengths of thread. Thread your needle with a single strand and knot one end. Do not double the thread. You don't need to wax basting thread.

c. (Bottom left photo) Use a small stitch or "pick" through the fabric layers, with about 1" (2.5cm) between picks. Take several small picks with a short draw of the thread between each stitch before pulling the full length of the thread through the cloth. This will reduce abrasion on the thread. (Right photo) To tie off, take one small extra stitch on top of the last pick rather than knotting the end.

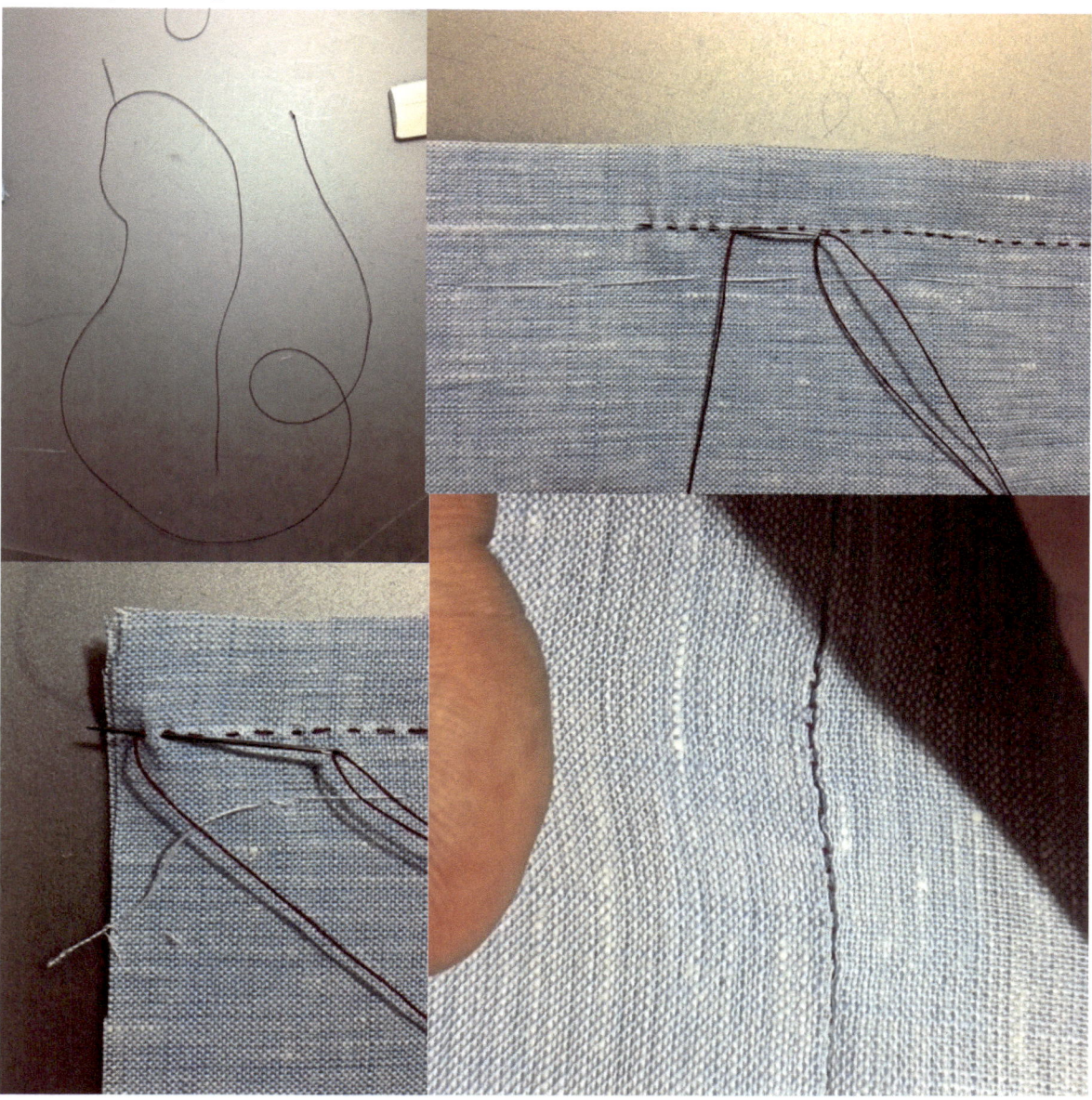

RUNNING STITCH: The running stitch, usually worked with size T-60 thread, is both fast and useful. Begin by first basting your pieces together a slight distance away from the stitching line with unwaxed basting thread (see above). The extra distance will prevent the basting from getting caught in your stitches as you work.

a. Cut off a length of topstitching T-60 thread that is no longer than your arm. Pull it through the beeswax and then press the thread to melt the wax into the thread (see above, under Beeswax). Thread the needle with a single thread, and knot one end.

b. Weave the needle in and out of the fabric in very small picks, as small as the fabric and needle will allow. Take several stitches at once before pulling the needle and thread through the fabric.

c. Continue in this manner until you are ready to tie off. To tie off, take three small stitches in the same place right on top of each other and cut the thread.

d. Once the seam is sewn, remove the basting thread.

Whip stitch a—wrong side

Whip stitch a—right side

Whip stitch b

WHIP STITCH: The whip stitch is used in two ways. The first way is for stitching seams open. This use of the whip stitch looks best on thicker fabrics. If the picks are very small on a fine fabric, it can actually weaken the fabric rather than strengthen it. The second use is to finish the edge of fabrics to prevent fraying.

a. **When stitching seams open, t**hread the needle with a single strand of waxed T-60 and begin stitching as shown in the photo above and to the left. The needle direction is always perpendicular to the edge that is being covered with whip stitch. The pick (the size of the stitch on front) is kept small, and the distance between stitches is governed by the fabric and garment needs.

b. **To finish the edge of fabrics,** simply insert the needle right to left through the edge to be covered, and draw it through. The next stitch should be fairly close to the first, with no more than 1/4" (7 mm) between stitches. You can take multiple stitches and then draw them all through, although this can collapse the edge if you are not careful. Pay attention to your tension, and do not draw up your stitches too tightly.

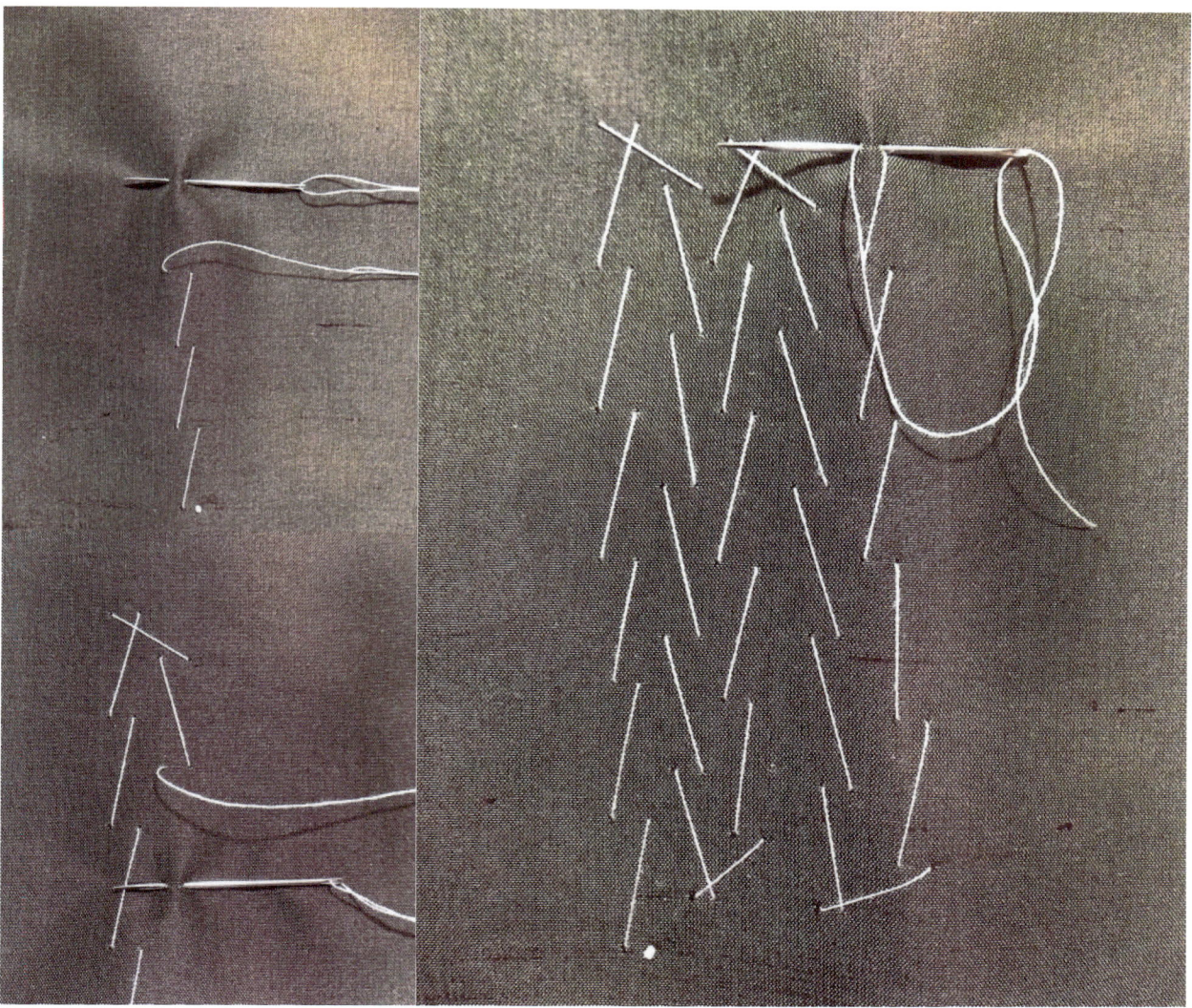

PAD STITCH AND DIAGONAL BASTING STITCH: The pad stitch and the diagonal basting stitch are the same stitch used for different purposes.

The motions used for the pad stitch and the diagonal basting stitch are the same as those used for the whip stitch, except that the stitches are worked on the flat surface of the fabric rather than on an edge. Like all basting, it is meant to hold multiple layers of fabric together. Diagonal baste is nearly always removed after it has served its purpose.

Pad Stitch: Pad stitching is the process of stitching multiple rows of diagonal basting, worked consecutively and without turning the work. When the end of the line is reached, you just move over to the location of the next row and work opposite direction. Most often, pad stitching is worked with the needle passing right to left and the line of stitching going up and down creating the characteristic "crows foot" appearance. Pad stitching is rarely seen on the outside of the work, but all the same, great care should be given to evenness and regularity of this stitch. It is most often used to sculpt layers of fabric into a curved shape permanently. In the garment presented here, pad stitching shows through on the outside of the garment only in the work of shaping the collar. It should appear as a series of offset dots.

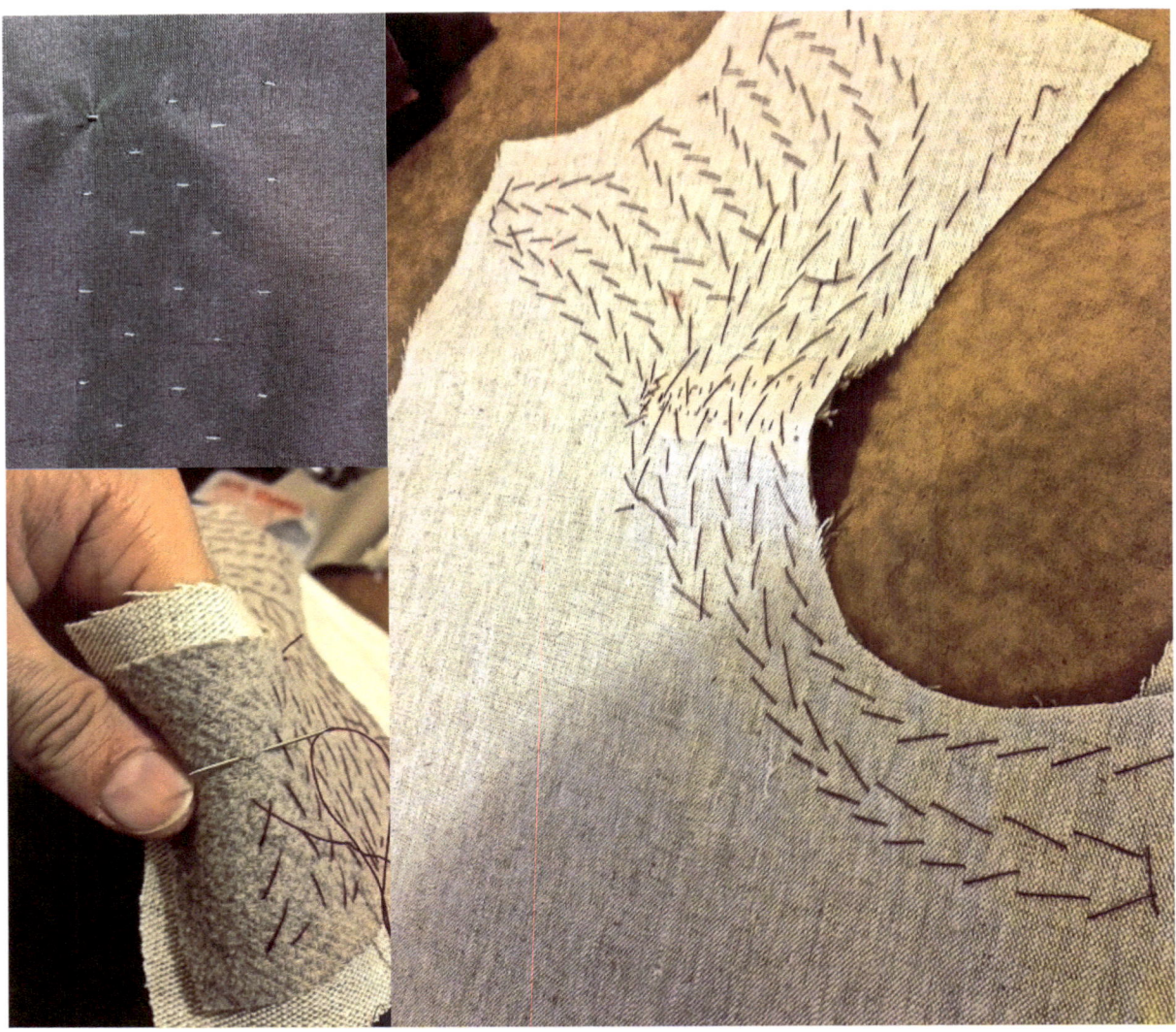

Simply learning how to execute the stitch is only half the battle. You must also train your hands to sculpt the layers intentionally as you work. In practice, rolling the fabric over the hand as you work row after row is enough to create subtle shaping. It can also be used more dramatically, as we will do for the shoulder and armhole area of the body canvas of the garment presented here.

Pad Stitching to Apply Padding and Stuffing

Pad stitching can also be used to apply fabric padding and stuffing, as the name suggests. The main difference between the stitches used for applying stuffing and those used to apply a padding fabric is the way in which the different rows are worked. In *offset pad stitching*, used when adding a layer of fabric as padding, your stitches create the aforementioned crow's foot pattern.

In contrast, *parallel pad stitching* is used to secure stuffing between layers of fabric. It creates a nice little square grid when done correctly, and is almost never used for any other purpose.

Men's padded doublet (T&D.180-1900). Courtesy of the Victoria & Albert Museum, London. © Drea Leed.

The padded lining shown to the left is quilted silk from a circa 1620 doublet. We are looking at the wearer's left armhole, with the garment front on the right side of the photograph. Observe the little gusset in the armhole; as we will be incorporating this feature into our doublet as well, though in a slightly different manner. The linings on the right are from a suit I made for a client in 2013. They are quilted in the same way.

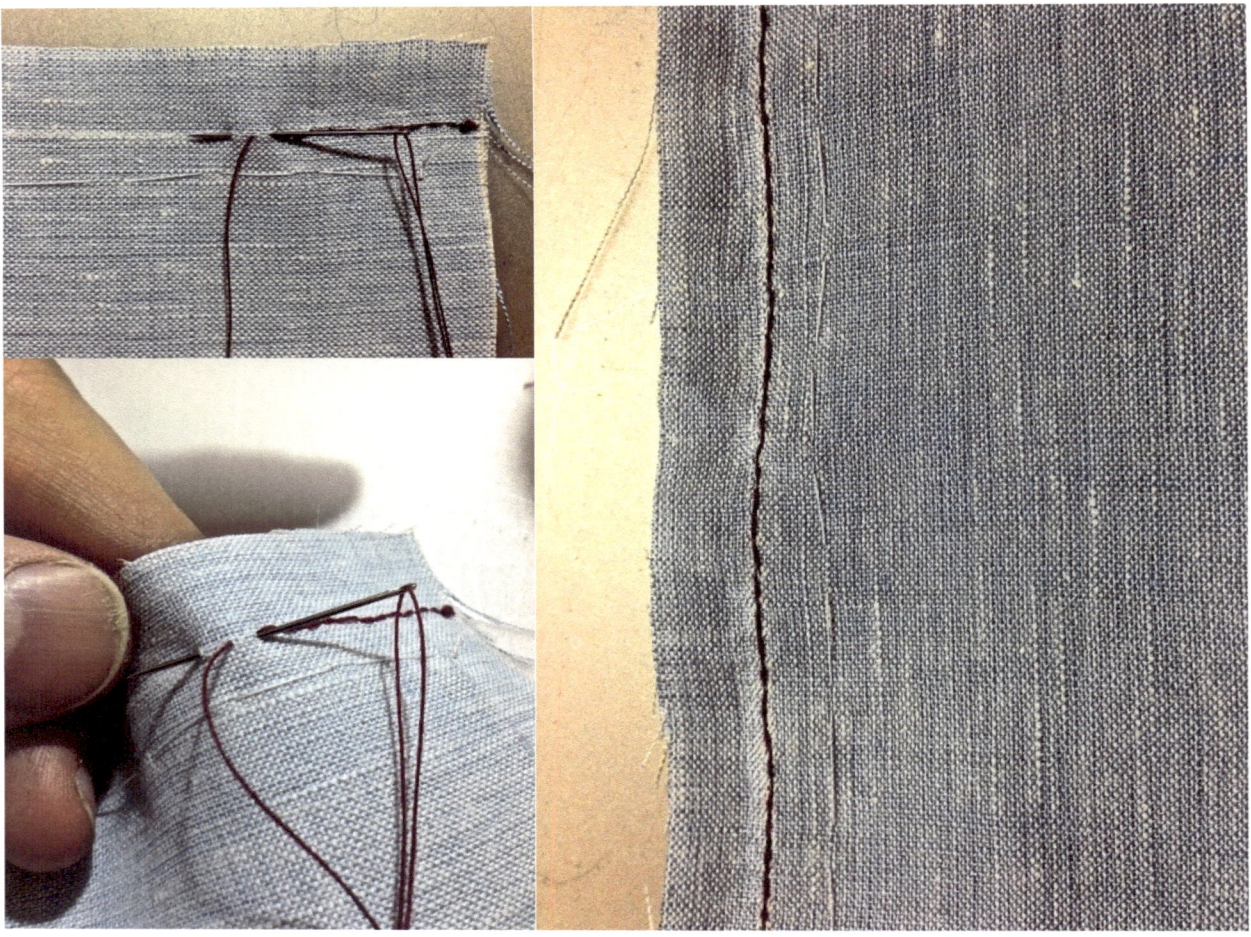

BACK STITCH: The back stitch is actually a family of stitches, all of which use the same backward stitching motion. In most cases, the distance between the needle's entry and exit points in the fabric is roughly twice the length of each finished stitch. (Both left photos)

The back stitch is an extremely strong stitch, good for seams that need to withstand abuse and strain. As it also requires the thread to be entirely drawn through the fabric with each stitch, abrading and damaging the thread more quickly, shorter lengths of thread should be used. Keeping the thread short also means that you can draw the thread through the fabric and begin the next stitch very quickly, whereas a long thread means a longer draw and longer arm motion. This wastes time and energy and increases the likelihood of a thread snarl, which will waste even *more* time in the untangling.

The back stitch is also used for top stitching in some surviving garments. This top stitching has an appearance very similar to the stitching seen today on the seams of blue jeans.

After exiting, the needle is re-inserted along the seam at a point *behind* the previous exit point of the thread—usually into the exit point of the previous stitch—and then comes out of the fabric ahead of it. This technique makes the stitch resemble machine stitching from the right side of the work. It does not resemble machine work on the wrong side.

PICK STITCH: This stitch has many uses. In the sample garment created for this book, it is used as a decorative element to stitch seams open after pressing. It is also used to install the linings in most parts of the garment.

At its most basic, it is a variety of back stitch in which you move only a tiny distance backwards before re-inserting the needle, rather than re-inserting it at the previous stitch's exit point.

The photo on the bottom left shows the back side of both the back stitch and the pick stitch. Both of these stitches, when used together, produce an extremely strong seam that will stand up to the toughest abuse.

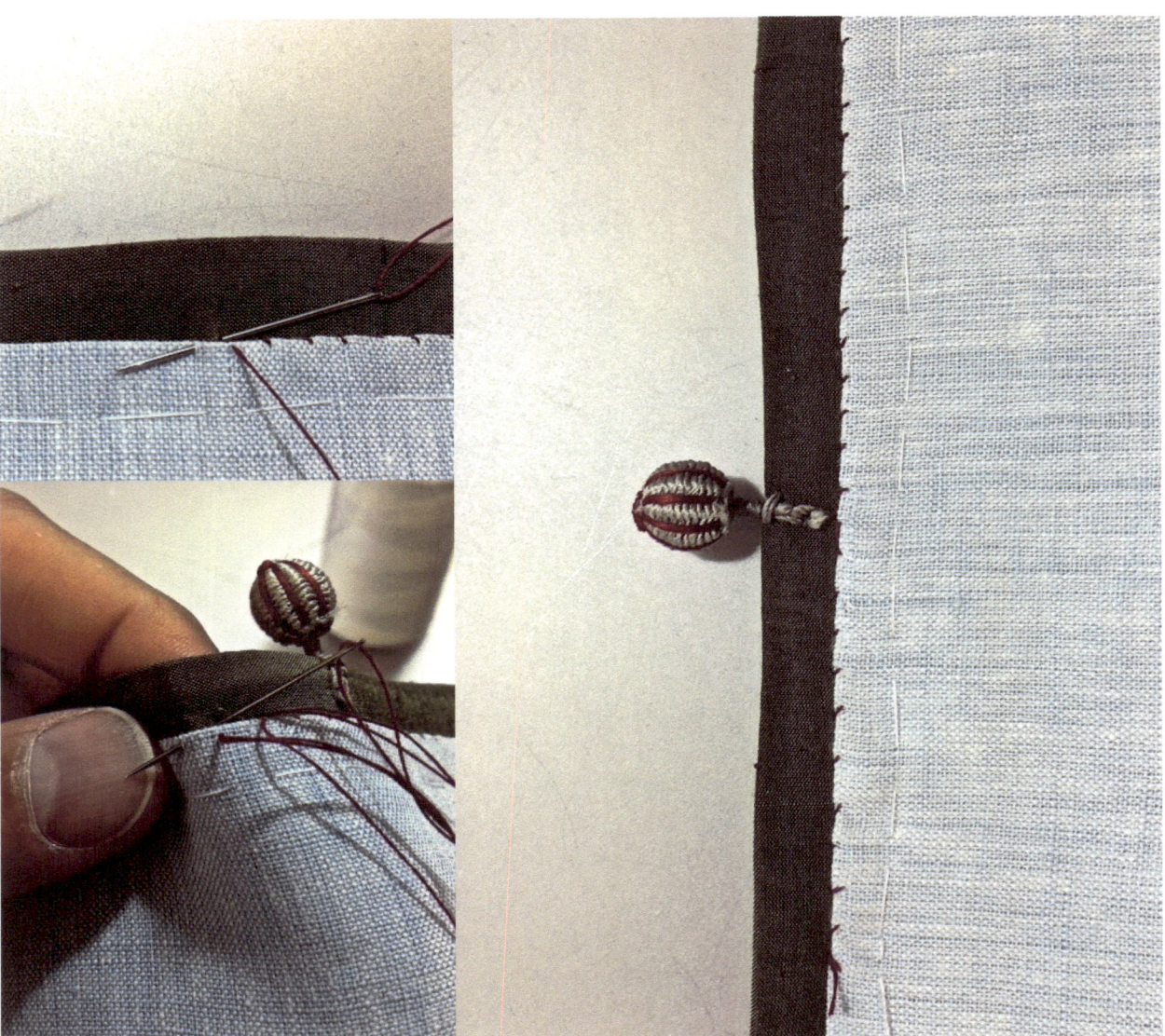

FELLING STITCH: The felling stitch is used mostly for installing linings or stitching seams that are sewn from the outside of a garment. Its movement is similar to the whip stitch. It differs from whip stitch in that the needle travels to the next location between the layers of fabric instead of on the surface. This stitch can be found in nearly all extant items of tailored clothing. Its ubiquity and usefulness cannot be overstated. If there is one stitch that you should learn above all others...this is it.

In the sample garment set forth in chapter 5, this stitch is used to finish bindings, hem linings, finish armholes and attach the collar lining. It is also used to stitch the side-back and shoulder/ neck seams. It is very strong even though it is remarkably simple in its execution. Make this stitch second nature and you will be able make even the most basic clothing look professional.

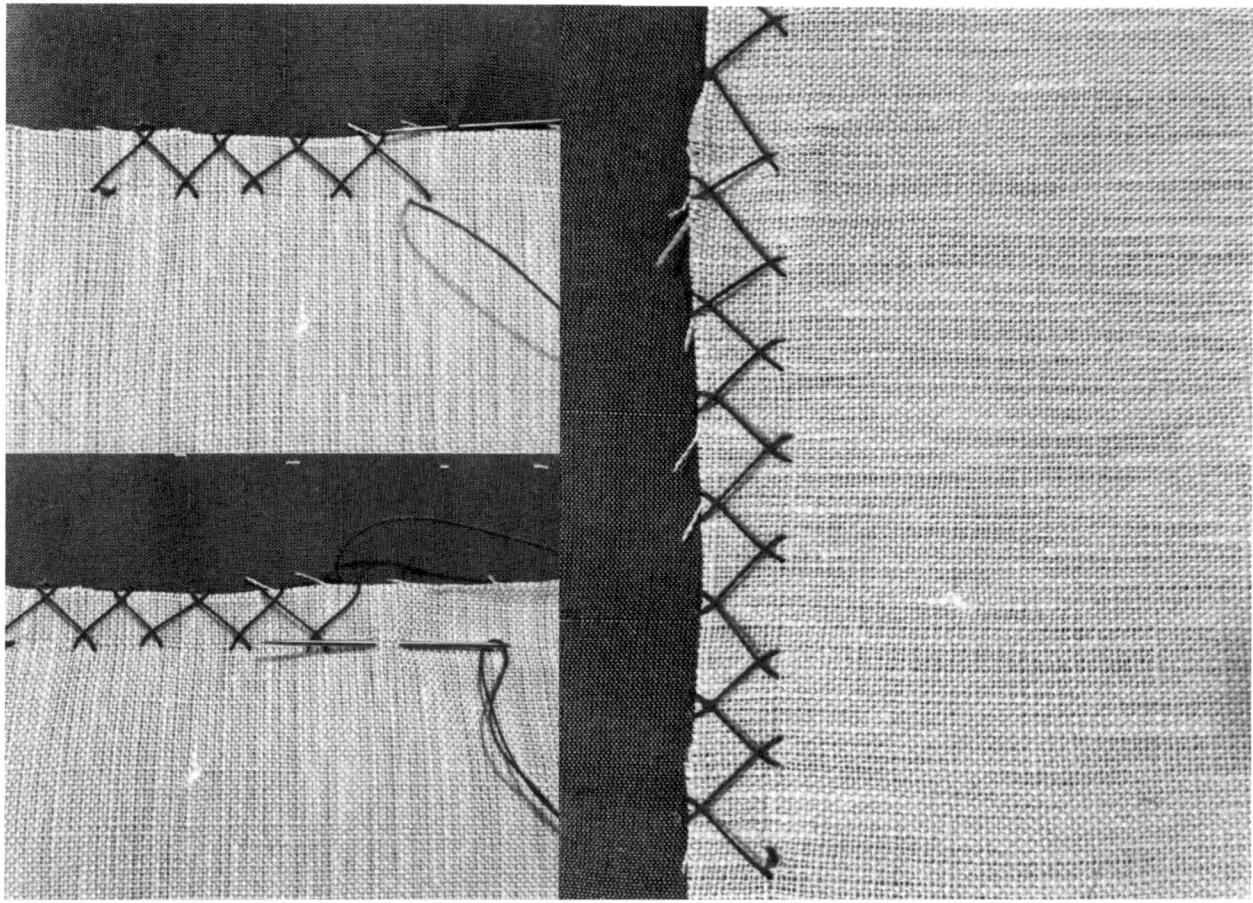

CROSS STITCH: The cross stitch is considered a relatively modern stitch. There are a few examples of its use in 17th century clothing; Zimmerman, in her analysis of the Gronignen excavation *Textiel in Context*, describes it as the "flannelsteek" (flannel stitch) used to finish the gores on hose.

The direction of this stitch creates the characteristic crossing pattern. The needle passes from right to left, alternating between the upper and lower layers of fabric. The direction of the line of stitching is from left to right, in the opposite direction of the needle's movement. In the sample garment of this book, we use this stitch to secure the silk facings in place behind the buttonholes before the holes are made.

The modern tailor often uses this stitch to hem trousers and skirts and to tack down the edges of fabric while simultaneously covering the edge with stitches as seen above. It is also used to stitch twill tapes and tailored canvases into modern coats in places where the canvas does not extend into the seam allowance. It is typically used inside garments and is not seen. However, when used to hem trousers or skirts, it is an attractive stitch that appears crisp and professional.

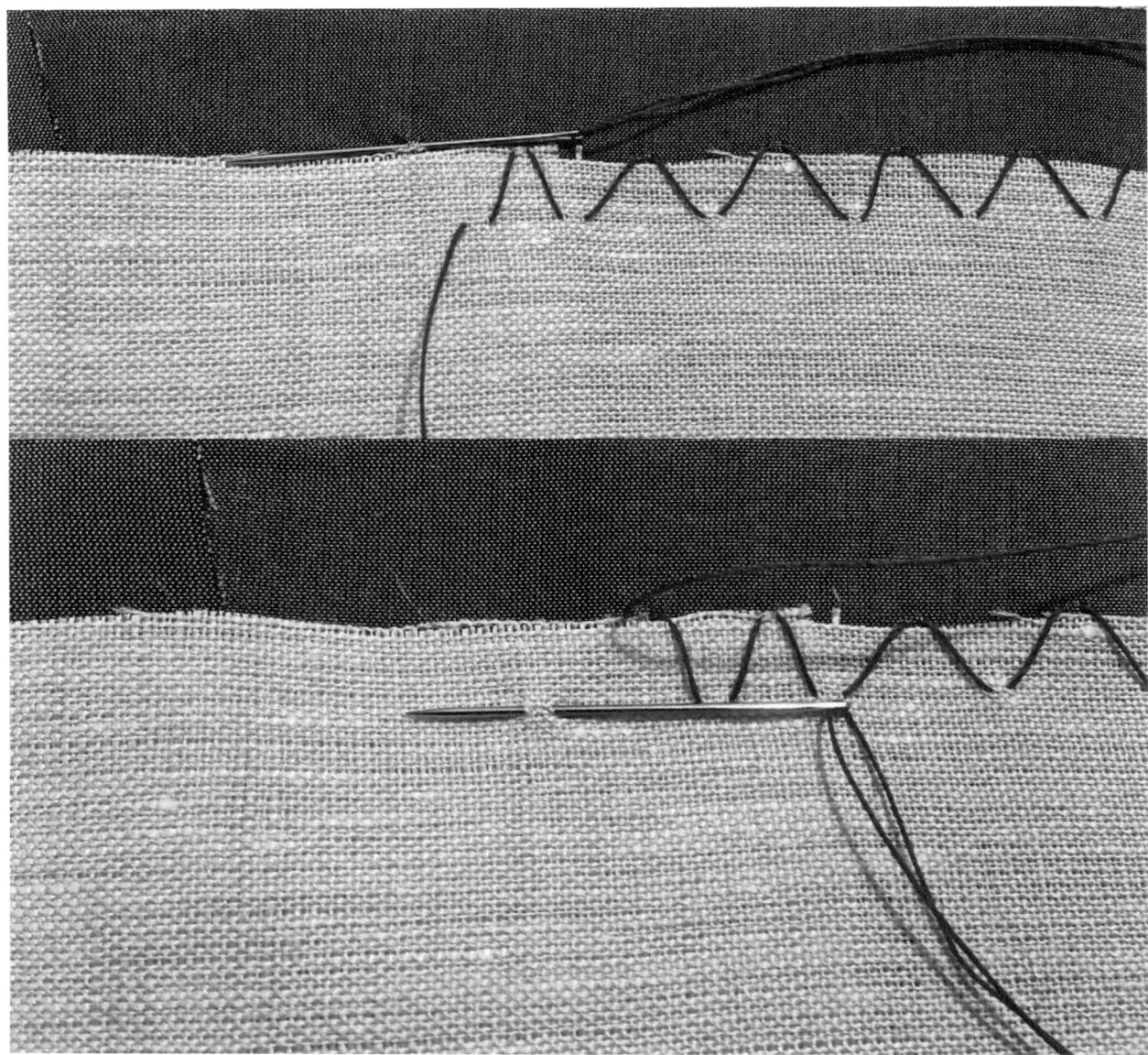

CATCH STITCH: The catch stitch serves the same function as the cross stitch, and is often substituted for the cross stitch where speed is necessary. It is faster to execute than the cross stitch, due to the direction of stitching. Like the cross stitch, it is rarely found in 16th and 17th century garments, but is handy when you need the layers of fabric to have slightly more freedom of movement.

The needle alternates between upper and lower layers in the same manner as the cross stitch, except that the direction of the work is right to left, rather than left to right. The change in directions creates the difference in the appearance of the finished stitch.

Buttonholes

One of the most challenging aspects of garment finishing is learning to make a perfect hand-sewn buttonhole. Many novice clothiers struggle with them for years. The *only* way to conquer the buttonhole is through repetition and practice, and even I, as a seasoned professional, still have moments when they frustrate me.

The stitches we see on the surface of a buttonhole are only the outer-most layer. There are several steps to creating a buttonhole that looks clean and attractive and will withstand the rough wear caused by repeated pushing and pulling of a button through it.

Brown wool doublet, c. 1625-1635 (T. 29-1938).

Men's quilted satin doublet and breeches (347&A-1905).

Men's red silk doublet, 1615-1620 (T. 147-1937).

Photos Courtesy of the Victoria and Albert Museum, London ©Mark Goodman.

Here are a few examples of buttonholes on surviving doublets. As you can see, they are quite utilitarian. The buttonholes on extant garments are, from a modern perspective, rather inexpertly worked; they may appear inconsistent up close, as in these photographs, but look neater from a distance. Despite their imperfect quality, these are some of the best constructed examples I've seen on extant garments. Of course, they've survived for 500 years, so it is safe to say that they were made to last.

The following steps describe my preferred method for make a buttonhole. Every tailor makes them differently. There are many variations of buttonholes appearing on surviving clothing, but they all share specific elements in common:

1. There are at least two and sometimes three layers of stitching.

2. There is often, but not always, a padding or support thread running under the stitches to keep the stitches neat and to prevent the hole from stretching over time.

3. The hole must be first cut and then stitched.

Boy's pink taffeta doublet and breeches, c. 1640 (T.4-1922).

Men's red silk doublet, 1615-1620 (T.147-1937).

Photos Courtesy of the Victoria and Albert Museum, London ©Drea Leed

4. There is nearly always some type of bar-tack at the ends to keep the buttonhole from tearing open. Rarely, as in the lower left photograph above, one will fine buttonholes with a bar at one end and a rounded appearance at the other. Neatness doesn't seem to be a top priority.

5. Tailor's buttonholes are always worked from the OUTSIDE of the garment so great care must be taken with their execution as they are quite visible.

The supplies that are needed are shown in the photo above, to the right. Moving clockwise, we have:

Beeswax

Weak white basting thread

Regular sewing thread in a color matching the garment

Buttonhole twist or #5 perle cotton for the final stitching (it can be a matching or contrasting color)

Sharp pointed scissors

Marking chalk

A size 5 or 6 between needle

A good thimble

A ruler (optional; I don't usually use one.)

When learning how to make buttonholes, first prepare a practice swatch. I usually use one or two layers of canvas between two layers of silk. For beginners, I recommend starting with one layer of canvas and working your way up to two, as learning can be more difficult with too many bulky layers.

Once the layers are stacked together, I usually overlock them or baste them together around the edges.

1. Using the chalk and the ruler, mark a line that's 1/2" (1.2 cm) from the edge where you want to put the buttonholes.

2. Measure the distance between the holes. I nearly always measure with my fingers. For many buttons, use one finger between marks; for fewer, use two, three, or even four. I prefer this method, as it is remarkably consistent as well as convenient—you're never without your measuring tool.

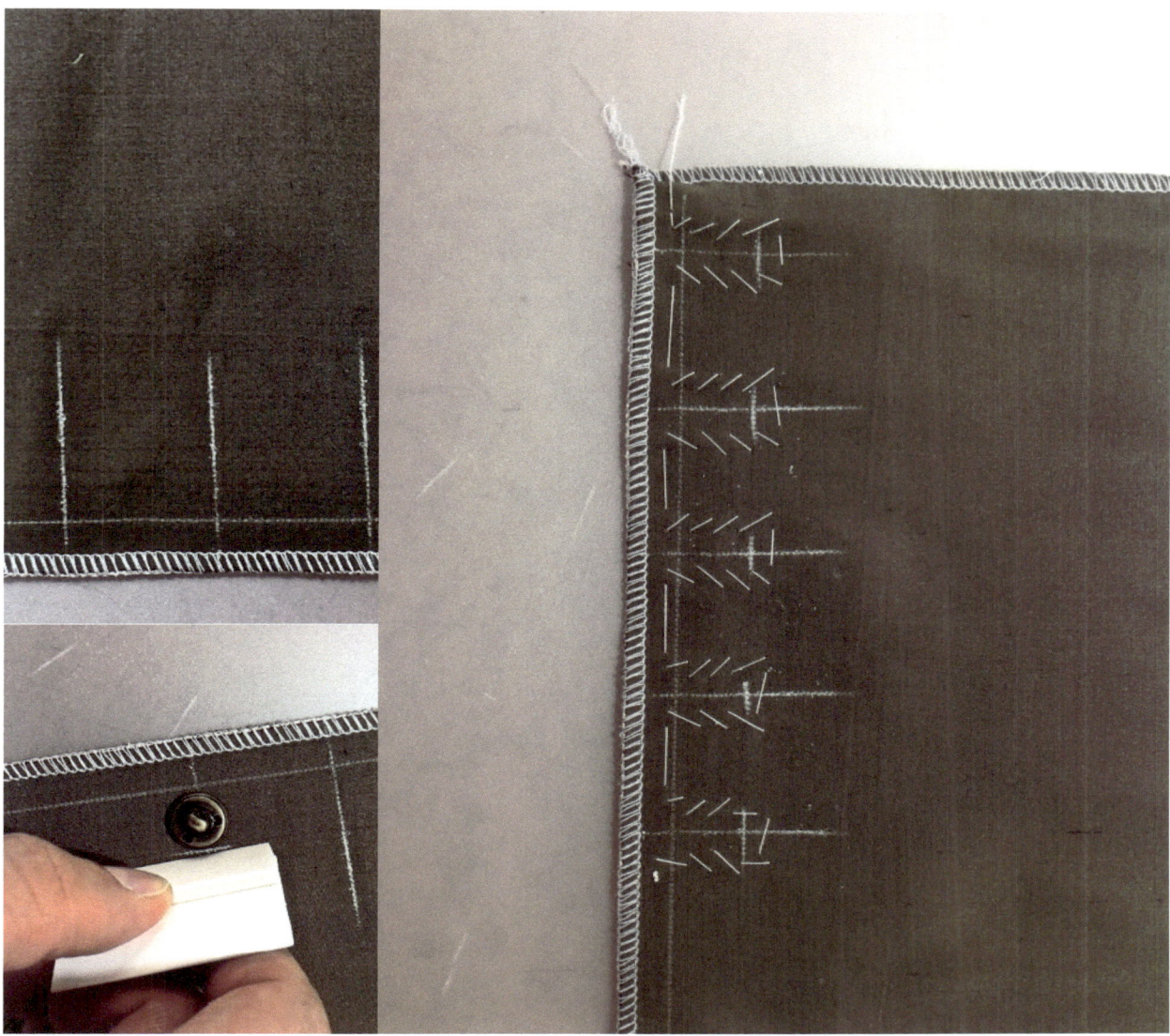

3. Use the button itself to measure the width of the hole. For round ball buttons, add 1/8" (3mm). This will make the spherical buttons much easier to push through the buttonhole.

4. With weak white basting thread, work a diagonal basting stitch (pg. 52) around the holes as shown above to the right. The stitches should be no more than 1/4" (7 mm) away from the cutting mark where the buttonhole will be, and no closer than 1/8" (3 mm). Keep these stitches firm and small, as they will be holding the layers of fabric firmly together while you work. There will be quite a bit of fabric handling while stitching the buttonholes, and this preparation prevents the fabric from shifting and making it harder to catch the layers on the inside of the garment.

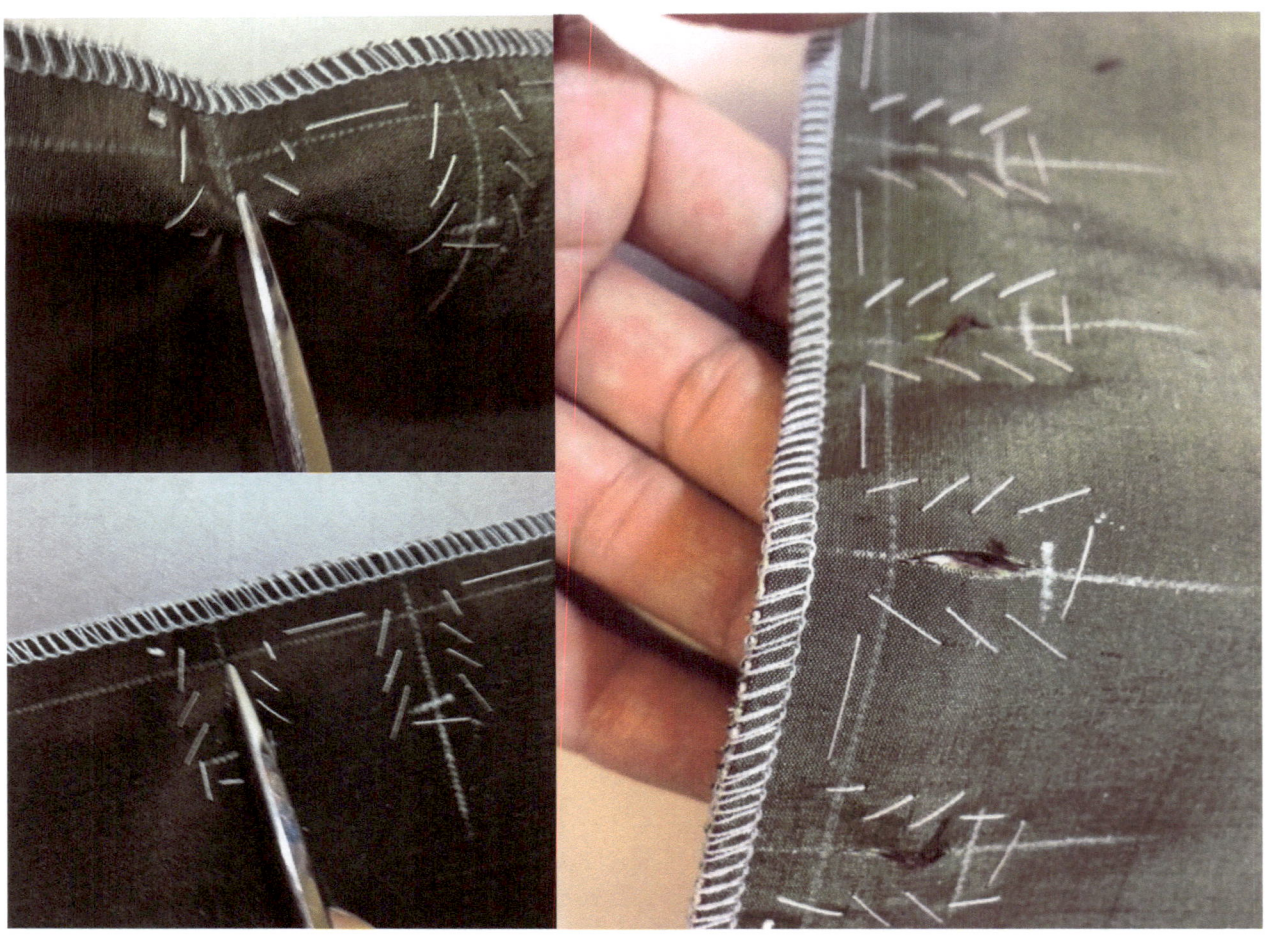

5. Cut each hole open with the sharp scissors. First, fold the fabric and make a small clip on the line, then use the snips to cut the hole to the end marks. Make sure you cut all the way to the ends, or your buttonhole may end up too small.

When I make a large number of buttonholes on a single garment, I find it very helpful to do the same step on all of them at the same time, so that the basting and cutting of all the holes happens together, followed by the remaining steps.

Grouping the tasks in this manner speeds progress and helps you master skills more quickly, as repeating one motion multiple times creates muscle memory, training your body in the right movements.

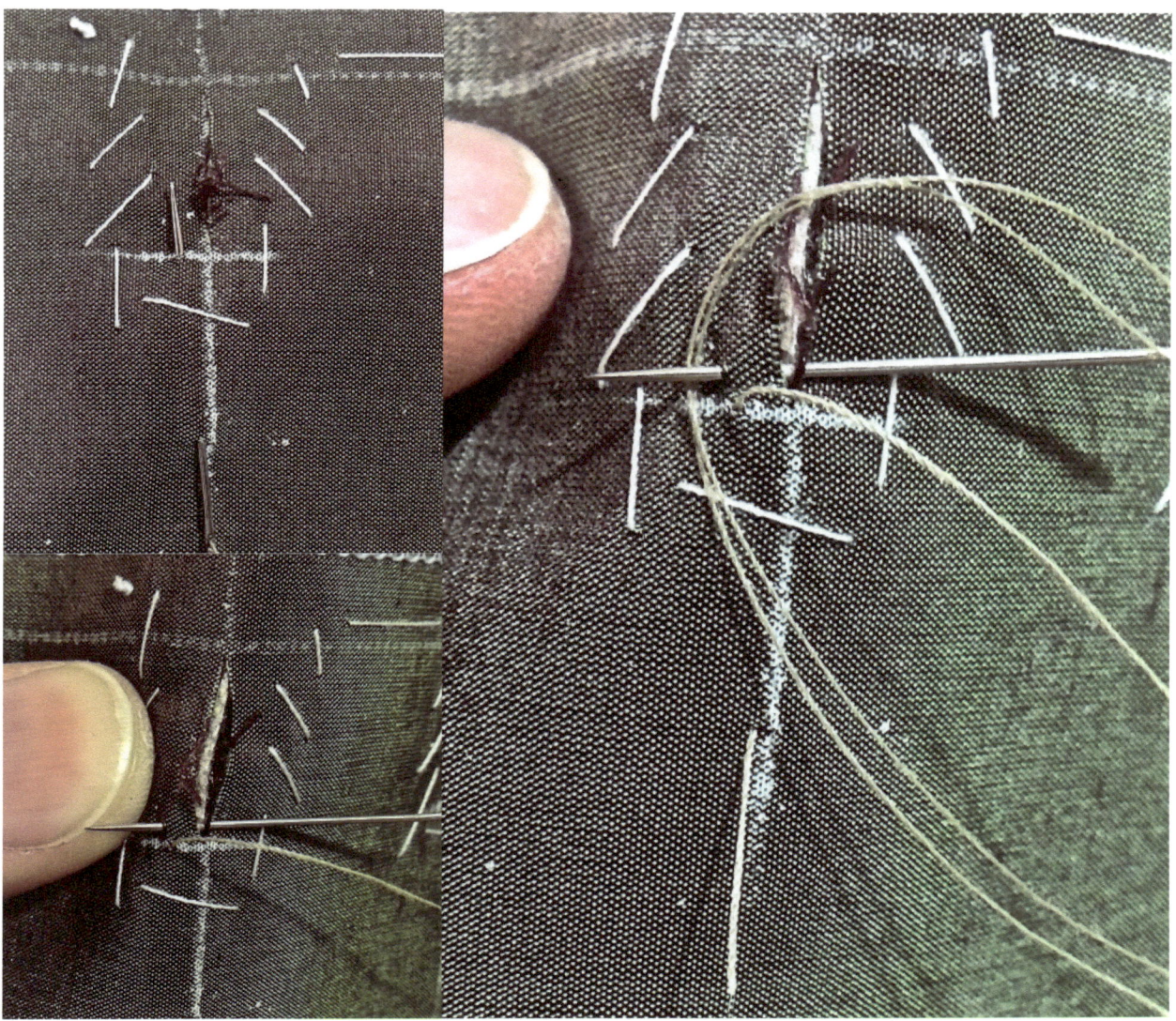

6. Next, cut off a workable length of the regular sewing thread and pull it along the beeswax. After waxing, take it to the iron and press it between two pieces of paper or scrap fabric to melt the wax into the thread. This important step binds the wax to the thread, preventing it from flaking onto the surface of the fabric and possibly leaving stains when the fabric is ironed.

7. No knots are used when making buttonholes. To begin, therefore, we insert the needle a short distance away from the end of the hole and leave a short tail about 1/2" (12mm) long.

8. The next line of stitches are called blanket stitches. It is a stitch that is usually mistaken for a buttonhole stitch. To make this stitch, insert the needle right to left, UPWARD through the layers from back to front as shown. Take the thread coming from the HEAD of the needle and wrap it COUNTERCLOCKWISE under the needle's point. Draw up the stitch and pull it snug, but not unnecessarily tight.

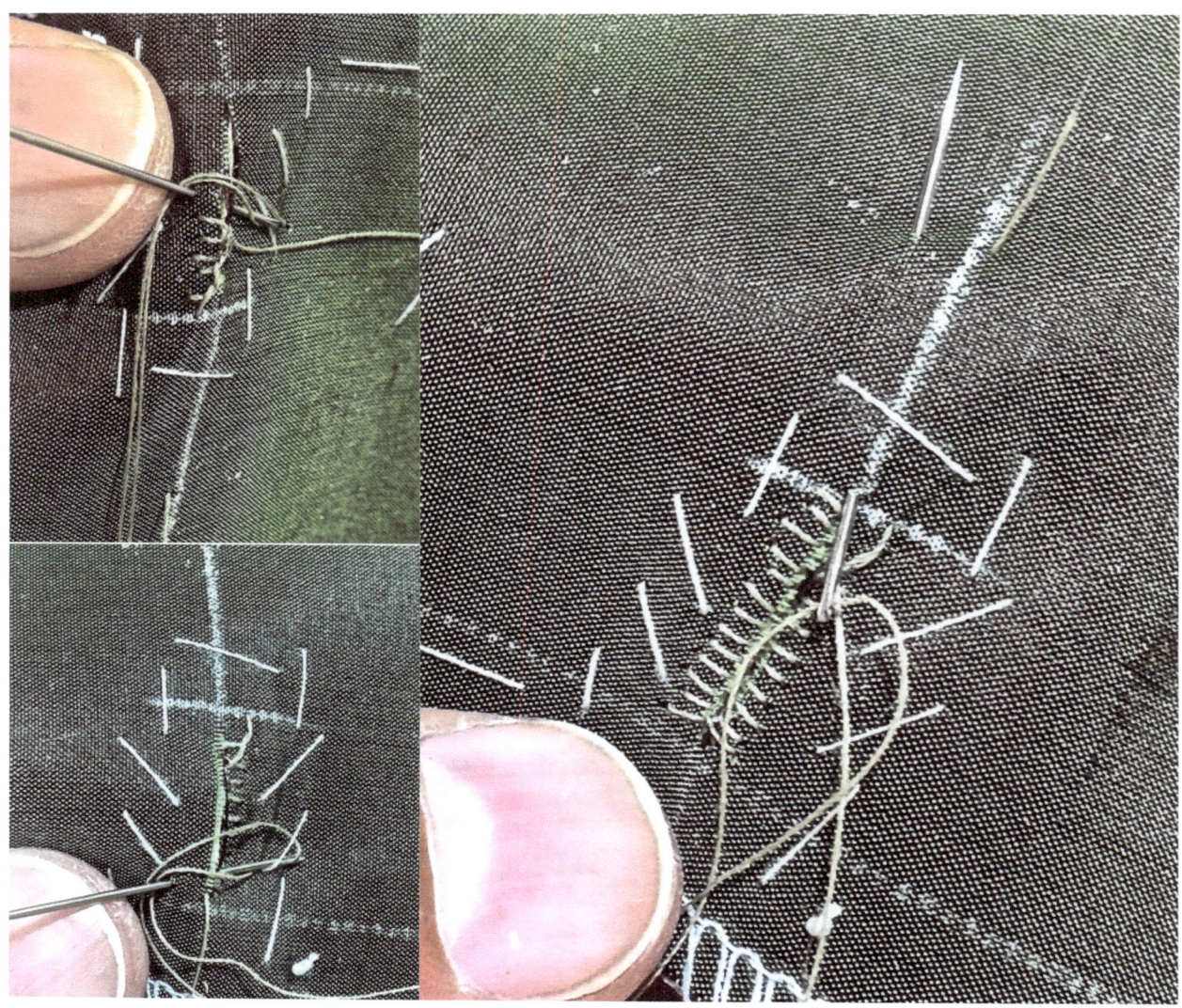

The next stitch will be made about 1/16" (1.2mm) away from the previous one. Continue in this manner until the opposite end of the hole is reached. Without doing anything at the end of the hole, simply turn the work and continue in the same manner along the opposite side of the hole. When the end is reached, tunnel the needle between the layers to a point some distance away from the hole, pull the needle out, draw snug and snip the end. The tension will allow the thread to self-bury. Repeat the same step on all remaining buttonholes before moving on to the next step.

Although modern couture hand-sewing and embroidery techniques avoid knots, knotted threads were the norm in extant garments of this era. In the case of buttonholes, however, the presence of a knot can create a wear point near the hole that might lead to premature degradation of the hard work you've put in to make a beautiful buttonhole.

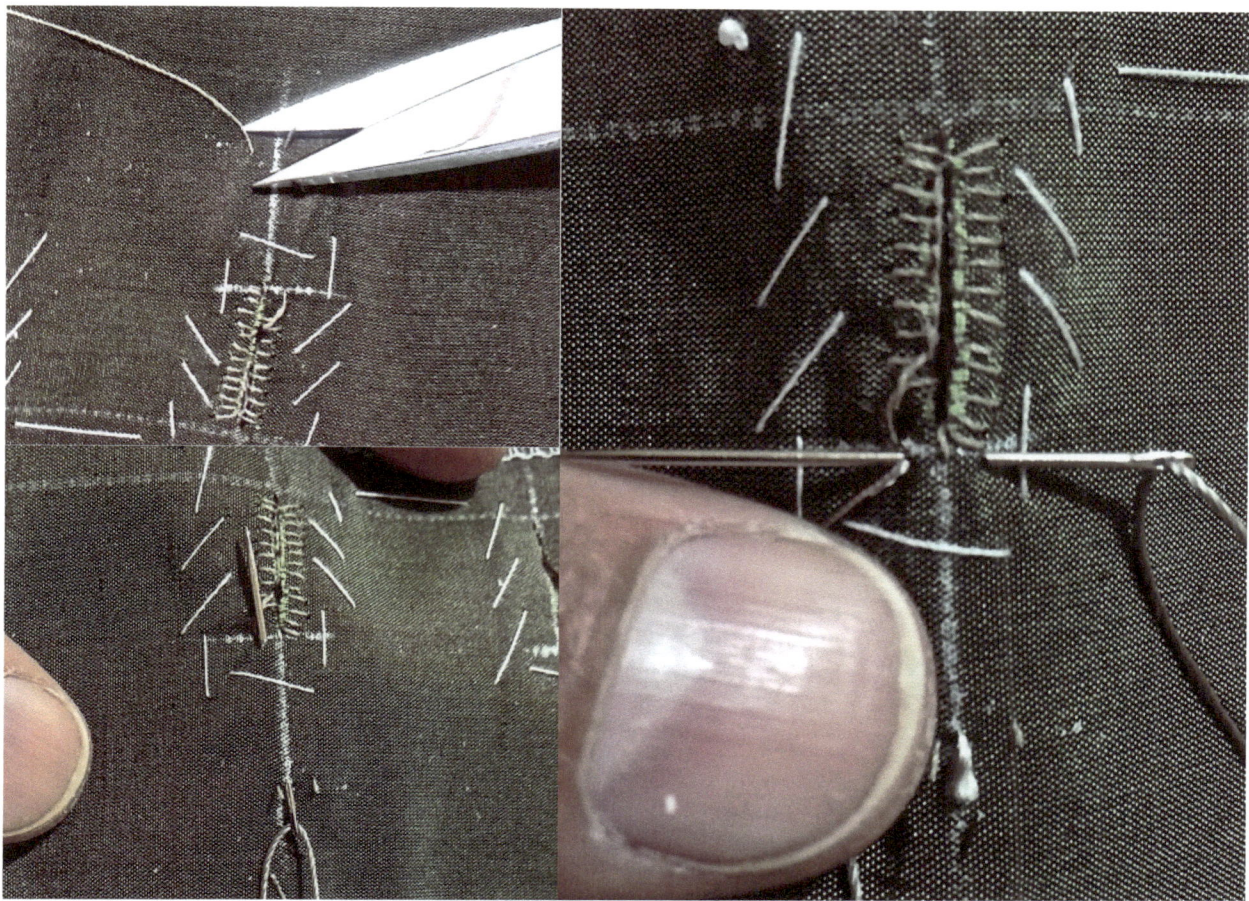

9. The next step is called "stranding the hole." In modern keyhole-style buttonholes with one rounded end, this is done with a separate, heavier gimp thread called a "choker" thread. The choker keeps the finished buttonhole from stretching with use. Alternately, you can use a more old-fashioned method, where the hole is stranded with long stitches that span the full width of the hole and cross the ends twice for each hole so that there are two strands lying along the cut. These threads serve both to preserve the size of the hole over time, and to give it a little padding. This padding shows off the shine of the silk and makes the stitches appear more even. These stitches should also be snug, but not excessively tight. Pull them too tightly and you will end up with a buttonhole that is too small.

Take an arm-length of buttonhole thread, and press it to set the twist in the thread. **Do not wax buttonhole thread**, as the waxing tends to remove the thread's sheen and diminish the fine appearance of the completed buttonhole.

Begin the same way as we did with the previous round of stitching: insert the needle some distance away from the hole, and have it exit where we need to begin stitching. To secure the thread, make one stitch across the end of the cut buttonhole. The next stitch is taken across the opposite end of the buttonhole followed by a stitch across the end where you began. Repeat so that there are two strands along each side of the hole. Do not pull these stitches very tight or it will distort the hole and the result may be too small.

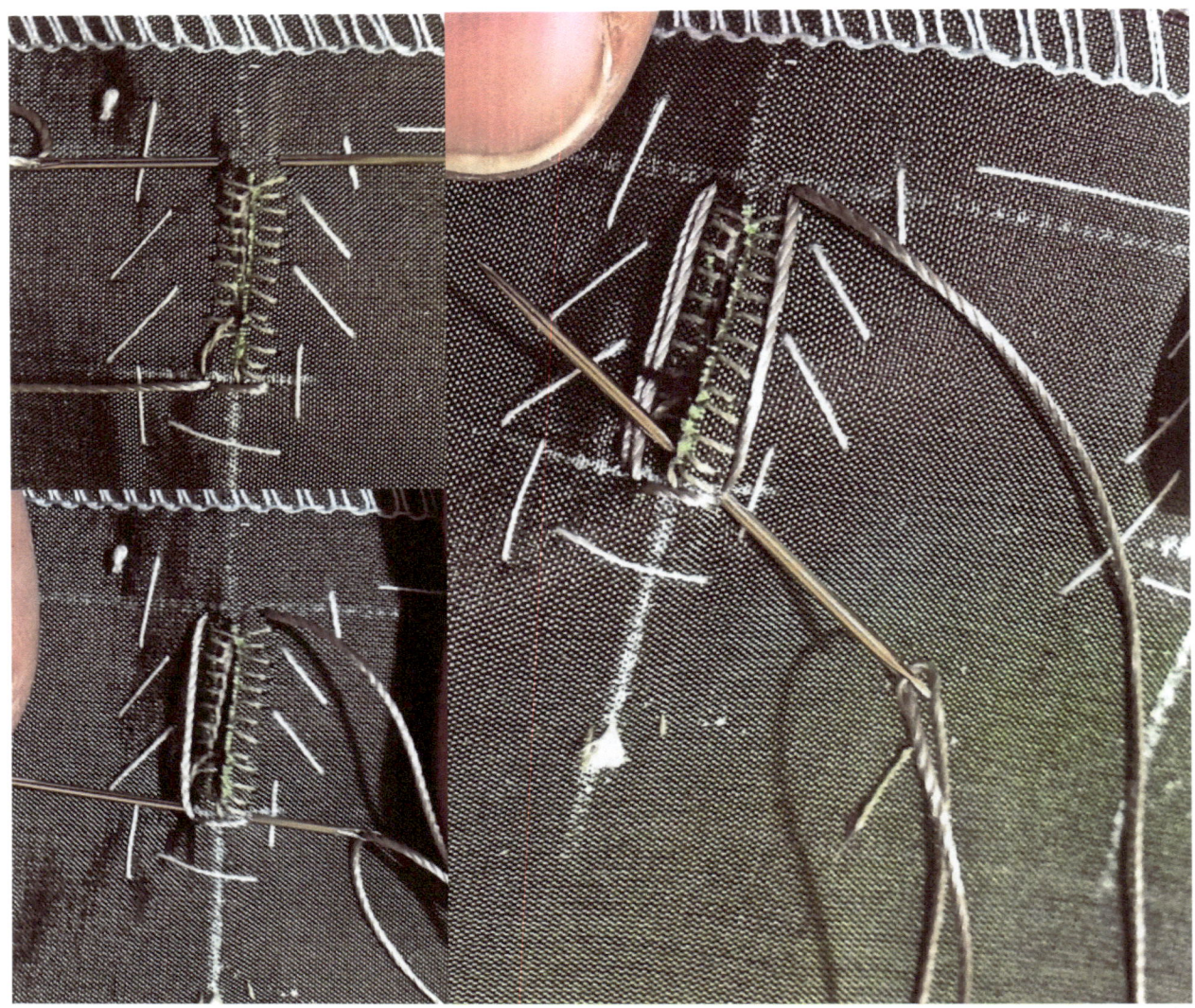

As you finish the final stitch across the hole, the needle should exit up through the cut as shown in the photograph to the right, above. This will put the thread in the perfect place to work the first stitch without distorting the stitch.

By now, you will have realized just how important those initial basting stitches are for keeping the layers together as the hole is worked. Without them, you would be unable to catch the inner layers of fabric as well and the buttonhole would start to look a little sloppy. I trust that at this point, you've also realized just how much practice it takes to make a buttonhole look neat and even; but if you haven't, just wait for the next step.

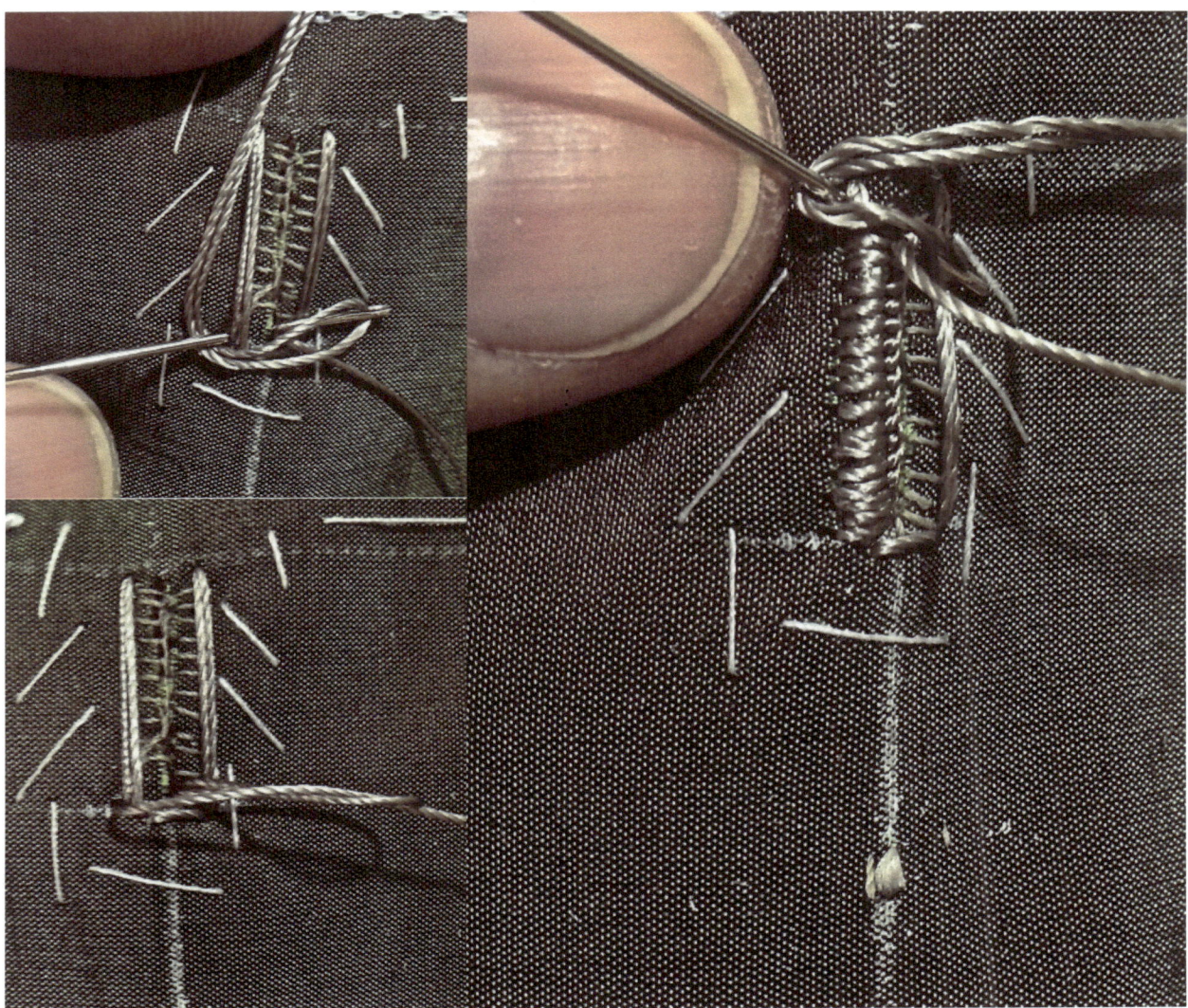

10. Now we begin the actual buttonhole stitch, a sturdy knotted stitch that tailors have used for centuries and which takes practice to master. It is similar in structure to the blanket stitch that we used earlier, but there is an extra twist at the top producing an extra little "purl" stitch which fills in the gap of the cut.

To begin, we insert the needle exactly as we did for the blanket stitch round. The BIG difference is that the thread from the head of needle is wrapped CLOCKWISE and under the needle tip. (See the photograph at the top left, above.) When you draw up the thread to tighten the stitch, always pull so that the stitch stays very flat the fabric and the "head" of the stitch ends up right in the center of the hole.

Continue these buttonhole stitches along the first side. This round's stitches must be very close together; not so close as to crowd the stitches, but close enough to present a smooth and satiny appearance. The goal in the end is to have the earlier layers of stitching hidden.

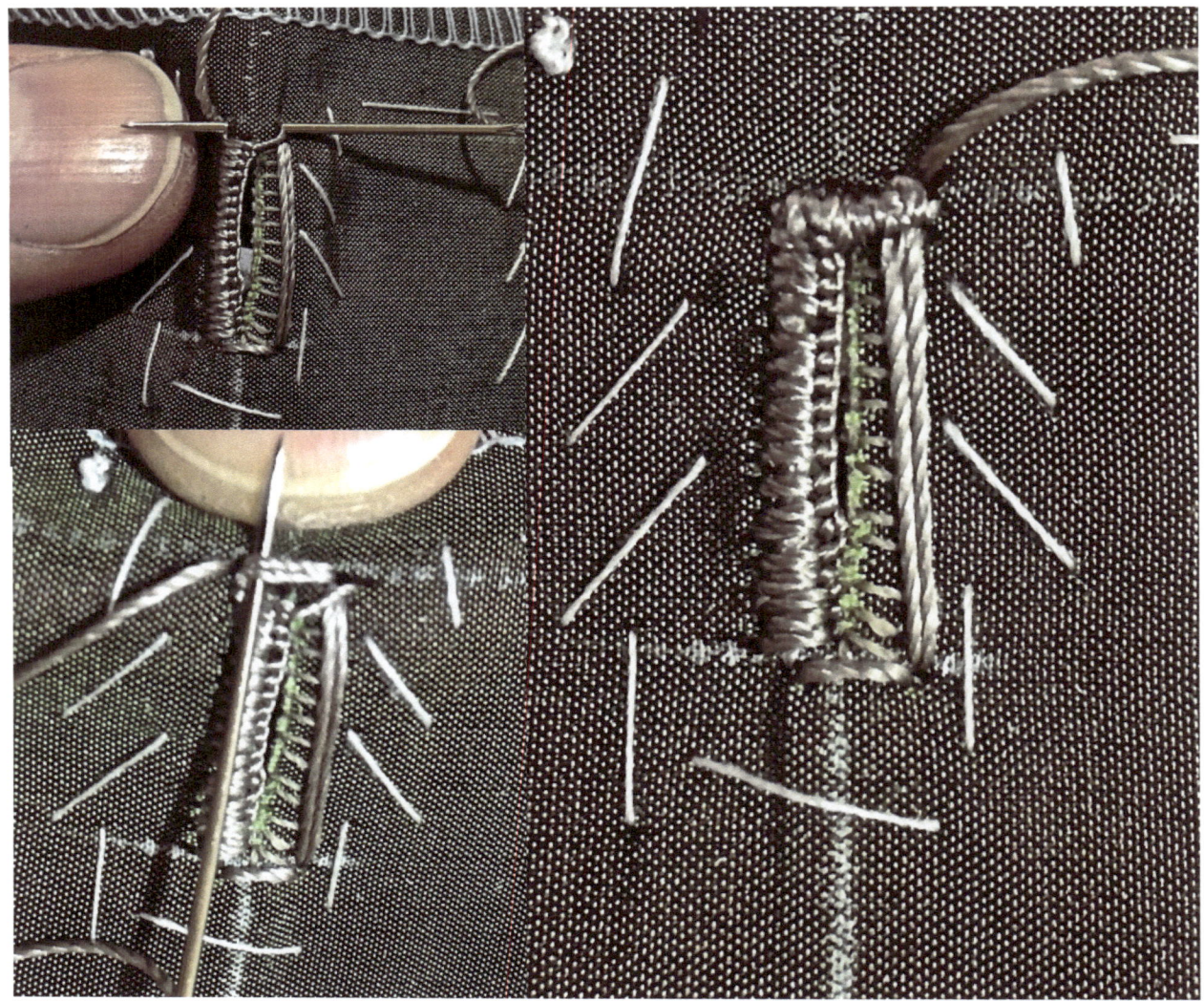

11. Once you're done with the first half of the buttonhole, make a bar tack at the end spanning the entire end of the buttonhole. Begin by taking two stitches across the end of the buttonhole. Next, turn the work and begin to make tiny whip stitches over the two strands of stitching you've just made. With each whip stitch, make sure that you catch some of the threads on the surface of the fabric. When you reach the center of the bar, take two stitches which go right into the cut and up from the back (upper right photo). These two stitches secure the end of the buttonhole, and add strength to one of its most major stress points. After these two stitches are taken, continue to whip stitch over the bar, making sure to catch small threads from the fabric beneath. When you reach the end of the bar, plunge the needle into the fabric at the end of the bar and exit through the cut, just as was done at the beginning of the hole.

11a. Work the second leg of the buttonhole just like the first.

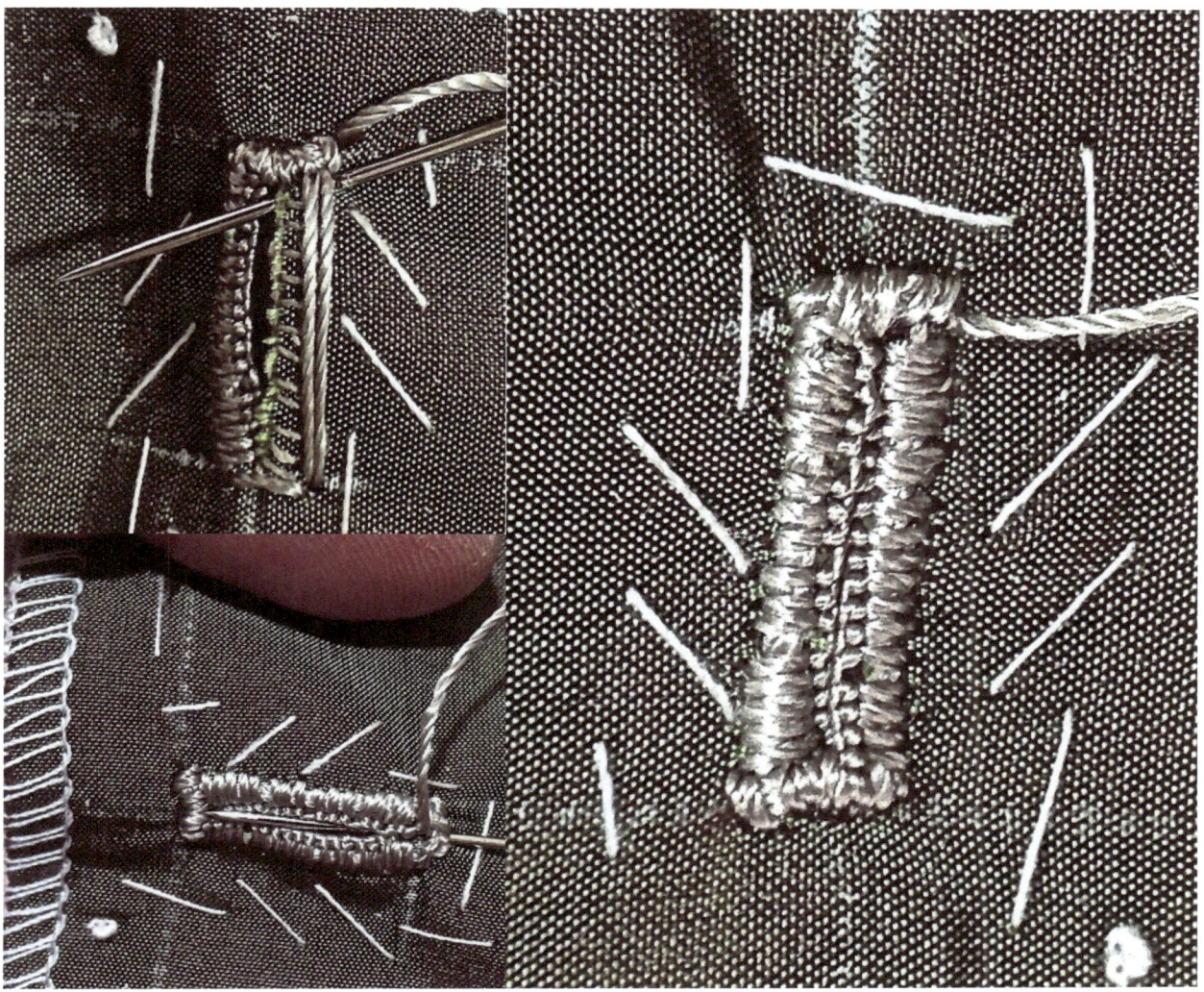

12. Once the second half of the buttonhole has been stitched, take two more bar tack stitches across the other end of the buttonhole. Whip-stitch them in the same manner as you did the previous end. Make sure to take two stitches around the bar and up through the cut when you reach the middle of the bar, and pull these two stitches rather tight.

13. As you complete the bar tack, tunnel the needle through the fabric between the layers to a point some distance away from the buttonhole. Pull the needle and thread out, pull tight and snip, again allowing the cut end of the thread to self-bury. Trim away the tail left from the start of the stranding.

14. Repeat these steps on all remaining buttonholes.

15. When all buttonholes are complete, remove the basting stitches and press well.

If you wish, you can use a piece of polished glass or bone, or even a teaspoon if you've got no other option, to lightly burnish the buttonhole. This will make the buttonhole shiner and will flatten the stitches somewhat, filling in the gaps.

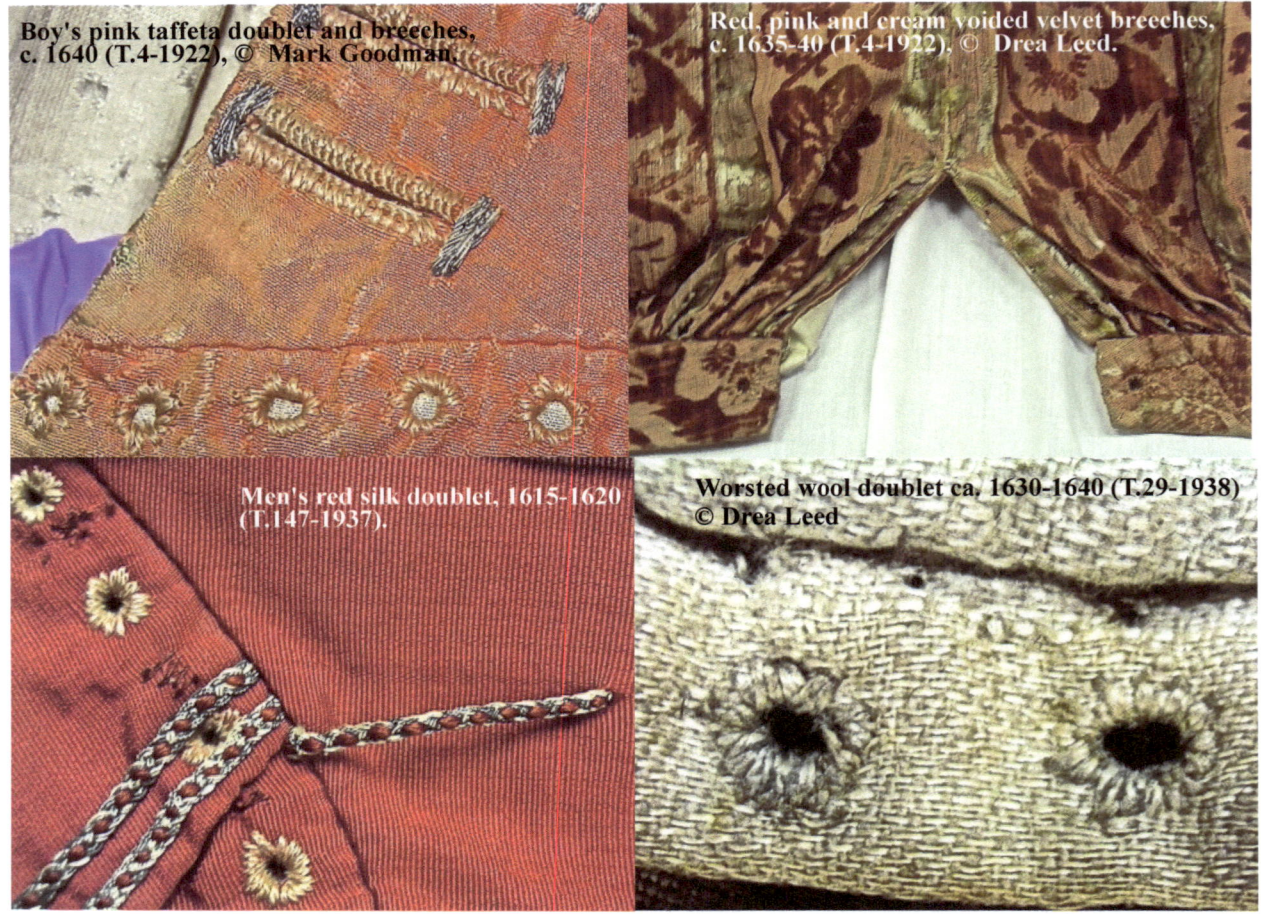

Boy's pink taffeta doublet and breeches, c. 1640 (T.4-1922), © Mark Goodman.

Red, pink and cream voided velvet breeches, c. 1635-40 (T.4-1922), © Drea Leed.

Men's red silk doublet, 1615-1620 (T.147-1937).

Worsted wool doublet ca. 1630-1640 (T.29-1938) © Drea Leed

Photos Courtesy of the Victoria and Albert Museum, London

Eyelets

Eyelets play an important role in historical clothing. In most cases they serve the purpose that zippers do in our modern clothing: they are easy to close and easy to open, but also—unlike our modern zippers—adjustable. Because they are so common in historical clothing, there are many tutorials available for creating various styles of eyelets. Some people insist on stitching them around metal rings for strength, although this type of eyelet appears in relatively few extant examples of men's clothing from this era. Others imply that they should be worked with a buttonhole stitch, in the same manner as an actual buttonhole.

In the many men's pieces that I have seen from the era, however, eyelets are quite simply made: the tailors simply stretched a hole with a tailor's stiletto and whip-stitched it open with sturdy silk thread. This simple and straightforward method is the one presented here.

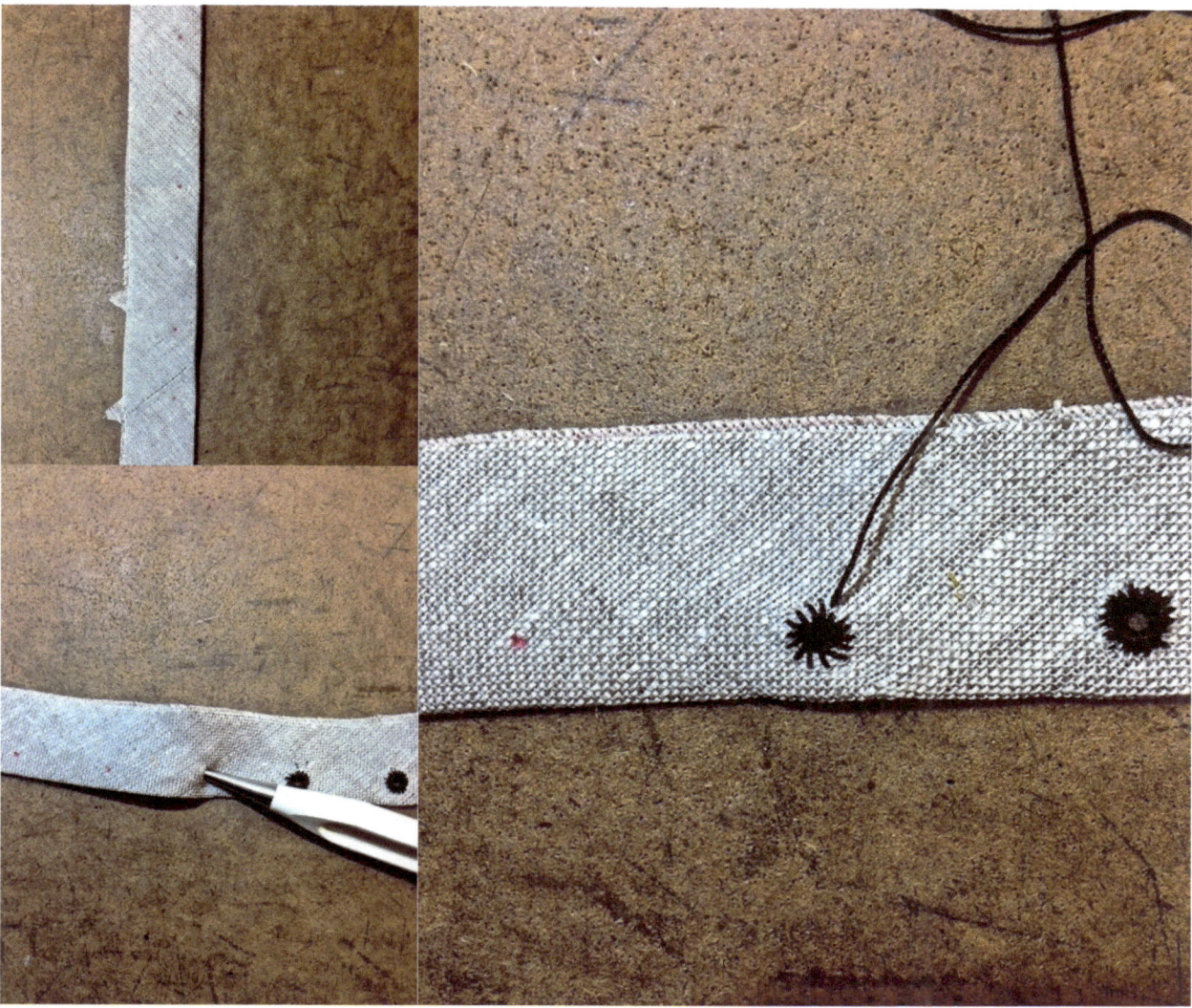

1. Mark the location of the eyelets with a marking pencil or piece of chalk.

2. Using a tailor's stiletto (a long tapered awl that you can get at your local sewing supplier), stretch a hole in your fabric. For regular tailoring, I usually just stretch the hole as large as it will go. For fine, thin fabrics and fewer layers, too much stretching can tear the fibers. In these cases I am much more careful about how large the hole is stretched.

3. Thread a needle with buttonhole twist, or #5 Perle cotton, and work a round of simple whip stitches through the hole. I use the same needle position and movement as for the buttonhole, as it is fast and feels the most natural. This first round can be fairly well spaced, as its job is simply to hold the hole open. Don't cut the thread after this first round.

4. Using the stiletto, stretch the hole a second time. Whipstitch around the hole a second time with a little more tension as you pull each stitch. Fasten off and cut the thread.

Men's red silk doublet, 1615-1620 (T.147-1937)
photo courtesy of the Victoria and Albert Musem

Buttons

These instructions create a simple wrapped bead button that effectively reproduces one of the more common buttons from the era. You will need:

1. Small wooden beads. Many people prefer to use unfinished wooden beads, although these are increasingly hard to find in the average craft store. Here I use a simple bead that's available at most craft stores.

2. Silk thread or embroidery floss to cover the buttons in one or two colors.

3. Size 5 or 6 sewing needles for working the button.

4. A small wooden knitting needle (the one shown is US size 3) for holding the bead as you work. NOTE: the size required may differ, depending on the bead you are covering.

5. Scissors

6. Thimble

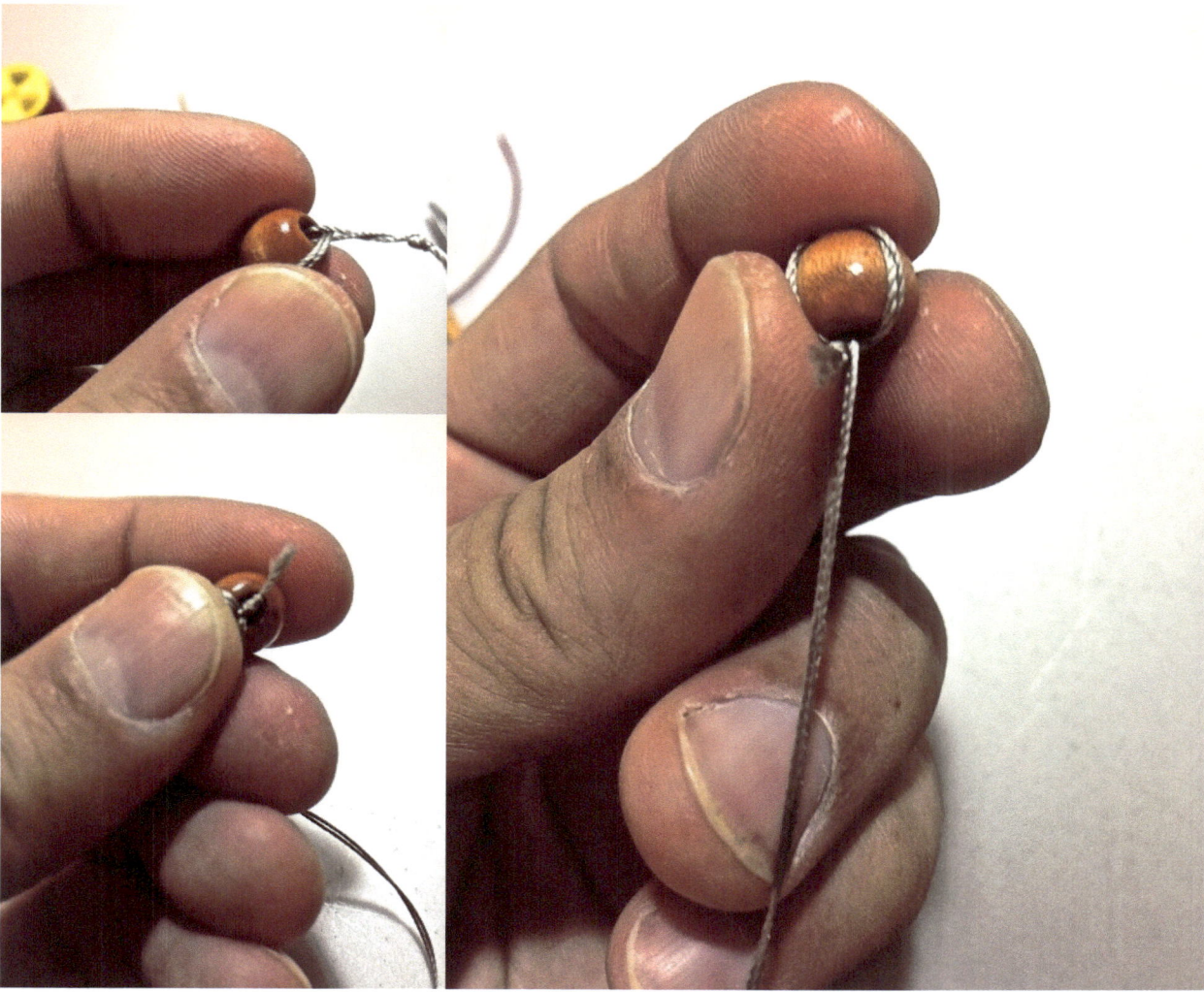

1. Begin by cutting off a length of the main color with which you will cover the bead. Make this length quite long (about 3 yards/3 meters), as there is a tendency to run out of thread. Press this thread well with an iron. This will set the twist and lessen the tendency for the thread to kink and snarl. Do not wax this thread, as waxing will dull the sheen of the thread. It will also make the button slightly sticky, making it harder to push through the buttonhole. Double the thread in the needle and knot the ends together.

2. Insert the needle through the center of the bead and pull most of the thread through. Insert the needle between the threads at the knotted end and pull the thread through, locking it around the bead.

3. Insert the needle down through the bead again, come out to the left of the thread, and draw tight. This will create a little nub similar to the top of a blanket stitch. Repeat this step 6 more times until are 8 total ribs around the bead.

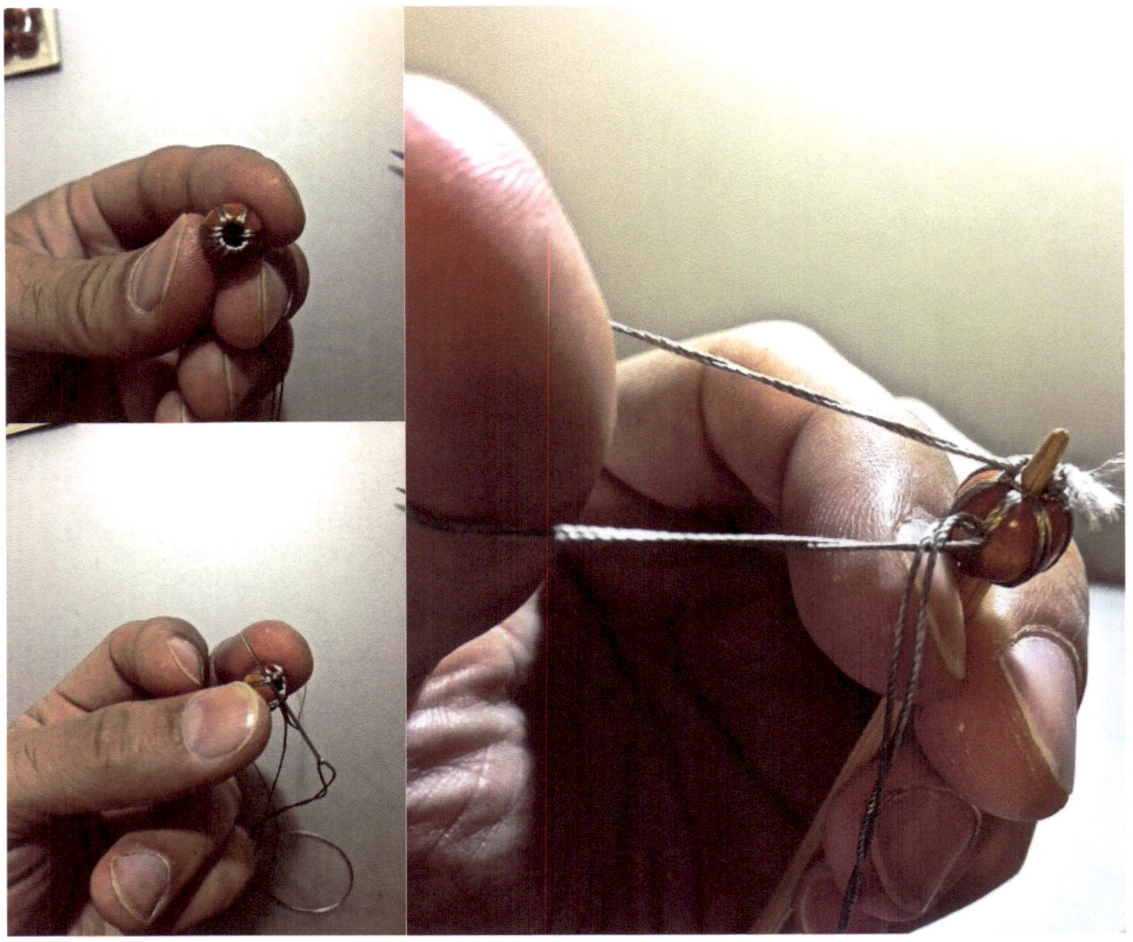

4. When all 8 ribs are made, slip the needle under the first rib that you made and pull the thread snug. This locks the ribs in place and ends the first round.

5. From now on, the end of the bead with the knot from the first step will be the top.

6. Now we will begin to wrap the bead. With the knot on top, move one rib to the right. The needle will pass right to left under this rib. Draw the thread up, but not too tightly. If you pull too tightly, your ribs will not stay evenly distributed and the button will become asymmetrical. After the first round of wrapping stitches, poke the end of the knitting needle through the center so that the button is stuck at the end. This will make it easier to manage and will tire the hands much less...very important when you're making dozens of buttons at a time. When you've got a few rounds complete, you can use the end of the needle to push the knot into the hole of the bead to hide it.

    With the needle giving the left hand more freedom, you can use the thumb to tension the thread after each stitch and help keep it from kinking.

    Continue in this manner, moving one rib to the right after each stitch, slowly covering all the ribs and the bead with rounds of thread.

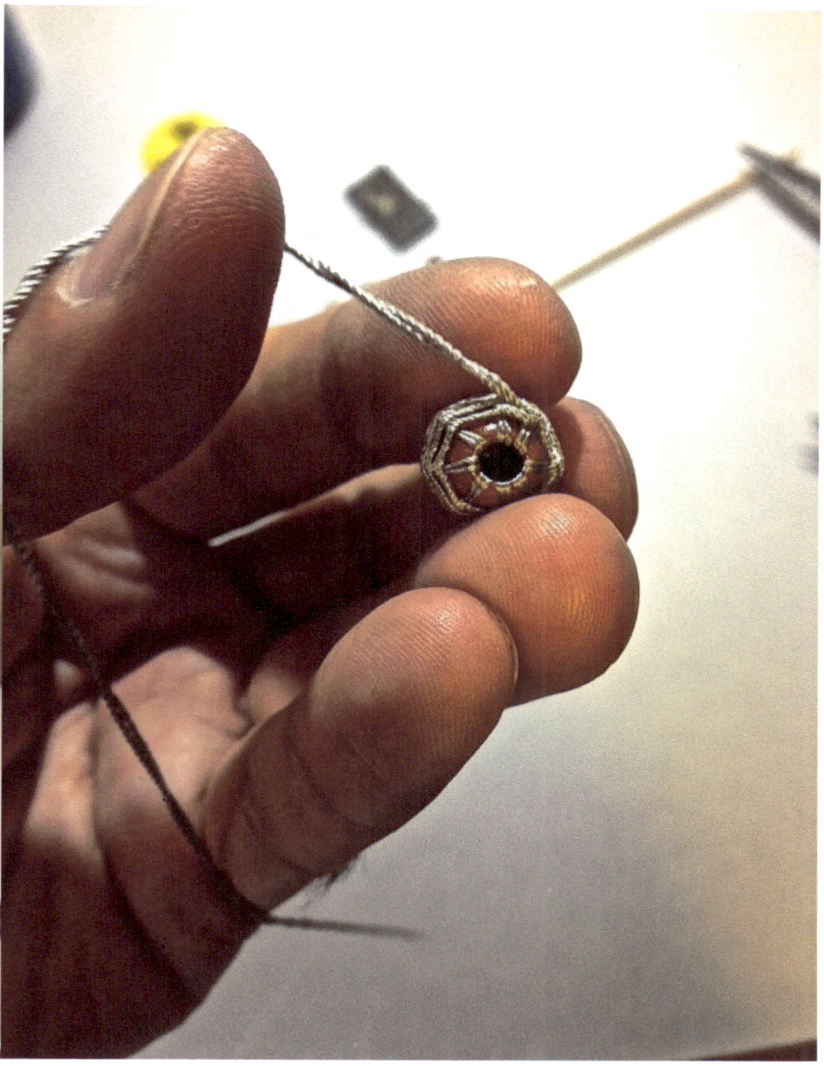

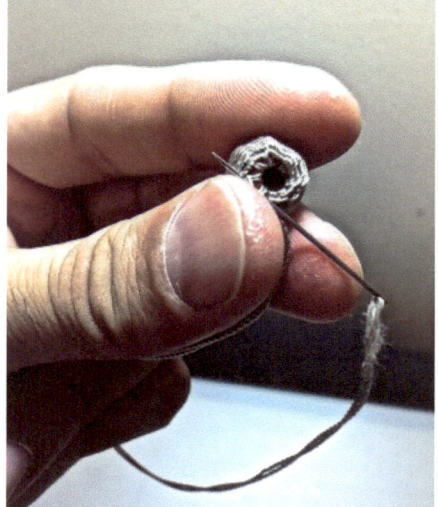

It is important to maintain even tension and to periodically remove the knitting needle from the center of the bead, to allow the stitches at the top to begin to sink into the central hole. You can push the knot into the hole as well and it will self-bury so that it cannot be seen.

When the work passes the middle of the bead and begins to curl around toward the bottom, remove the knitting needle and work only with your fingers. Continue the stitches in the same manner. When the bead is fully covered, take a few whip stitches along the round at the bottom and cut the thread.

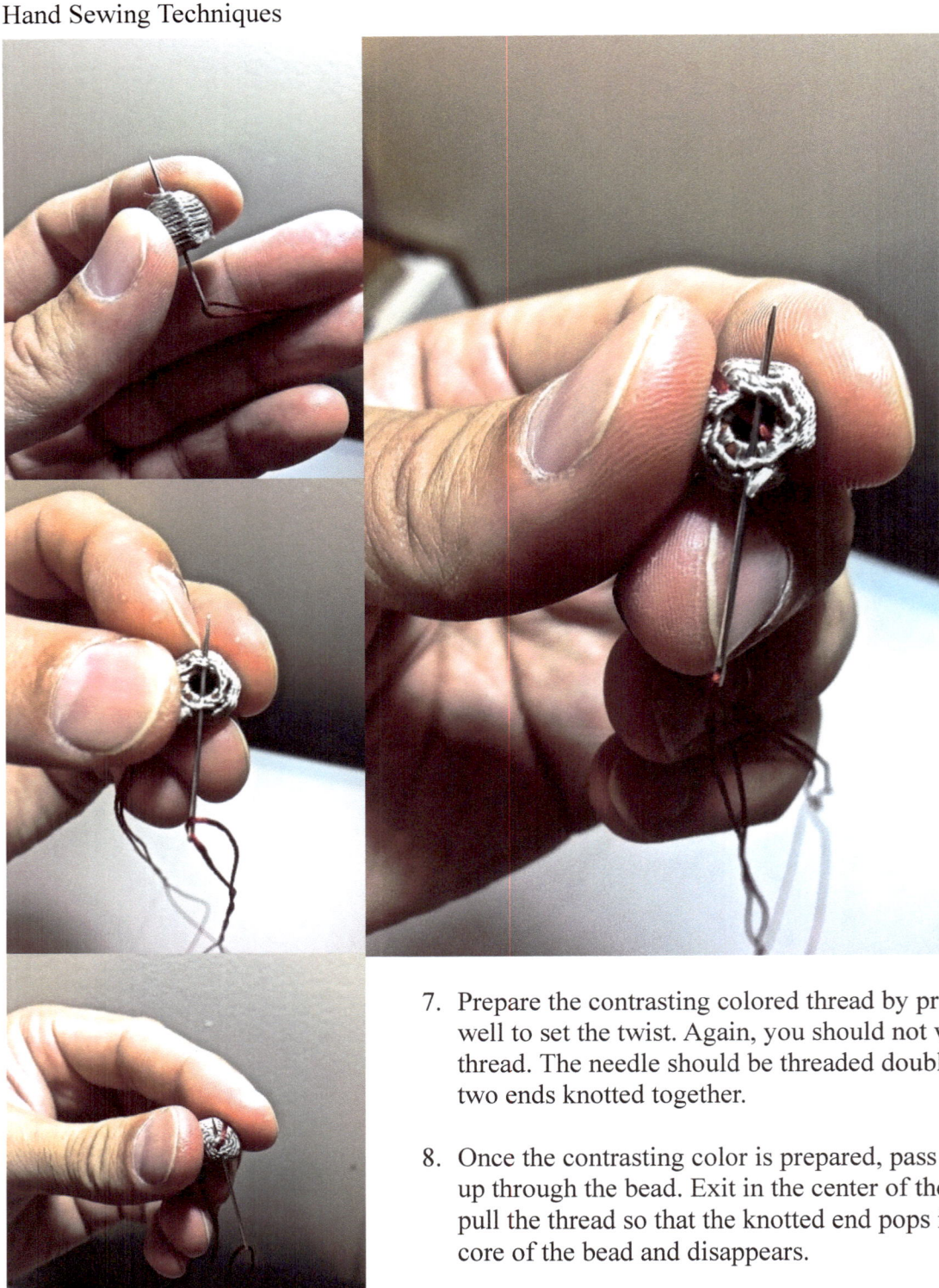

7. Prepare the contrasting colored thread by pressing it well to set the twist. Again, you should not wax this thread. The needle should be threaded double and the two ends knotted together.

8. Once the contrasting color is prepared, pass the needle up through the bead. Exit in the center of the top and pull the thread so that the knotted end pops into the core of the bead and disappears.

9. Follow the "valley" between the ribs around to the bottom of the bead and cross the opening as shown, exiting at the base of the valley on the opposing side of the bead.

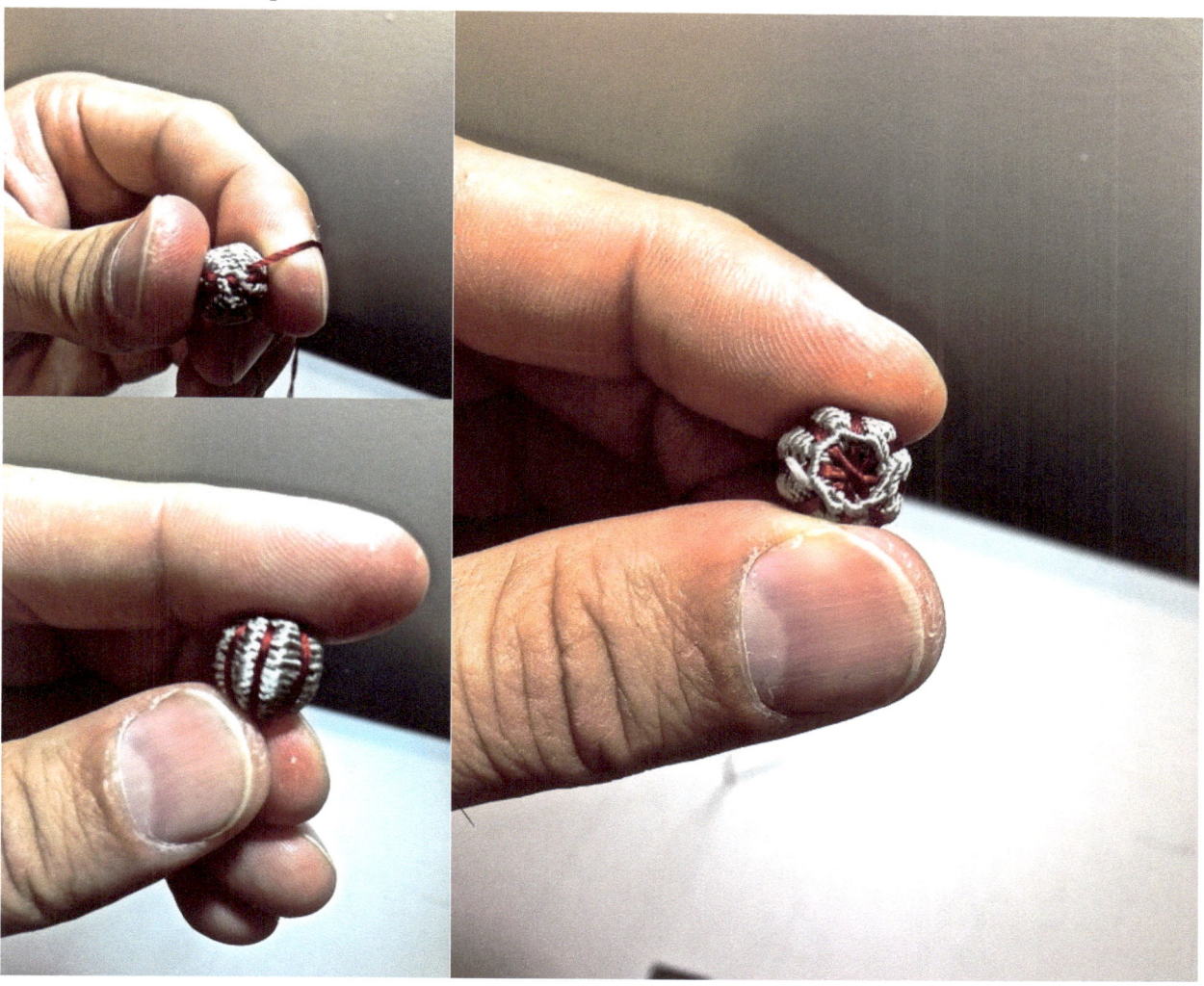

10. Follow the valley up the bead and insert the needle through the stitch at the top. Pass the tip of the needle under the first pass of the contrasting color, and exit with the tip at the top of the next valley to the left of the first. When you turn the bead over, cross the bottom as you did before and follow the next valley up to the top of the bead.

Continue in this manner until all valleys have been filled with ribs of the contrasting color.

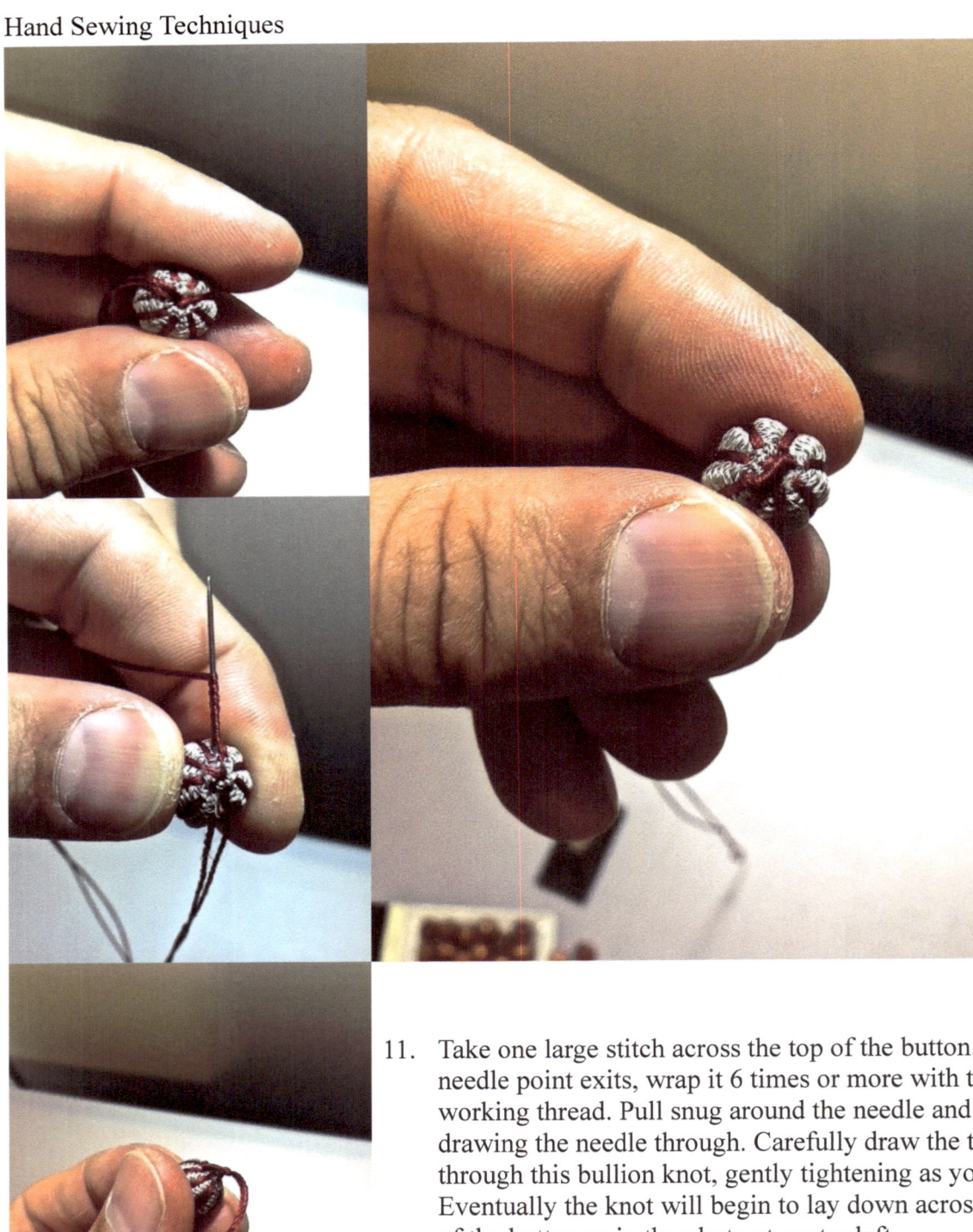

11. Take one large stitch across the top of the button. As the needle point exits, wrap it 6 times or more with the working thread. Pull snug around the needle and finish drawing the needle through. Carefully draw the thread through this bullion knot, gently tightening as you go. Eventually the knot will begin to lay down across the top of the button as in the photo at center left.

12. Once the knot has been pulled into place, insert the needle beneath it and through the center of the button and out the bottom. Use several stitches in one place on the bottom of the button to secure the thread, and cut.

13. Mark the placement of the buttons at the edge of the garment receiving them.

14. With a doubled WAXED and ironed thread, come up through the fabric and through one of the stitches on the bottom of the button.

15. Draw up the thread, leaving about 3/8" (9 mm) of distance between the garment and the button. This extra length will become the wrapped shank for the button. Insert the needle up through the fabric in the same place, and through a different stitch in the bottom of the button. Repeat this process, slowly working your way around the stitches of the bottom of the button and maintaining the distance from button to garment. There should be a minimum of 6 passes between the button and the garment.

16. Wrap the shank about 8 or 9 times with the working thread. Make these wraps quite tight so that the shank has some stiffness and strength to it. End the wrapping at the bottom of the shank.

17. With the needle, take three or four stitches around the threads on the inside of the garment, making sure to catch some of the garment fabric with each stitch. Tunnel the needle between the layers of fabric to a point some distance away from the button, draw the thread tight, and clip the thread so that the end will self-bury.

6

Making Up

Stitching up a doublet by hand can be done in a variety of ways. Each tailor had a different method of assembly and interior construction, some preferring a softer line and others a more structured approach. Additionally, the interior structure of a doublet changes dramatically through the eras.

The doublet constructed in this chapter follows a simple, softer line that would have been worn by the common man of about 1618. This garment is not heavily padded, moves easily and, if the construction steps are followed well, it will last for decades.

Making Up

Here is a brief description of the process:

1. Canvases are constructed and shaped
2. Exterior fabric is applied to canvases
3. Main seams are sewn, leaving shoulders open
4. Skirting and lacing strip are applied
5. Front facing and buttonholes are worked
6. Lining is installed, back lining first and then front
7. Exterior shoulder seams are closed
8. Collar is stiffened and pad-stitched
9. Collar is lined
10. Shoulders of the lining are closed
11. Neckline of lining is closed
12. Front bindings are applied
13. Buttons are attached
14. Sleeve facings and sleeve buttonholes are worked
15. Sleeve seams are sewn
16. Sleeves are lined
17. Shoulder wings are applied to sleeves
18. Sleeves are set into the armhole
19. Armhole binding is applied
20. Sleeve buttons are applied

This order of operations can be modified to suit the needs of your work environment and the number of individuals working on a single garment. For example, the right half and left half of the body can be made by separate teams, as well as right and left sleeves. With multiple teams working on different parts of a doublet, a fully hand-sewn garment can be made in an astonishingly short amount of time.

Each worker in the tailor's shop should be given tasks suited to their skill level. The Master Tailor of a shop should be well-versed in assessing the skills of people working in his or her establishment.

If, as is likely the case, you are a lone individual making the entire garment yourself, make sure to take the time to work samples of each stitch with the correct fabrics and layers to "tune" your hands to the style of stitch used for each step. This method of sampling is essential for one person executing the many different steps, as each type of stitching has different hand movements and different tension requirements. You must give your body the opportunity to 'reset' to a new motion, rhythm, and stitch size. It is for this reason that in larger shops with multiple workers, one person does the same task all day long. This repetition enables the person to become an organic machine, accelerating their stitching to astonishing speeds and unheard-of levels of accuracy. As an individual, you can work in a similar way by grouping the various steps of the construction so that the whole garment will show remarkable consistency.

BUILD THE CANVASES

1. Cut a slash into the canvas halfway between the bottom armhole notch and the shoulder point. Make the slash about 3-4" (7-10 cm) long. Using the small rectangle of canvas cut for the fronts, begin working a running stitch (pg. 49) from the bottom of the slash to the armhole edge, approximately 1/4" (7 mm) from the cut edge of the slash as shown in the photograph at the top left.

2. Without turning the work, use a whip stitch/overcast stitch (pg. 50) from the armhole edge back to the bottom of the slash.

3. Repeat this process on the other side of the slash, making sure to spread the slash open at the armhole edge by 1 inch (2.5cm).

4. Once this step is complete, you may trim away the excess canvas. Leave a 1/4" (7 mm) margin on the interior, and trim the piece even with the edge of the front canvas at the armhole.

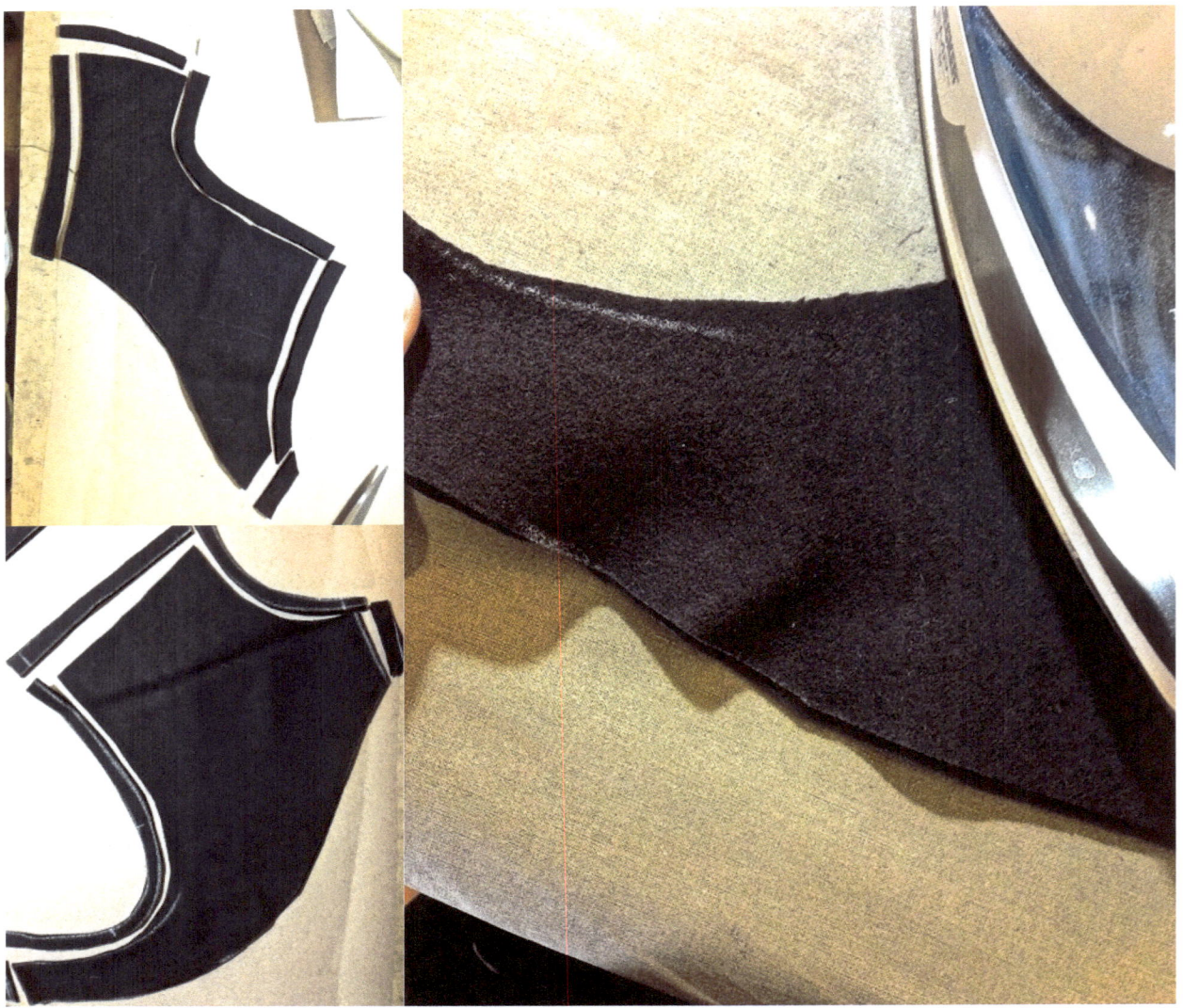

5. Repeat this step with the other front canvas, making sure to create a mirror-image of the piece just worked so that there are clear right and left sides to the garment.

6. Next, take the layers of heavy wool padding that were cut and trim away all seam allowances. Remember that the allowances are different on different edges of the piece. Be careful not to trim away too much.

7. Using an iron with steam or a damp cloth, stretch the armhole by about 3/4 of an inch (1.8cm) in the same area where you've put the gusset into the canvas. This will require some diligence and may be a little difficult, as this part of the armhole is mostly on the straight of grain. You may put one or two small cuts in the armhole edge if it will not stretch. Don't worry if you over-stretch the wool, as you can shrink it back down with lots of steam if necessary.

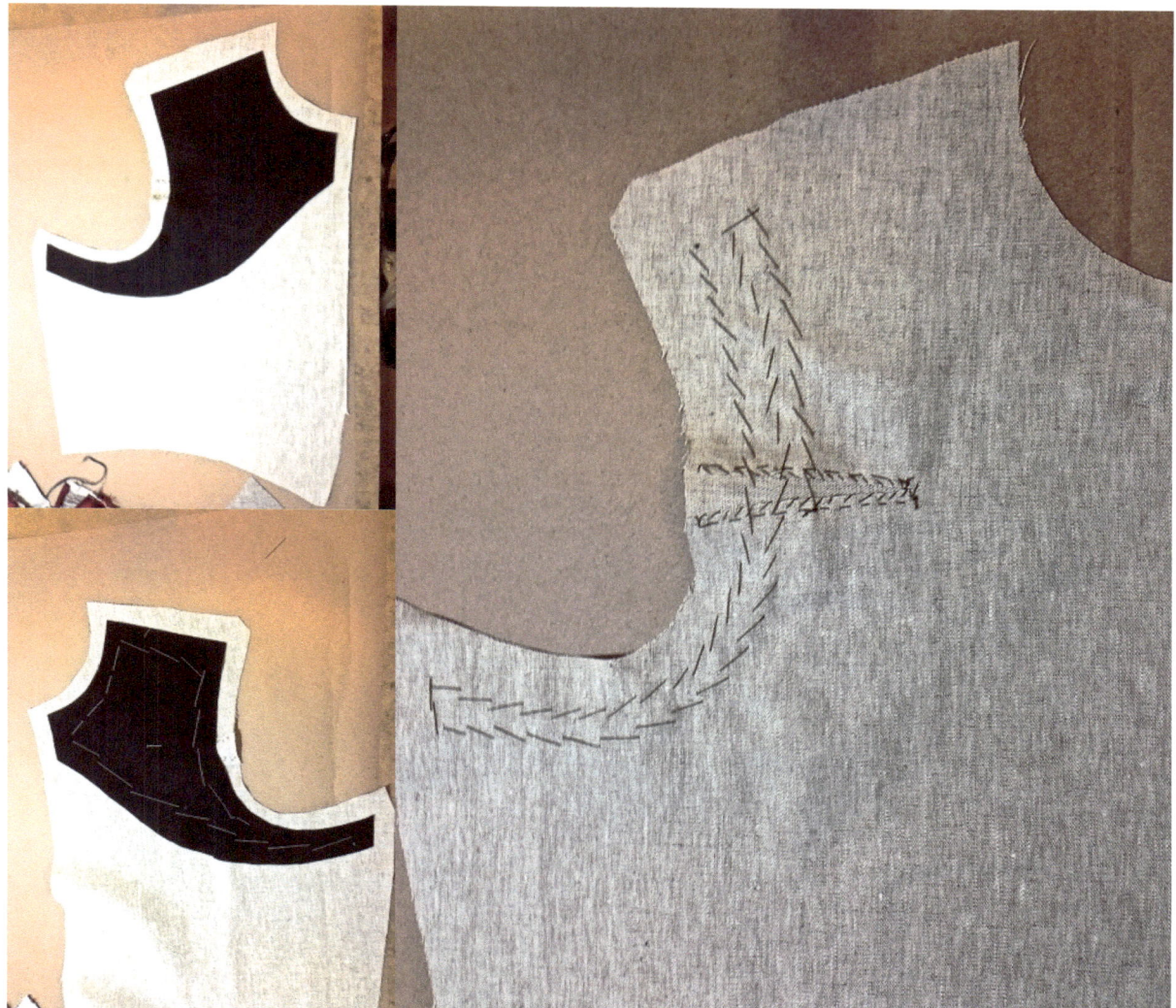

This step is essential for creating the doublet's tailored shape. Unlike most other types of costume and clothing construction, real tailoring is invisible. It involves stretching and manipulating the flat surface plane of the fabric into a three-dimensional form, enabling the garment to flow naturally over the contours of the body without needing to be moved into place by the wearer.

8. Lay the stretched front padding on the front canvas. The raw edges of the gusset should be face up for this step. As you lay the wool onto the canvas, make sure to leave wide enough margins around the outside edge. If you recall, when cutting out the pattern we cut the front canvas LARGER than the pattern to allow for manipulations. Eventually, this excess will be trimmed away. Using weak white thread, baste (pg. 48) smoothly around the edges of the padding as shown above.

9. Begin pad-stitching (pg. 51) on the CANVAS side. Work three lines of pad-stitching around the armhole. The stitches should be about 1/2 to 3/4 of an inch (1.2-1.8 cm) long. After the third line, follow the photograph on the following page and curve the next three lines of stitching towards the neckline. At the end of these 6 lines, you should be almost to the end of your gusset. End the 6th line of stitching at the neckline.

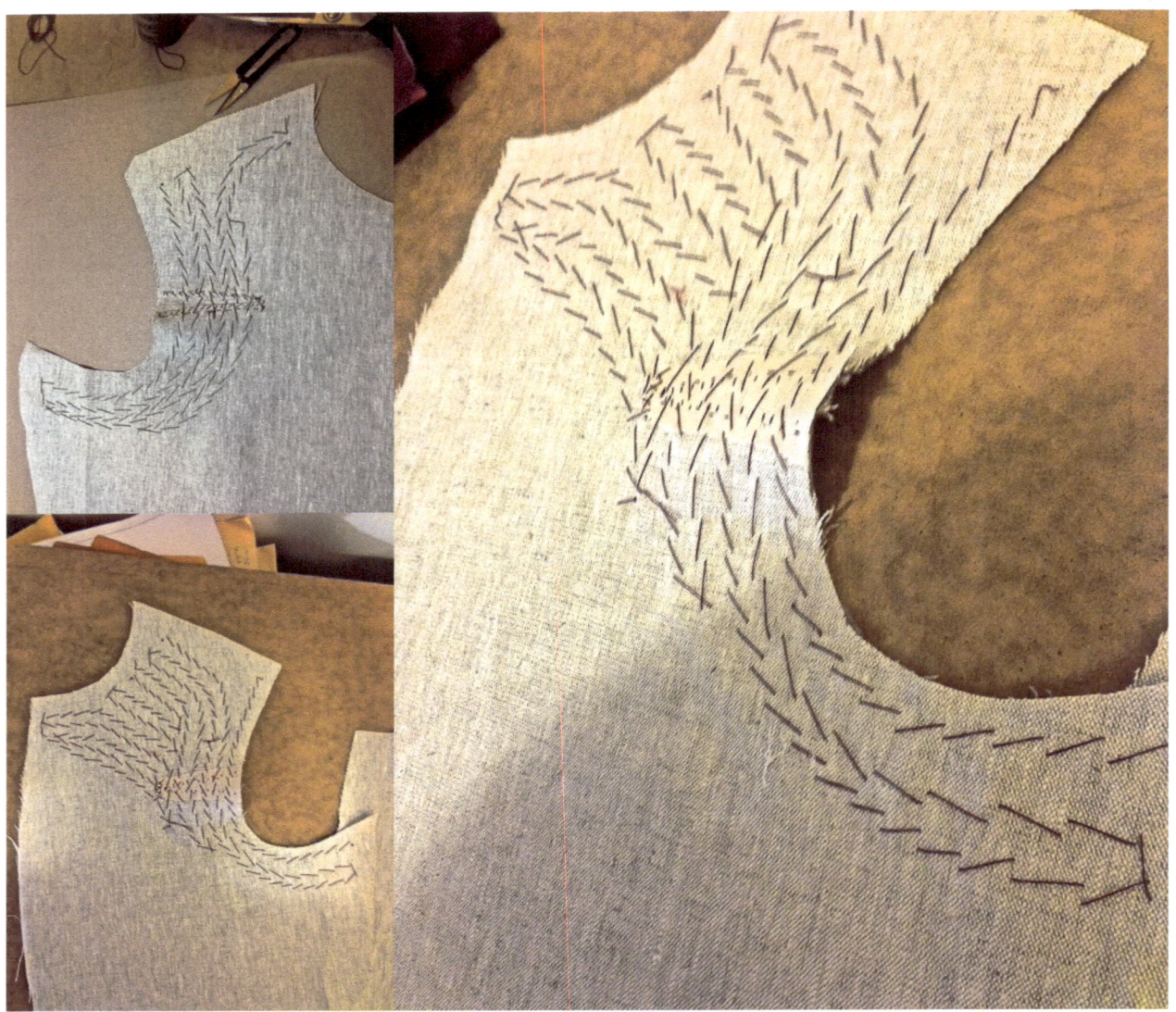

10. Next, turn the work and begin working lines parallel with the shoulder. As you work each successive line, roll the shoulder towards the padded wool side of the piece to allow for an easier grip in the hand. This motion also subtly shifts the layers of wool and canvas against each other. As each line of stitches is sewn, this shift in layers is made more permanent. Pad stitching in this manner and location sculpts the surface of the fabric in a way that plain sewing will not achieve. It should be noted that firmer tailoring can be achieved by simply making the stitches smaller and closer together. Once the pad stitching is complete, remove the white basting stitches from the wool padding.

11. Next, take the back canvases and place the wool on them as shown. Baste in place with large white stitches as you did for the front, as shown to the left above. Unlike the front, where the pad-stitching was worked from the canvas side, the pad stitching of the back is worked on the wool side of piece.

Begin at the armhole, as you did for the front. Work five lines of pad stitching along the armhole, ending at the bottom edge of the wool. Turn the work and pad stitch along the bottom toward the center back. Work the stitches in parallel lines across the back, gradually working up towards the neck. Once you reach the bottom of the back collar, reduce the size of the stitches and increase their frequency. It is important that the work be quite firm in this area of the doublet, as this type of collar needs good support to avoid collapsing with wear.

Repeat this step with the second half of the back. The photo on the bottom left, above, shows the proper position of the piece when pad stitching the back neck. You must carefully curl the work towards the canvas side of the piece with each row of stitching to create a well-formed curve to the back collar. This will create a well-fitted, durable collar that will be the envy of anyone familiar with the art of doublet making.

12. With the left front canvas laid wool side up, lay the bias cut strip of canvas along the front edge about 1/4" (7 mm) from the cut edge. Trim the strip about 1/2" (1.2 cm) inside the cut edges at the top and bottom. Pad stitch this strip in place with three lines of stitching as shown in the bottom left photograph. These stitches will not be removed, and need not be particularly small; they are merely to hold this fabric in place until the buttonholes are worked.

13. Once all the pad stitching is complete, use a hot iron with either lots of steam or a damp cloth laid between fabric and iron to press these garment pieces. Make sure to preserve the shaping as you press, as you do not want to undo all your careful pad-stitched sculpting work with sloppy pressing. When complete, the front canvas should have a significant bump in the armhole, as shown in the lower left photo.

14. Stretch the doublet body front exterior pieces. The best way to achieve this is to stack both fronts on top of each other, WRONG sides out. Lay them on the ironing board and use the same technique used to stretch the armhole of the wool padding for the canvas. The exterior fabric is lighter in weight than the canvas, so it isn't necessary to use as much force. A lot of steam and a little pressure will gently stretch the front armhole by about 1/2"-3/4" (1.2-1.8 cm).

You can check whether you have the proper amount of stretch by laying the piece onto the completed front canvas and observing whether the amount of fulness stretched into the front exterior armhole lays smoothly over the shape of the canvas. The next step will be to baste the exterior to the canvas and we will be stretching the exterior fabric in this area.

See page 93 for more photos of the results of the stretching.

Stretch carefully in this area with an iron and damp cloth before applying to canvas

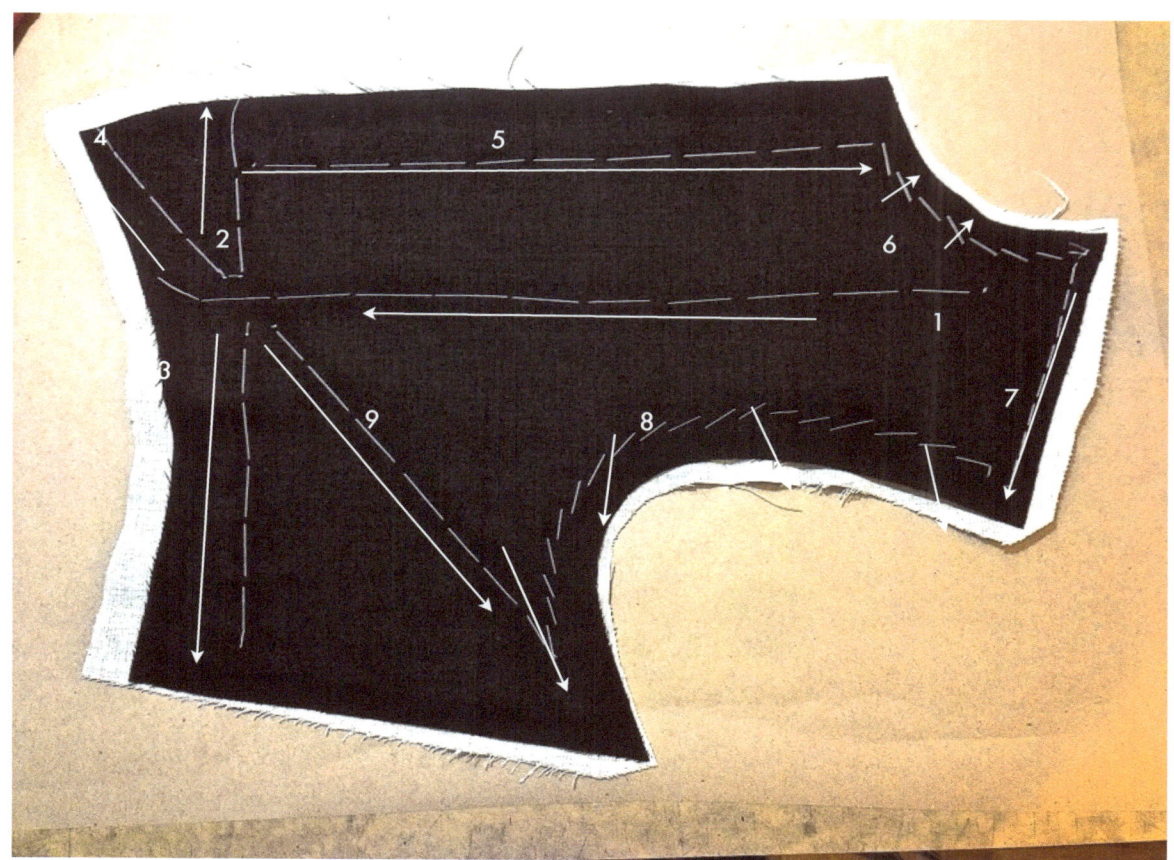

BASTING

This tremendously important step gently stretches the exterior fabric onto the canvas. The lines of basting are worked in a specific order using weak white thread that will be removed later. Gently smooth the fabric in front of the needle as you work these basting stitches. The front does not need to stay in the position shown in the photo. You will need to turn it different directions to put your hands in the correct orientations for smoothing the fabric.

15. Baste along line number 1 from the shoulder to the bottom using a long running baste.

16. Follow line number 2 along the waist. It is worked straight towards the center front, perpendicular to line number 1.

17. Work line number 3 in the opposite direction of number 2; outward from line 1 towards the side back edge of the front panel.

18. Work line number 4 at an angle from the intersection of 1, 2, and 3 and smooth down toward the center front point. Be gentler here, as you don't want to overstretch the fabric along the bias.

19. Work line number 5 upward from the front waist toward the neck. As this line is worked, the fabric should be smoothed toward the center front.

20. Work line number 6 as a diagonal baste along the neckline, gently smoothing the fabric towards the cut edge of the neckline and slightly towards the upper neck point.

21. Line number 7 holds the shoulder in place. Work this line of basting carefully smoothing the fabric toward the armhole and slightly up into the shoulder.

22. Work line number 8 with a diagonal baste along the armhole. The fabric should be smoothed straight out toward the cut edge of the armhole canvas. The smoothing should be quite firm, and the stitches small and strong.

23. Work line number 9 diagonally from the intersection of lines 1, 2, and 3 towards the back point of the armhole.

24. When all basting is complete, steam-press gently from the back. **Do not smash it flat. You must be very careful to preserve the sculpting that you have achieved.** At this point in construction, it is very easy to accidentally rotate the fullness from the gusset out of the armhole and into the center front. Avoid this by pinning the center front edge to the ironing board or table and checking it against the pattern.

25. Baste around the perimeter and trim away excess canvas.

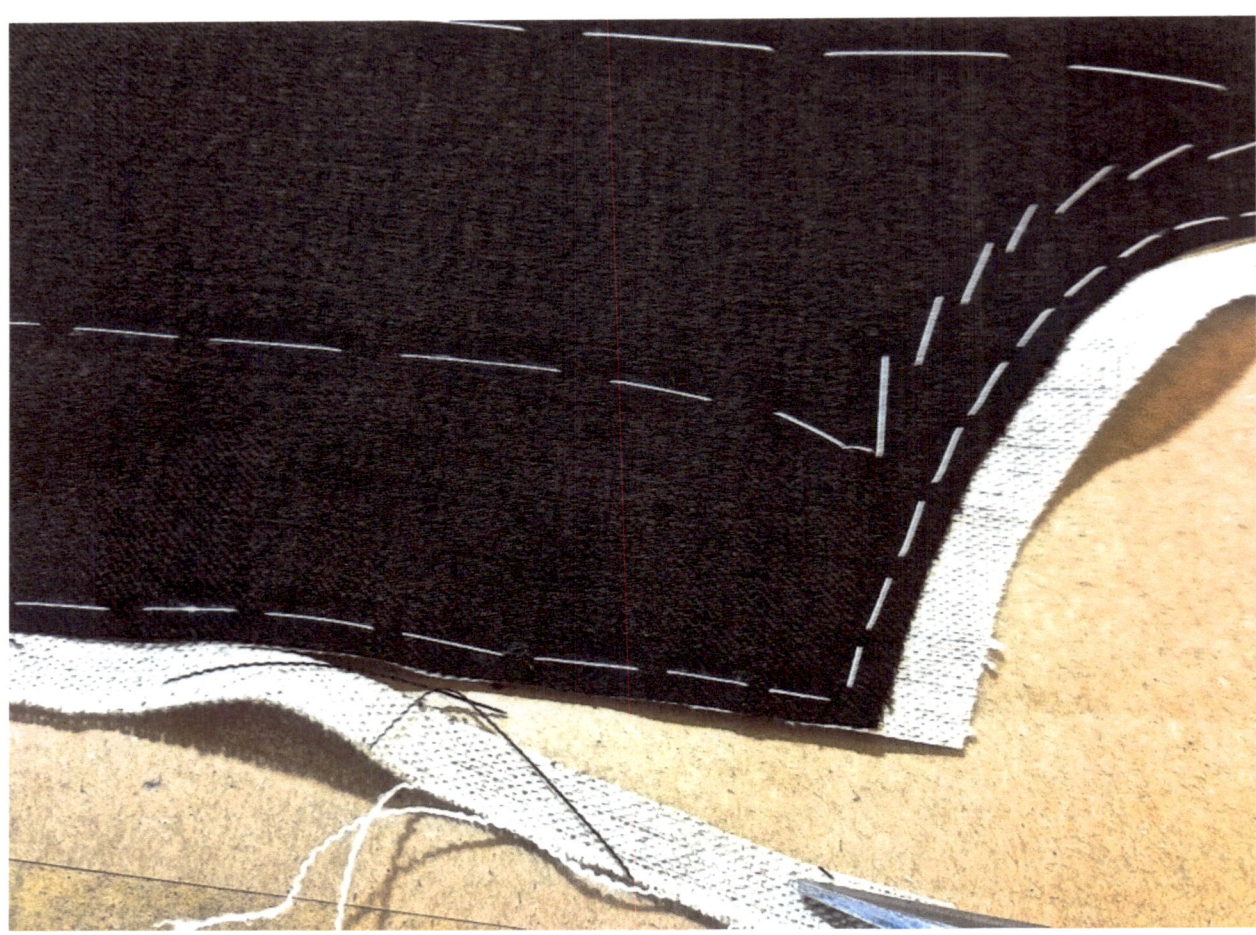

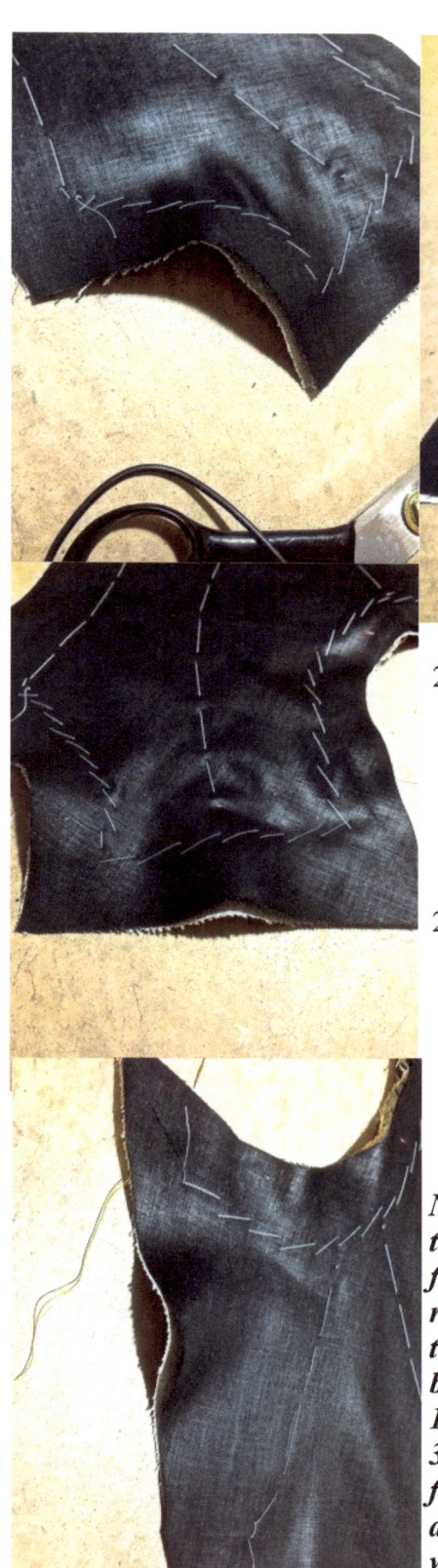

26. Using an iron, stretch several edges of each front panel. The shoulder is stretched until it is about 1/2" (1.2 cm) longer than the shoulder of the pattern. The neckline is stretched until it is about 3/8" (9 mm) longer than the pattern. The side back should be stretched by about 3/4" (1.8 cm).

27. Basting the remaining pieces is *much* simpler than basting the fronts. Simply lay the exterior fabric pieces onto their canvases (with the padding layer face down for the backs) and, working out from the center of the piece, pin the exterior fabric to the canvas and baste around the perimeter. Repeat the same process for all remaining pieces.

Now that the basting and stretching are complete, it is a good time to take a break, clean up your workspace and get ready for the next step: sewing seams. Stretch and get your hands relaxed and warmed up with a few runs of test stitching. The two stitches we will be using in the next several steps will be back stitch and pick stitch. The back stitches should be about 1/4"(7 mm) in length and the pick stitches should be about 3/16" (5 mm) apart. Please note that the thickness of your fabrics and your own strength and skill will make these distances vary. The distances given reflect the stitches that were used for the samples in the photographs.

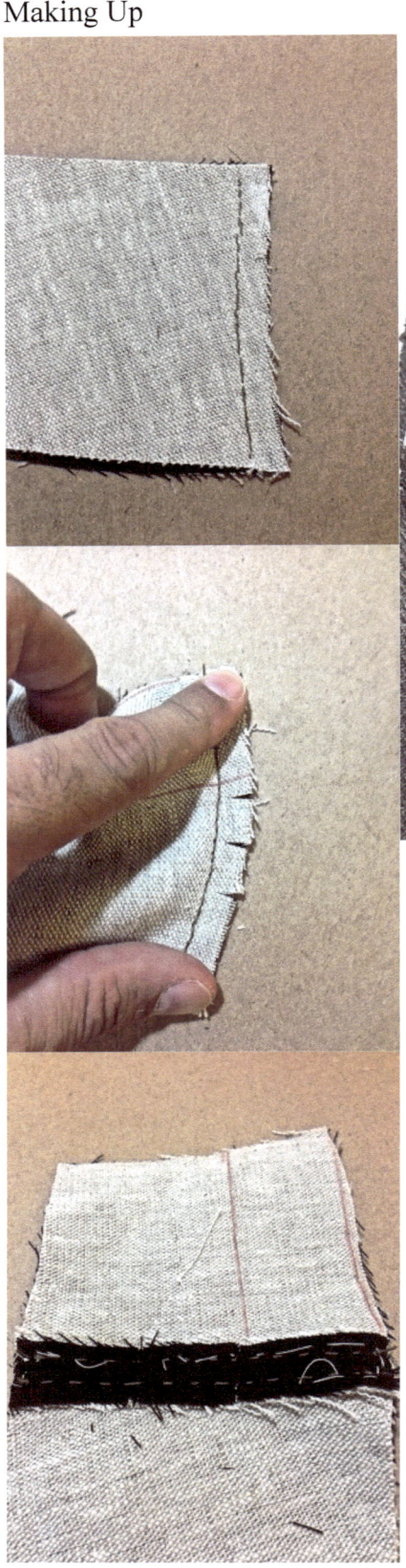

ASSEMBLY OF THE COLLAR

28. First we stitch the front collar seams. Since the front collar is made from two pieces, we must stitch the seam and pick stitch (pg. 55) the seam allowances open. Thread of a contrasting color was used in the photographs for clarity, but surviving examples use matching thread.

    Each front collar consists of a front and side front. Lay out both left and right fronts before stitching to prevent the tendency to make two lefts or two rights. Using a strong topstitching-weight thread or a more authentic heavy linen thread, work a back-stitched (pg. 54) seam with a 3/8" (9 mm) seam allowance. Secure the thread well at both ends of the seam. Next, clip three notches into the seam near the center as shown. Make sure these clips are cut almost all the way to the thread, as otherwise they will not release the curve enough for the collar to lay correctly.

    Once the seam is sewn and clipped, press it open and begin pick stitching the seam allowance into place from the outside. Pick stitches are best worked approximately 1/8" (3 mm) from the seam. Pick stitch both sides of the seam. Repeat for the opposite collar front.

29. Lay the completed front collar onto the neckline and, using weak white thread, baste in place 1/2" (1.2 cm) from the cut edge. As you baste, make sure that the back half of the collar is lightly eased into the neckline, as the front neckline is approximately 1/4" (7 mm) shorter than the collar itself. As the seam is back stitched, the neckline will stretch to accommodate the extra length in the collar. Any fullness can be steamed out with the iron after the seam is sewn. Using a firm back stitch, sew the collar with a 3/8" (9 mm) seam. Once the seam is complete, remove the basting.

Clip the neckline seam allowance with 5 evenly spaced clips to allow the neckline to lay down smoothly. It is not necessary to clip the collar side. Press well with the steam iron from the wrong side only. From the right side, pick-stitch both sides of the seam allowance in the same manner as for the collar. Repeat this process with the opposite front.

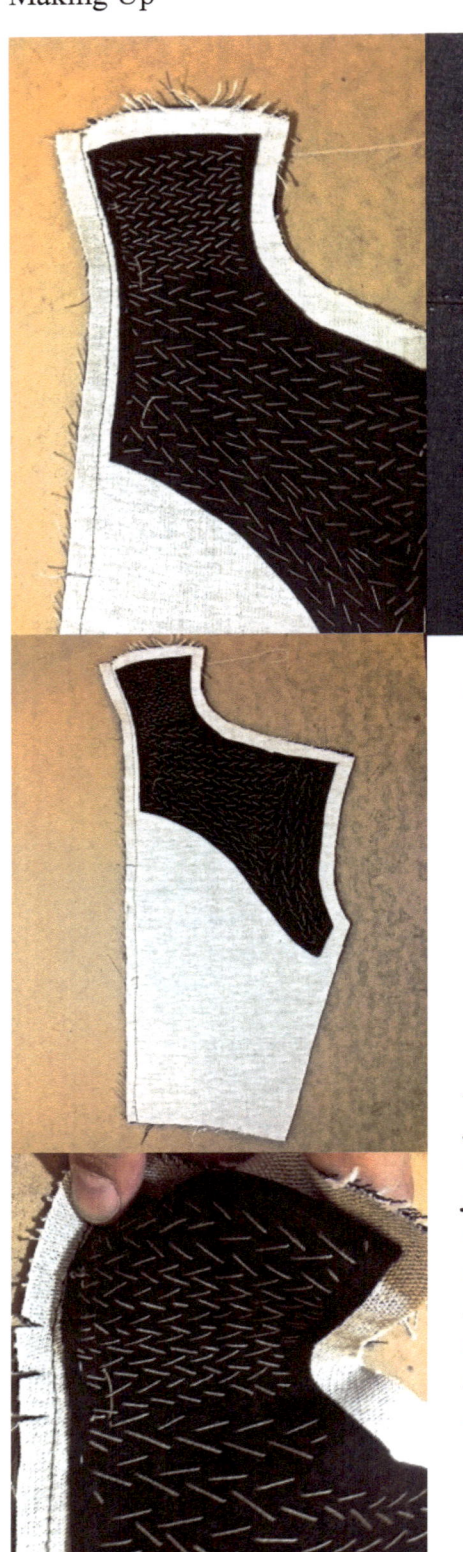

CENTER BACK SEAM

30. Using the same method as for applying the front collar, baste the two back pieces together with weak white thread. Back stitch the seam with firm stitches and either strong linen or top-stitching thread. After the seam is sewn, remove the basting and clip three times where the back neck curves into the back collar. Press the seam open from the wrong side only. Then, from the outside, pick stitch the seam open.

As you become accustomed to the rhythm of the stitches, your back stitching and pick stitching will be much faster and your stitches more even. The center back seam is, so far, the longest seam we have stitched. For an inexperienced novice, this seam can feel like it takes an eternity to sew. Many people choose to work the main seams of the collar, neckline and center back by machine and work the pick stitching by hand to speed the work and save precious time. As your skill improves, it will seem less intimidating to work all of these seams by hand.

SIDE BACK SEAMS

30. Cut a 1 1/4" (3.1 cm) bias strip from the scraps of the exterior fabric. Press this strip in half along its length and baste it to the side back edge of the back panel. The basting should be 3/8" (9 mm) from the cut edge of the fabric.

31. On the front panel, press the side back edge under by 3/8" (9 mm).

32. Lay the front onto the back as shown and begin pick stitching the seam together FROM THE OUTSIDE.

It is frequently evident in surviving garments that certain seams were, in fact, sewn from the outside of the garment. In the case of this side-back seam, about half of the pieces I have seen are sewn in this manner. The small folded piece of bias that is inserted as a decoration and reinforcement is more common towards the middle of the 17th century, although it does occasionally appear in 16th century specimens as well. I include it here as interesting optional design detail; it is not structurally mandatory.

The side back seam as seen from the interior, immediately after sewing, and the final appearance of the back after both side back seams have been completed.

THE SKIRTS

33. Lay out the skirting pieces of both the exterior and the lining in left and right halves. Each skirt half consists of two pieces, a back skirt and a front skirt. Using a firm back stitch, sew the joining seam for front and back skirts of both the skirt exterior and the skirt linings. Press open.

34. Turn up the bottom and center back edges of the exterior skirts by 1/2" (1.2 cm). Using a cross stitch (pg. 57) or a catch stitch (pg. 58), secure the hems in place.

35. Next, take the skirt linings, turn them up, and press the center back and bottom edges in by 5/8" (1.5 cm).

36. Lay the lining right side up onto the wrong side of the exterior skirts, aligning the seams and matching the cut edges. Using white thread, baste the lining onto the exterior about 3/4" (1.8 cm) from the finished edge of the skirt.

37. Pick-stitch the lining into place. You may alternately use a felling stitch along the edge, if you prefer.

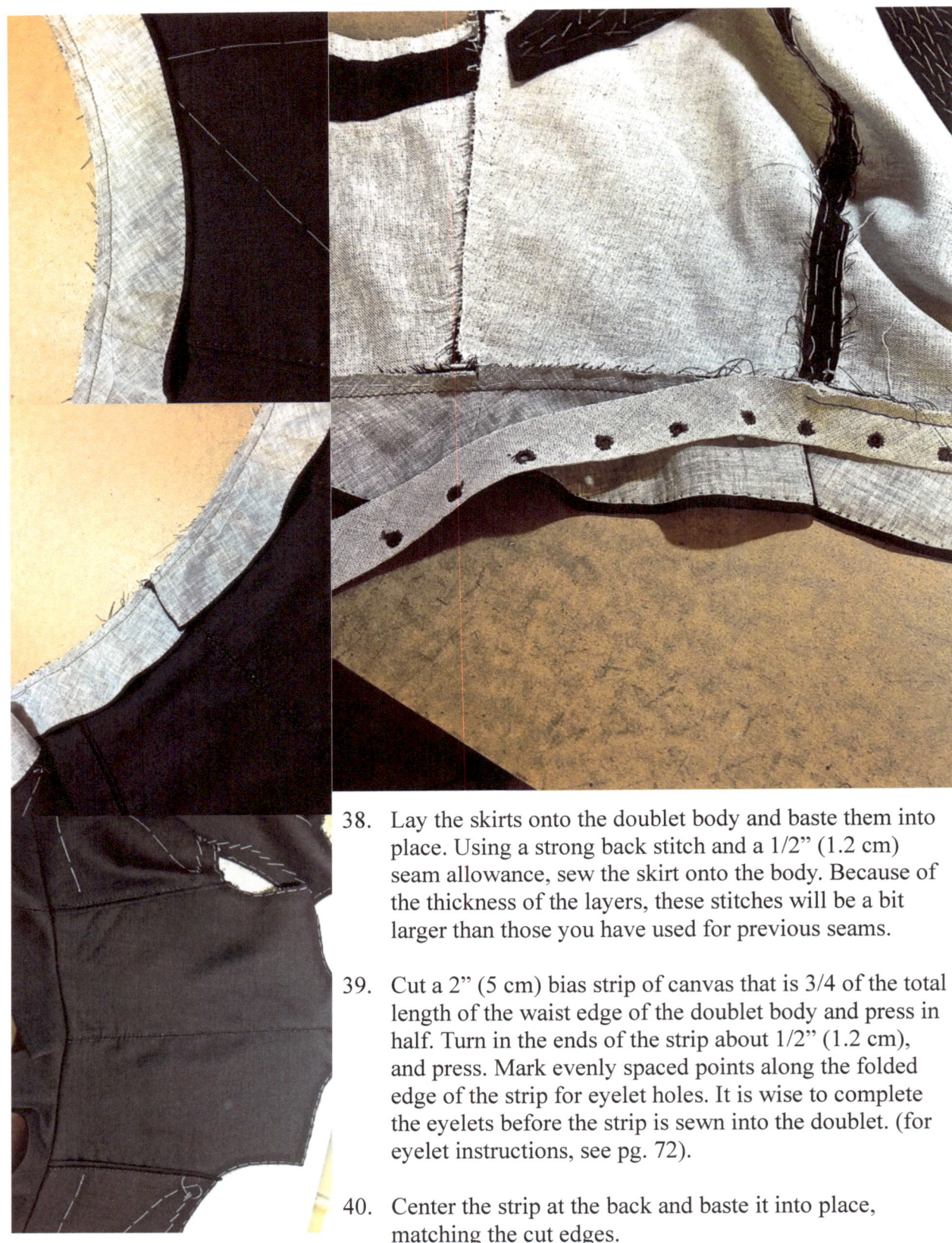

38. Lay the skirts onto the doublet body and baste them into place. Using a strong back stitch and a 1/2" (1.2 cm) seam allowance, sew the skirt onto the body. Because of the thickness of the layers, these stitches will be a bit larger than those you have used for previous seams.

39. Cut a 2" (5 cm) bias strip of canvas that is 3/4 of the total length of the waist edge of the doublet body and press in half. Turn in the ends of the strip about 1/2" (1.2 cm), and press. Mark evenly spaced points along the folded edge of the strip for eyelet holes. It is wise to complete the eyelets before the strip is sewn into the doublet. (for eyelet instructions, see pg. 72).

40. Center the strip at the back and baste it into place, matching the cut edges.

41. Again using a back stitch, sew the strip into the waist of the garment. These stitches will also be quite large, due to the thickness of the layers of material.

42. Once the strip is sewn in place, carefully press the entire seam allowance up into the body of the garment. You will need to do this from the outside of the garment, so be certain to use a press cloth to avoid leaving shine marks on the exterior fabric, especially if you're working with wool. Pay special attention to the bulky side back seams while pressing to make sure that you've pulled the seam tightly up and pressed it very well.

43. After the seam allowance has been pressed into position, use a strong thread and secure the seam allowance into the body with a whip stitch (pg. 50). These stitches should be firmly secured to the canvas. There are surviving garments where these stitches come through to the outer fabric as a small pick visible on the outside, but this is not the norm.

Pressing the seam allowance up into the body takes patience and skill. If you get it wrong, press it back down and try again. Mastery comes with repetition.

LEFT FRONT FACING

44. The following steps are to be worked ONLY on the left front of the garment, which will have the buttonholes. Cut a bias strip of silk 2 1/2" (6.3 cm) wide and the length of the full length of the body, from the top of the collar to the bottom of skirt plus a couple of finger-widths for a little extra leeway. I highly recommend a silk taffeta or shantung for this piece, as it is the buttonhole facing and must be both tightly woven and thin. Linen fabric tends to come loose from the buttonholes with even a small amount of wear, which weakens the front of the garment and lessens its beauty.

45. Pin the silk in place on the left front of the garment. Baste along the front edge from the neck to the hem, using small firm stitches in white thread about 1/8" (3 mm) from the edge. Where the collar joins the body, ease the silk onto the body to allow a little extra fabric in this area. This will prevent the facing from pulling on the collar and ruining the curvature.

46. Using a cross stitch or a catch stitch, secure the inner edge of the silk facing in place. These stitches should be very shallow and should not show on the outside of the garment. To keep the silk flat at the neckline, it may be necessary to clip the inner edge of the silk slightly to allow it to sit smoothly inside the garment.

BINDING THE FRONT EDGES

47. Cut a 2" (5 cm) wide piece of bias silk that is long enough to cover the full length of the front from the top of the collar to the bottom hem. Press this piece of silk in half along its length. Again, silk is recommended for its thinness and durability.

48. On the outside of the garment, beginning at the top of the collar and with all cut edges aligned, use a small running stitch to apply the folded silk to the body.

49. Once the first pass of the front binding is complete, turn the garment over and fold the silk around the edge of the front. Stitch the fold of the silk down onto the facing with small, even felling stitches (pg. 56). Stitch the entire length of the binding in place.

50. For the opposite front edge of the garment, again cut a full length bias strip of silk that is 2" (5 cm) wide. This time, however, don't press it in half. Simply lay it onto the right side of the doublet, matching cut edges. Use a small, firm running stitch to sew it in place.

51. Fold and press the bias strip around the edge of the doublet, leaving the raw edge to extend into the body of the doublet. Baste it into place from the waist seam all the way to the top. At the bottom on the front of the skirt, fold the raw edge of the bias under and hem it invisibly to the lining of the skirt.

52. It is at this point in the process that the buttonholes and eyelets of the fronts are worked. See page 59 for buttonhole instructions. This is a long process that is often difficult for novices. PLEASE make sure to work up buttonhole trials on a separate piece of sample fabric with the correct layers to perfect your technique before attempting to work the holes on the actual garment. The buttonholes on this garment are worked in contrasting color for emphasis. Although contrasting buttonholes are commonly seen on surviving doublets, I recommend choosing buttonhole thread similar in color to the outer fabric until until you've mastered the art of a cut-sewn buttonhole.

The photograph on page 133 shows the 13 buttonholes on this example doublet as well as the three eyelets on both fronts at the waist, with one eyelet below and two above the waist seam. You, of course, can have as many buttonholes as you like on your doublet.

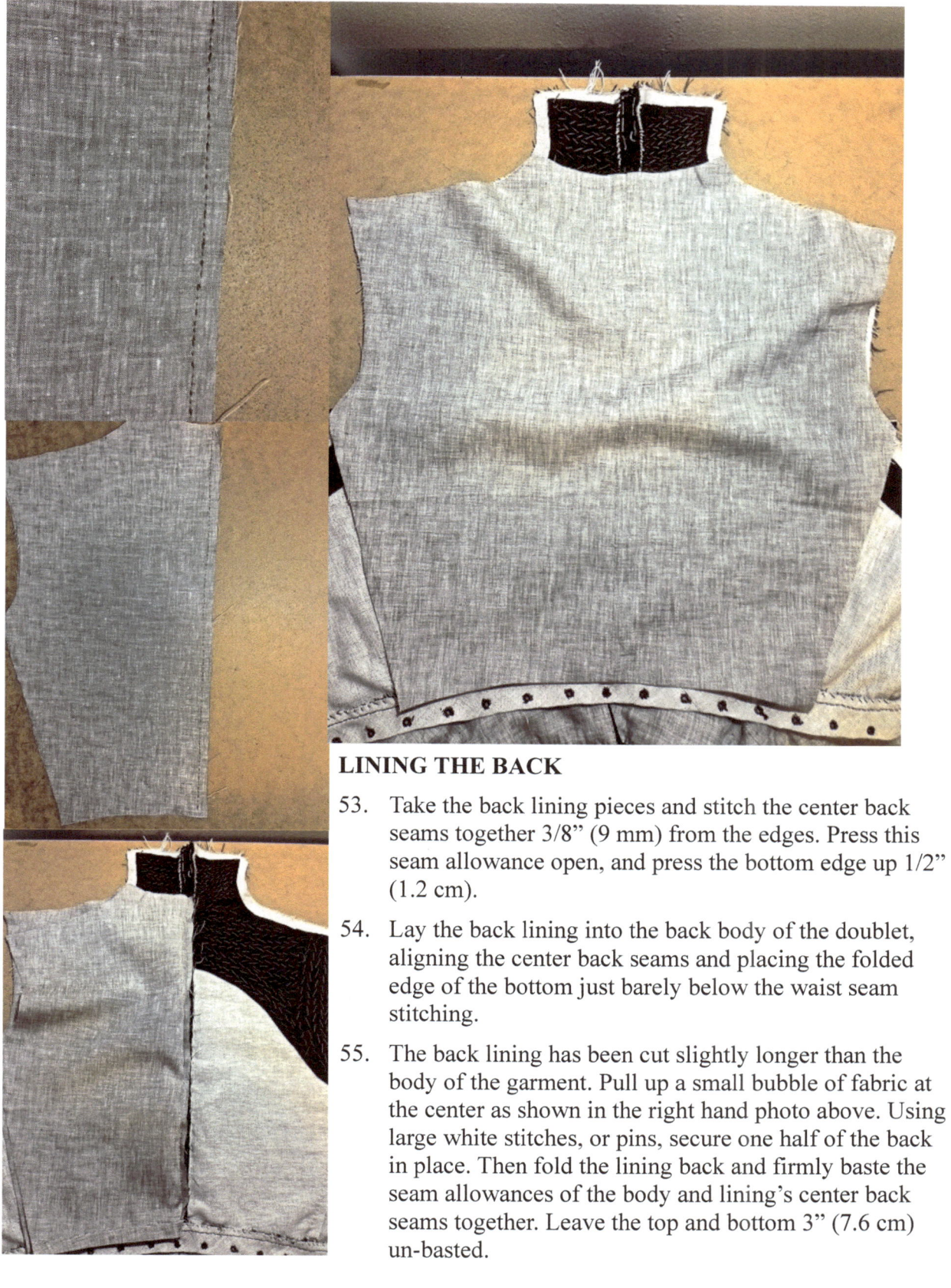

LINING THE BACK

53. Take the back lining pieces and stitch the center back seams together 3/8" (9 mm) from the edges. Press this seam allowance open, and press the bottom edge up 1/2" (1.2 cm).

54. Lay the back lining into the back body of the doublet, aligning the center back seams and placing the folded edge of the bottom just barely below the waist seam stitching.

55. The back lining has been cut slightly longer than the body of the garment. Pull up a small bubble of fabric at the center as shown in the right hand photo above. Using large white stitches, or pins, secure one half of the back in place. Then fold the lining back and firmly baste the seam allowances of the body and lining's center back seams together. Leave the top and bottom 3" (7.6 cm) un-basted.

56. Using a pick stitch or a felling stitch, close the bottom of the back lining.

57. Using the same color thread as the exterior, baste the lining allowance to the body seam allowances at the side back and up the armhole, stopping about 4" (10 cm) from the top of the shoulder.

Installing the lining in this manner allows the entire garment to move freely, preventing the lining from shifting inside the doublet and distorting the line of the exterior. The lining is left loose at the top of the armhole, to facilitate closing the shoulder and completing the collar before the lining's shoulder is closed and its neckline hemmed.

LINING THE FRONTS

58. Line the left front first. Lay the left front lining into the doublet, carefully turning back the seam allowance 3/8" (9 mm) at the side back seam. Using large white stitches, baste the lining into place. You will need to turn back the center front until the fold is just behind the buttonholes (right photo above). Because we cut the lining to a slightly different shape than the exterior, it is necessary to ease the excess length of the side back seam as we hem the front lining in place (upper left photo). Using a pick stitch or a felling stitch, hem along the center front until you are about 2" (5 cm) below the neckline. Close the bottom and side back as well, and then baste the armhole up to a distance of 4" (10 cm) from the top of the shoulder.

59. Repeat this process for the opposite front, but set the folded edge of the lining about 1/4-3/8" (7-9 mm) from the finished edge of the binding. At the eyelets at bottom of the body, fold the corner of the lining back a little farther to keep the eyelets exposed.

60. Liberally clip at LEAST five clips at the deepest curve of the back shoulder/neckline junction, ALMOST the full depth 3/8" (9 mm) of the seam allowance. This will allow the seam allowance to be pressed back without distorting the shape. Fold and press the seam allowance.

61. Baste a line on the front shoulder/side neck that is 3/8" (9 mm) from the cut edge.

62. Lay the back onto the front, matching the folded edge of the back with the basting line on the front. Using white thread, baste the back shoulder into place. **NOTE: the back shoulder is cut 1/2" (1.2 cm) longer than the front shoulder. The excess shoulder length MUST be eased onto the front in the shoulder area only, NOT into the side-neck area. To do so will destroy the shape of the collar.**

63. Using a firm pick stitch or felling stitch and strong thread, sew the shoulder seam. When the seam is complete, remove the white basting thread and press well from the outside, using a press cloth to protect the garment from iron-shine.

64. On the interior of this seam, clip the curvature of the side neck at least three times to permit the allowance to spread smoothly.

65. In the same manner as for the waist seam, use a whip stitch to secure the seam allowance to the canvases of the doublet. These stitches should be shallow and strong and should not be visible on the outside of the garment.

66. Repeat these steps for the opposite shoulder.

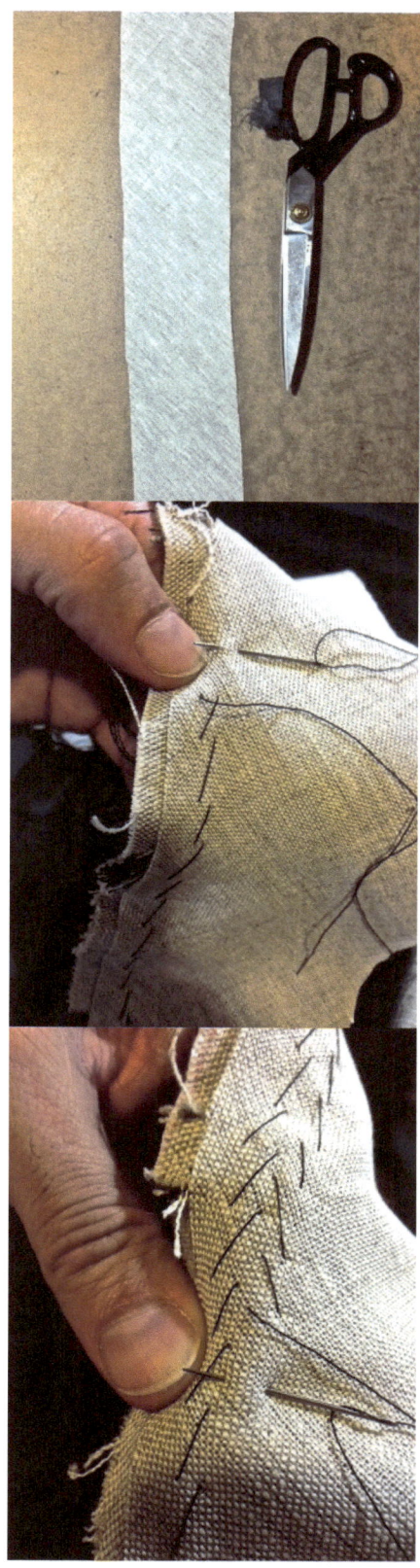

TALORING THE COLLAR

66. With the shoulders of the exterior closed, it is time to stiffen the collar with an additional piece of bias-cut canvas. Cut a rectangle of canvas long enough to extend past the ends of the collar from center front to center front. Its width should be equal to the height of the finished collar.

67. Take this piece of canvas to the iron and, using lots of steam, shrink one of the long sides while simultaneously stretching the other. The resulting shape should be rather curved.

68. Lay the canvas into the collar with the wider curved edge at the top of the collar. Make sure to position the canvas so that it does not extend past the buttonhole facing. Begin pad stitching the canvas to the inside of the collar, using small frequent stitches for stiffer collars and larger less frequent stitches for softer collars. As each successive line of stitching is worked, curl the collar more and more over the hand. This technique creates an elegantly flared and well-formed collar that will hang beautifully and maintain its shape for years to come.

   These pad stitches SHOULD show through on the outside as a series of small even pricks. For this reason, this stitching is ALWAYS worked in the same color thread as the outer fabric.

69. Press the collar well with steam, taking care to preserve the shaping. After pressing, trim all excess collar canvas so that no canvas extends below the neckline seam.

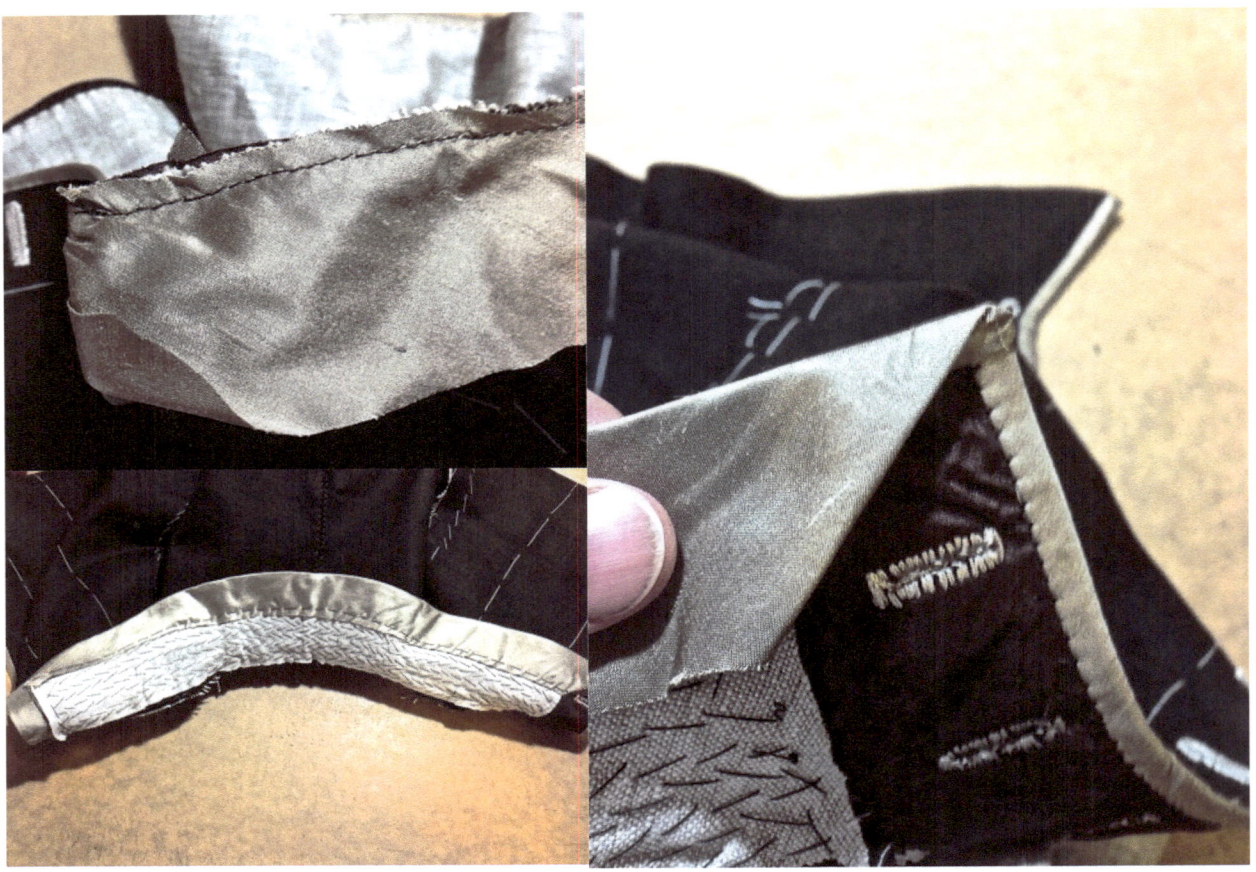

FINISHING THE COLLAR

70. Cut a 2 1/2" (6.3 cm) bias piece of silk long enough to go around the entire top edge of the collar.

71. In the same manner as the right doublet front binding, stitch the collar binding to the top of the doublet using a 1/4" (7 mm) allowance. Wrap the binding around the edge of the collar and press well. At the front edge with the buttonholes, turn the edge under at an angle to create the appearance of a mitered corner at the top of the buttonholes. Baste the raw edge of the binding in place and press one more time.

72. Take the collar lining pieces and stitch the center back seams together. Press the top edge under by 1/2" (1.2 cm).

73. Lay the lining into the collar, using white thread to baste it into position. Again, be certain to keep the left front edge from extending over any of the buttonholes by folding the excess away or by trimming away just enough to leave a small allowance to turn under.

74. Once the basting is complete, carefully use a felling stitch or a pick stitch to sew the lining in place in the collar. Once the outer edges of the collar lining are sewn, the basting stitches can be removed.

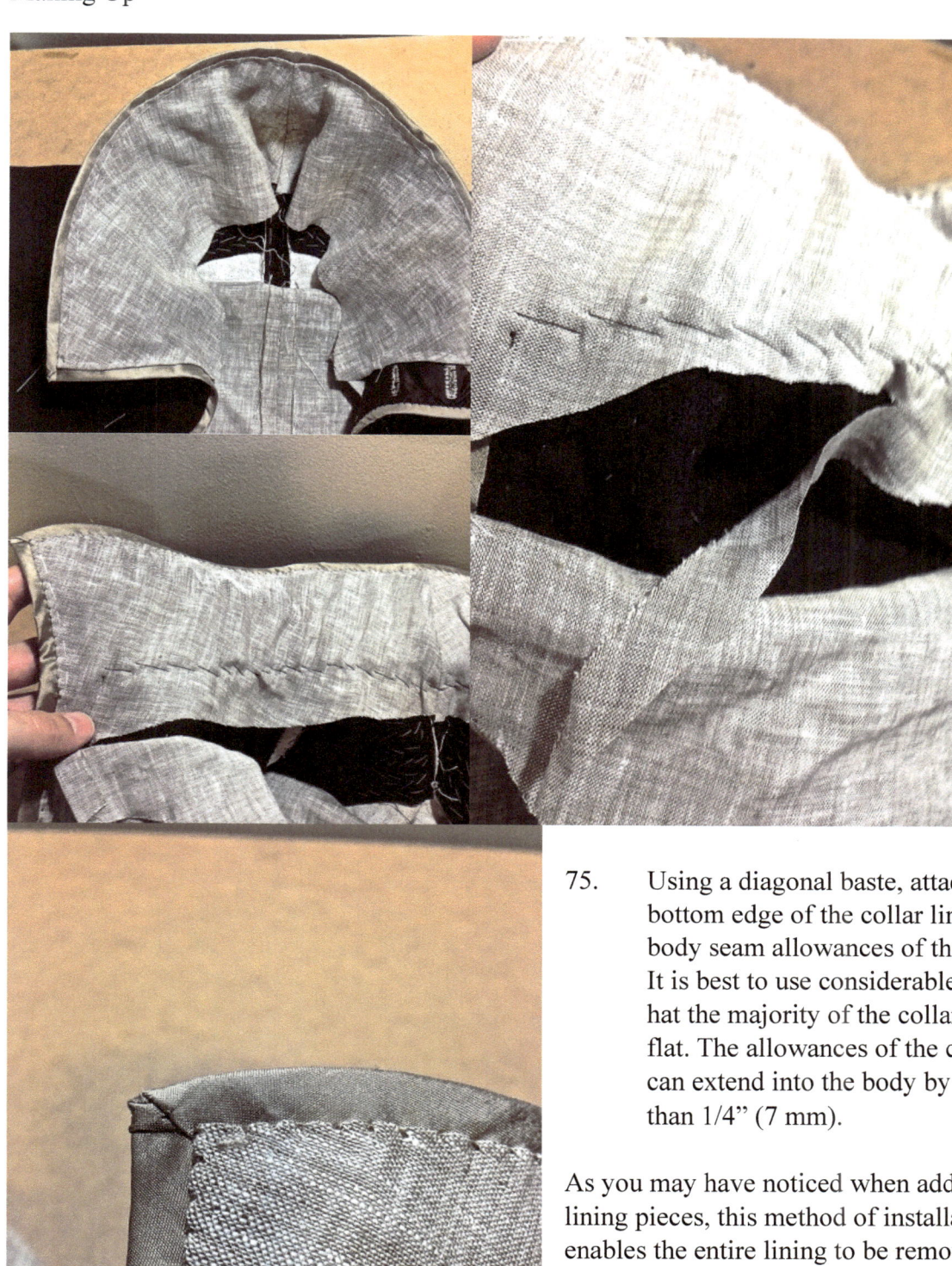

75. Using a diagonal baste, attach the bottom edge of the collar lining to the body seam allowances of the neckline. It is best to use considerable ease, so t hat the majority of the collar lining lays flat. The allowances of the collar lining can extend into the body by no more than 1/4" (7 mm).

As you may have noticed when adding the lining pieces, this method of installation enables the entire lining to be removed and replaced without affecting the buttonholes or eyelets at the front waist. Doublets often changed hands over the course of their life and were expected to withstand decades of use. For sanitation and longevity, the linings had to be easily replaceable.

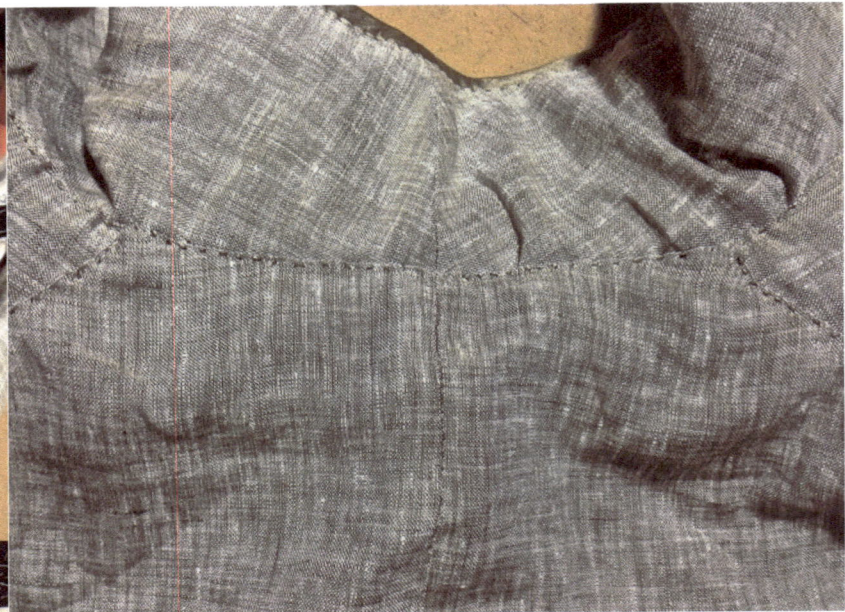

CLOSING THE LINING

76. Next, we close the lining shoulder. Hem the front body lining onto the collar lining as shown. These stitches should be deep enough to catch the seam allowance of the body exterior but should not go completely through to the outside of the garment. Use this step to close the remainder of the center front lining at the neckline.

77. Baste the front shoulder lining onto the seam allowance of the body shoulder. This stitching should be strong and firm, but no more than 1/4" (7 mm) from the cut edge of the fabric. Repeat this step for the opposite front.

78. Turn the back shoulder and neckline allowances at the shoulder and neckline. Baste them in place in one pass.

79. Using a pick stitch or felling stitch, sew the back shoulders and back neckline in place. The stitches should not penetrate to the outside of the garment.

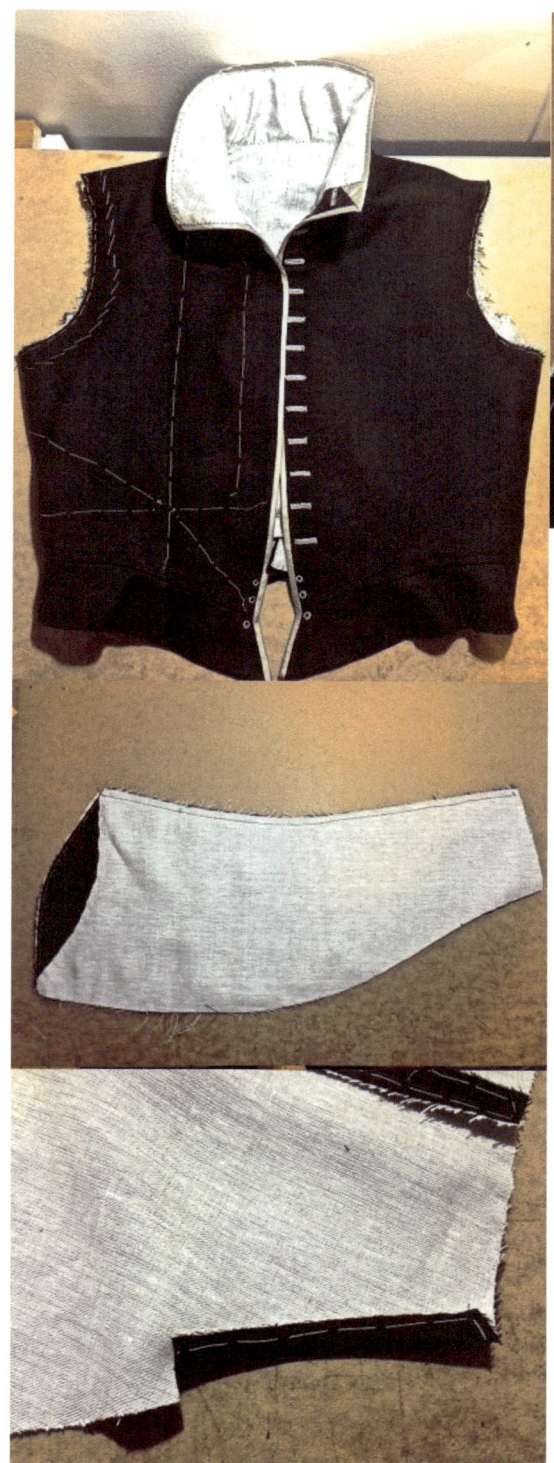

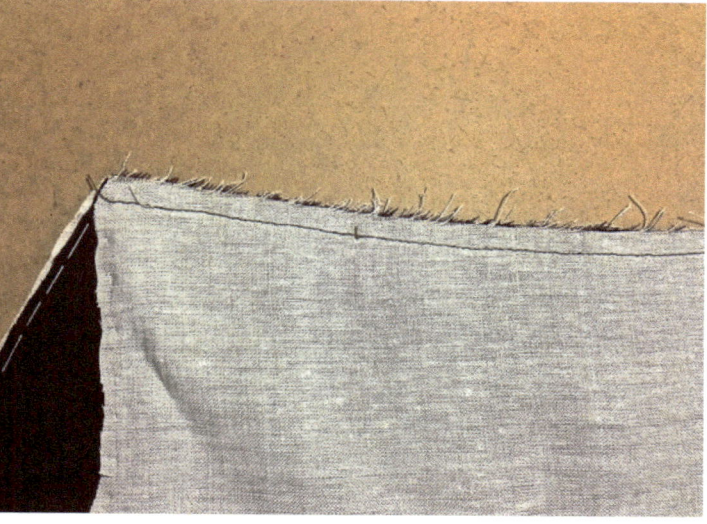

The top left photo is approximately what your garment should look like at this point. The left front shows the bastings removed.

SLEEVES

80. Begin by stitching the fore-seam of the sleeve with a firm backstitch and a 1/2" (1.2 cm) seam allowance. Repeat for the second sleeve.

81. Press the seam allowance open and pick stitch the seam allowances down. Repeat for the second sleeve.

82. About 5" up from the cut edge of the bottom of the sleeve, make a small clip to mark the top of the vent. Repeat this step on the second sleeve.

83. On the out-sleeve only (that's the sleeve half without the armpit cut out), turn up and press 1/2" (1.2 cm) between the clip and the end of the sleeve.

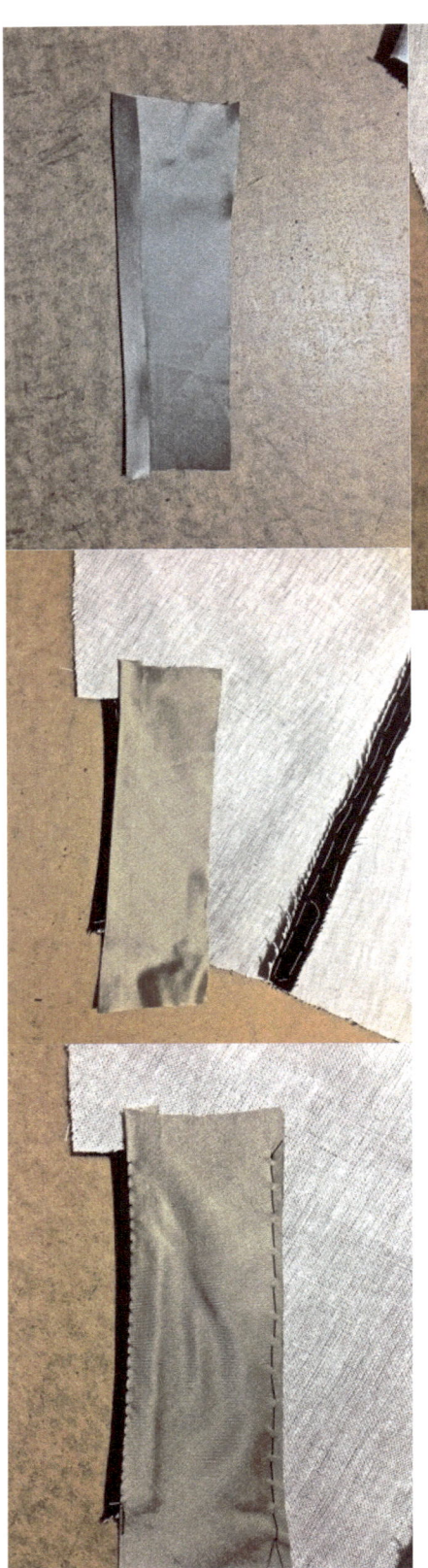

84. Using a small scrap of bias silk, create a facing as shown. Set the edge of the facing back approximately 1/8-1/4" (3-7 mm) from the edge of the fold. Hem in place using a felling stitch. On the inner edge of the facing, use a catch stitch or a basting stitch to secure the facing into place. Repeat for the second sleeve.

85. On the opposite side of the cuff, turn in the 1/2" (1.2 cm) allowance, and catch stitch in place.

86. On the side which has the facing, mark and work three or four buttonholes. The specific number of buttonholes is up to you. Surviving examples have anywhere from one button to almost a dozen going up toward the elbow. In keeping with the simplicity of this doublet, its sleeves have three buttons each.

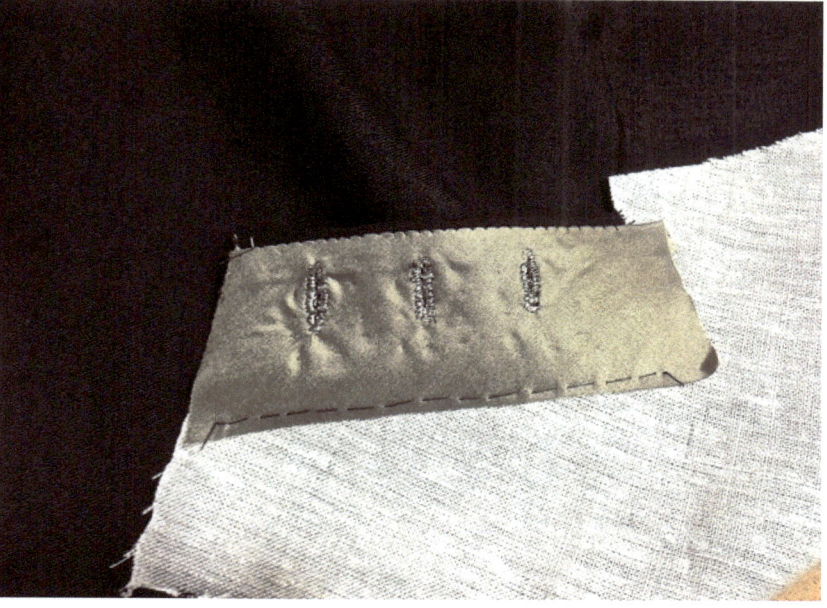

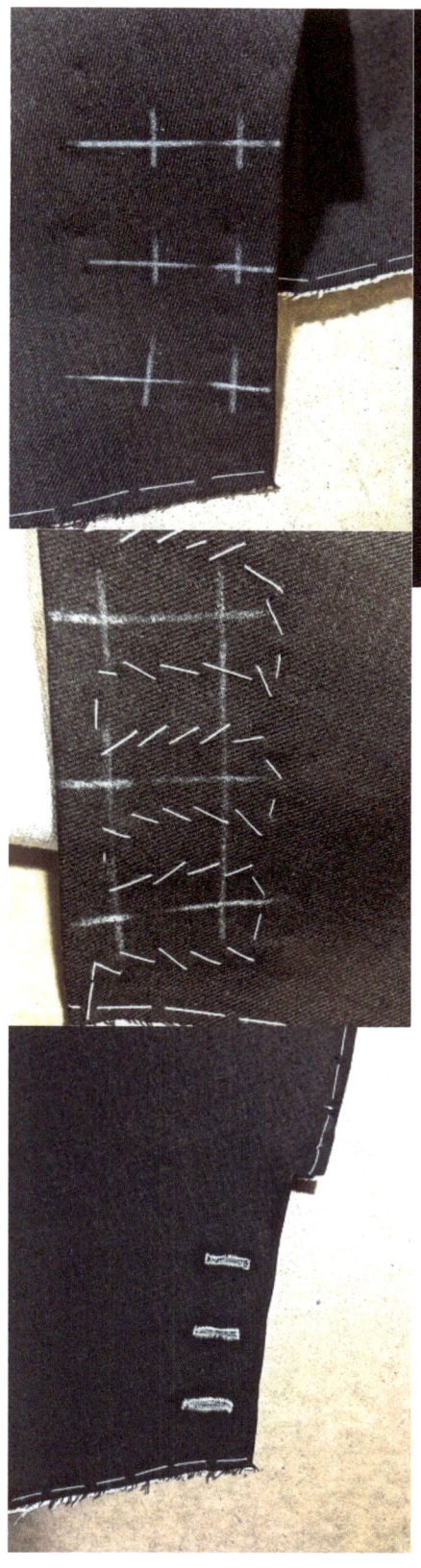

87. Once the buttonholes are complete, stitch the hind-seams of the sleeve halves together. Press the seam open and pick stitch the seam allowances down.

88. Trim the outsleeve lining as shown (see photograph on page 117, top left) to allow for the faced buttonholes, and then press a 1/2" (1.2 cm) allowance under before it is hemmed in place.

89. Sew the fore and hind-seams of the sleeve lining. Make sure that on the hind seam, you stop 5" from the bottom to allow for the vent.

90. Turn the sleeve inside out. Hem the lining in place around the buttonhole area. See the photo on the top right of page 117.

91. Once the vent is secured with the lining, baste the fore-seam and hind-seam seam allowances of the lining and exterior together. Use a diagonal baste and weak white thread, which will allow for a small bit of give and flexibility in the sleeve lining. See the center and lower left photos on page 117.

This technique of attaching the linings to the outer sleeve's seam allowances is still practiced today in all modern suit making. It is even more important in historical clothing. The majority of historic sleeve linings are made of linen, which catches on linen undershirts and causes undue wear and degradation if not properly attached at the allowances. The can lead to the extra expense and hassle of premature replacement.

That said, however, this is one of the steps that I am most likely to skip if pressed for time.

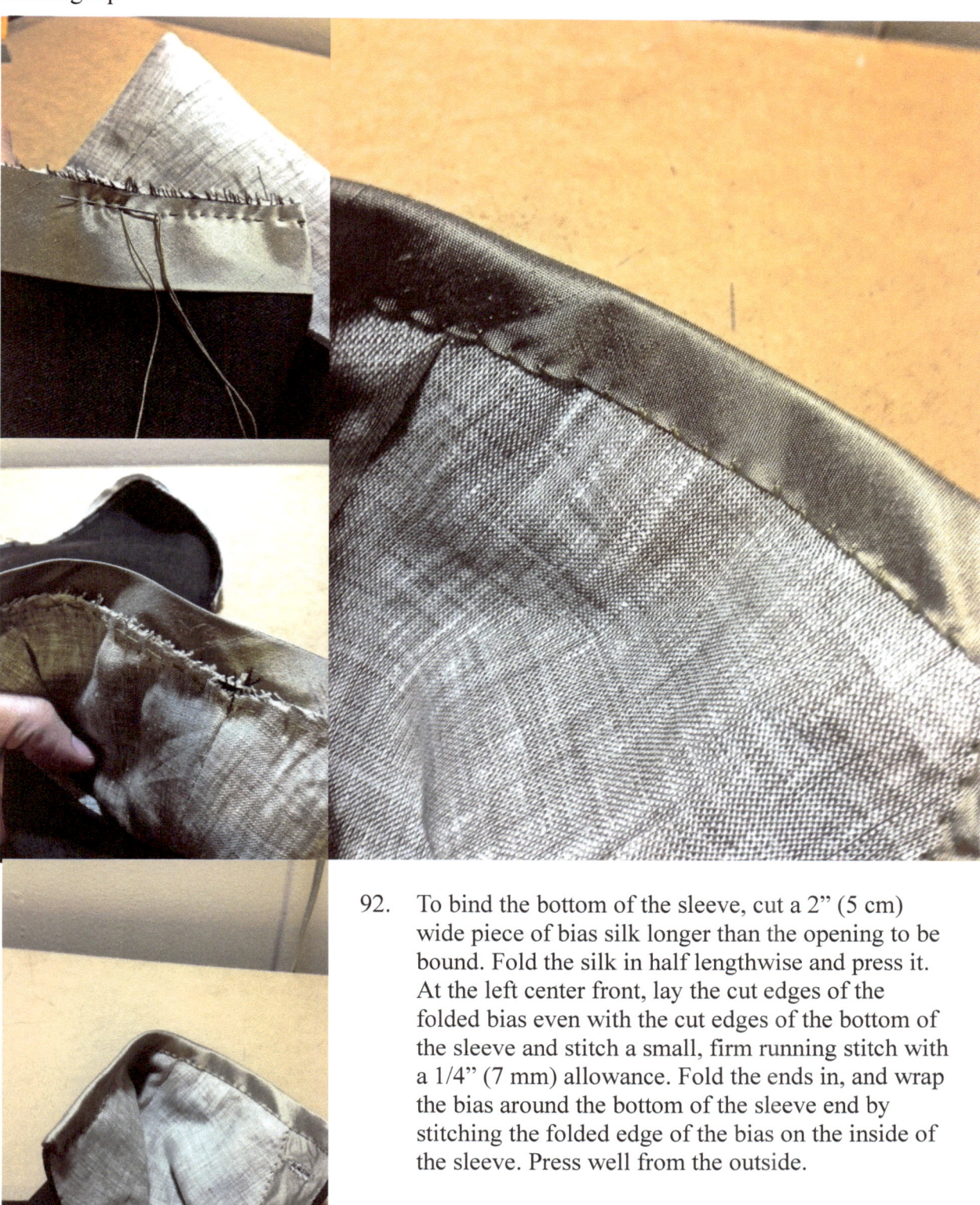

92. To bind the bottom of the sleeve, cut a 2" (5 cm) wide piece of bias silk longer than the opening to be bound. Fold the silk in half lengthwise and press it. At the left center front, lay the cut edges of the folded bias even with the cut edges of the bottom of the sleeve and stitch a small, firm running stitch with a 1/4" (7 mm) allowance. Fold the ends in, and wrap the bias around the bottom of the sleeve end by stitching the folded edge of the bias on the inside of the sleeve. Press well from the outside.

   Repeat with the second sleeve.

93. Once the sleeve end is finished, baste the lining to the exterior at the top of the sleeve.

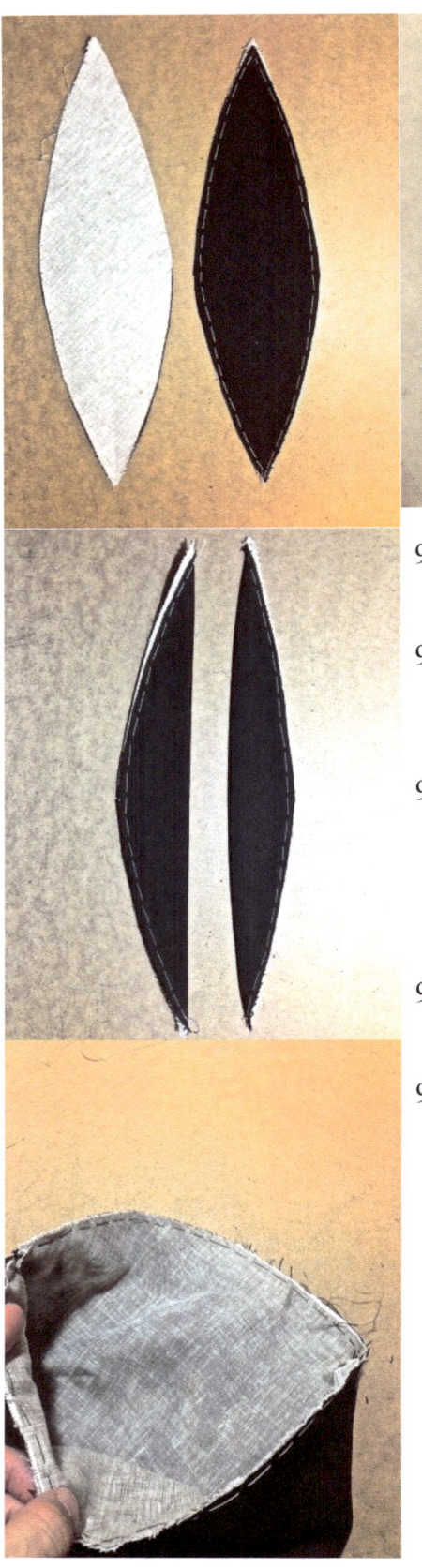

94. Take the epaulettes and press them in half along their length.

95. Once the epaulettes are pressed in half, baste them closed and trim away any excess interlining fabric that protrudes.

96. After the epaulettes are prepared, match the notches on the epaulette with the notch at the top of the sleeve cap and baste the epaulette to the sleeve. The epaulette is designed to only extend around 2/3 of the circumference of the top of the sleeve.

97. To avoid confusion later on, take a minute and lay out the sleeves so that there is an obvious right and left.

98. Next, match the top and bottom notches of the left sleeve with the left armhole. Baste the sleeve into the armhole with white thread about 1/2" (1.2 cm) from the cut edges.

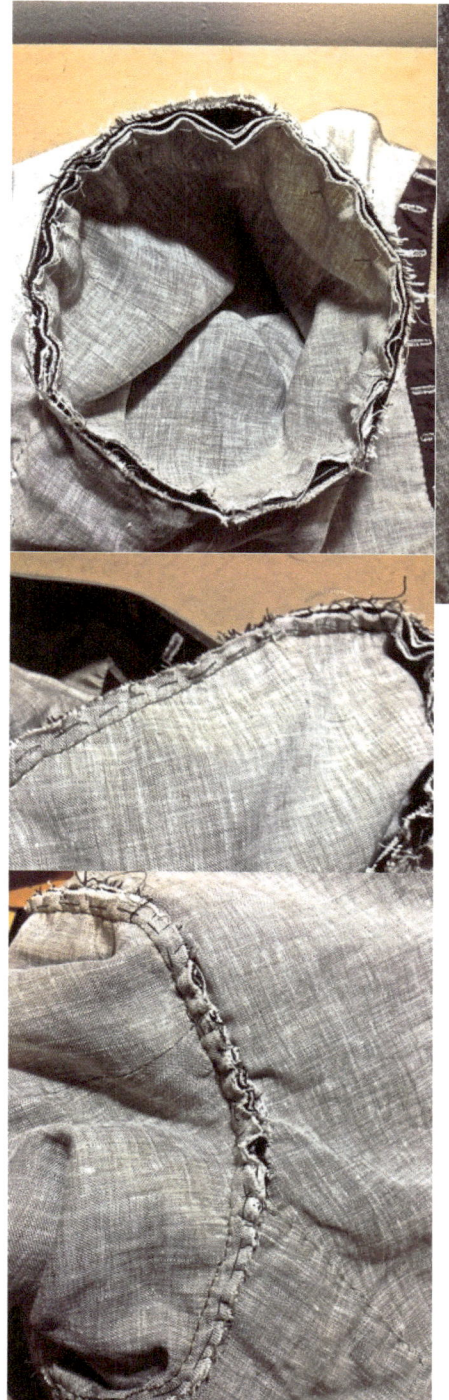

99. Working with the sleeve on top and the body on the bottom, begin to backstitch the sleeve into the armhole. The seam allowance is 3/8" (9 mm). Keep in mind that this is one of the thickest parts of the garment, so your stitches will be correspondingly large. There will be a slight amount of ease as you approach the top of the sleeve cap. As you stitch, use the thumb of the non-needle-holding hand to gently push excess fabric into each stitch, carefully avoiding any appearance of puckers or gathers. As you approach the front of the sleeve in the area where you've stretched the front armhole, take extra care to keep the work taut in your hands as you work. This will counteract the tendency for a back stitched seam to pull the fabric shorter. You certainly don't want to undo all your hard shaping work with sloppy, overly tight stitching at the very end of the process.

100. Turn the entire sleeve seam allowance toward the body of the garment and stitch it into place with a whip stitch, just as you did the waist seam. However, unlike all of the other curved seams in this garment, this is the ONE place where we will not be clipping allowances before we stitch them down. Because the armhole of a garment is subject to so much stress and wear, we do not want to weaken the armhole and create a potential point where it might tear.

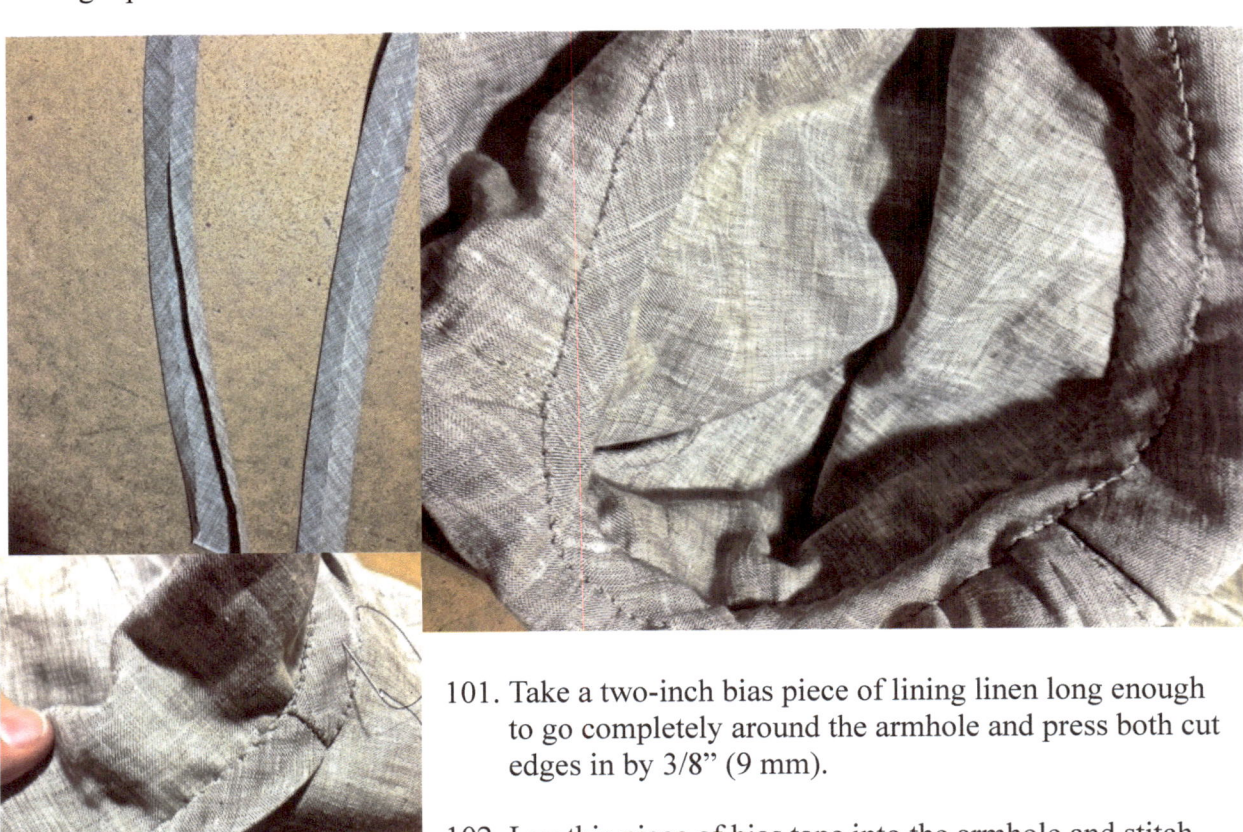

101. Take a two-inch bias piece of lining linen long enough to go completely around the armhole and press both cut edges in by 3/8" (9 mm).

102. Lay this piece of bias tape into the armhole and stitch both sides carefully down onto the lining. This will cover the bulky seam allowance and allow for more comfortable wear.

103. Now that the sleeves are complete, return to the front of the garment and mark the button placement on the edge of the right front binding. Unlike modern buttons which sit on the surface of the fabric, 17th century buttons usually extended from the edge of the garment.

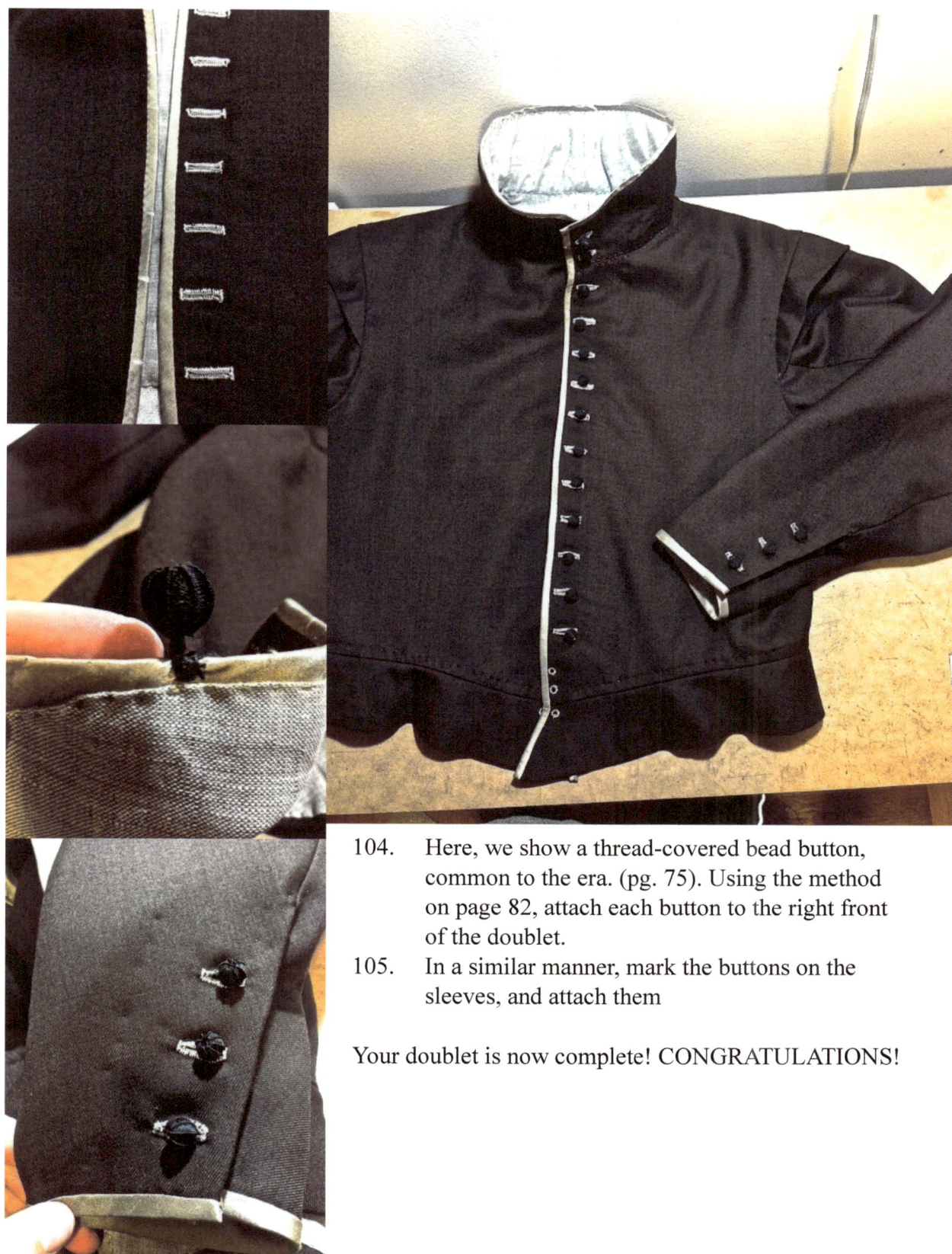

104.   Here, we show a thread-covered bead button, common to the era. (pg. 75). Using the method on page 82, attach each button to the right front of the doublet.

105.   In a similar manner, mark the buttons on the sleeves, and attach them

Your doublet is now complete! CONGRATULATIONS!

Here are some photographs showing the finished doublet. You can see, in the lower left photo, how substantial the collar is. When worn, however, the collar's bulk is not noticeable.

The most interesting photographs are of the inside layers, where all the work is done. For as much labor as we put into a garment of this quality, completely sewn by hand without the aid of a sewing machine, it is important to recognize that much of your work is invisible. The *results* of your work are beautifully visible in the drape and hang of the final doublet, but the interior structuring can only be felt and not seen.

Stamped and pinked white satin suit 348&A-1905 Photo
Courtesy of the Victoria and Albert Museum, London

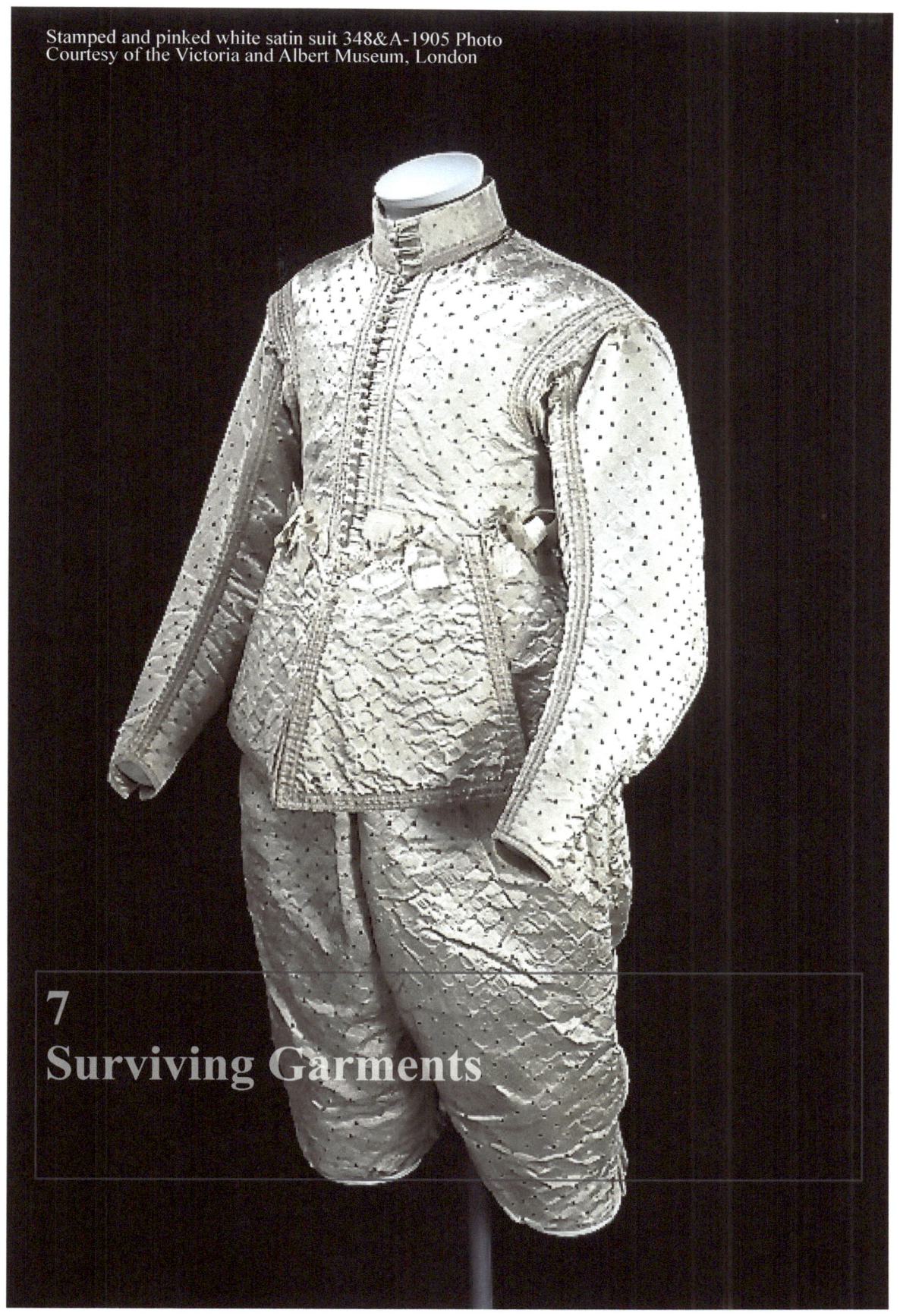

7
Surviving Garments

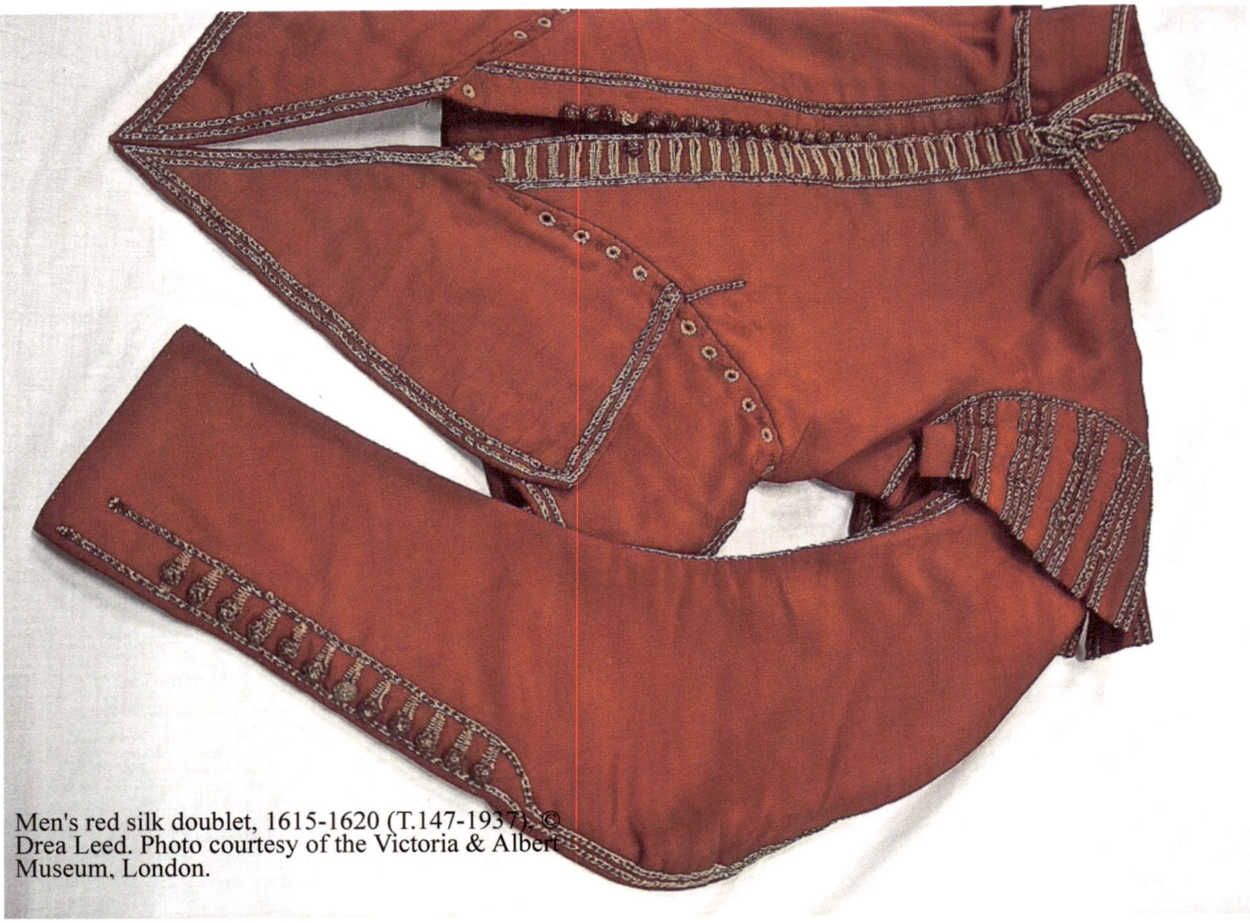

Men's red silk doublet, 1615-1620 (T.147-1937). © Drea Leed. Photo courtesy of the Victoria & Albert Museum, London.

Stamped and pinked white satin suit 348&A-1905 Photo Courtesy of the Victoria and Albert Museum, London

Many surviving examples of early modern menswear are housed in museums around the world. Although people have analyzed them over the years, I have noticed that very little attention is given to the nature of their tailoring and that tailoring's impact on the garment. When examined, I see clear evidence of stretching, shrinking and other manipulations typically found in a modern tailored jacket. These bits of evidence are hard to see if you're not trained to know that they are there. What follows are photographs that corroborate the techniques described in this book and that support my assumptions. I hope they will help you see and appreciate the quiet subtlety of how tailoring affects the fit and drape.

Men's quilted satin doublet and breeches (347&A-1905).

Doublet and breeches of slashed white satin over blue taffeta, c. 1618 (T.28&A-1938), © Mark Goodman.

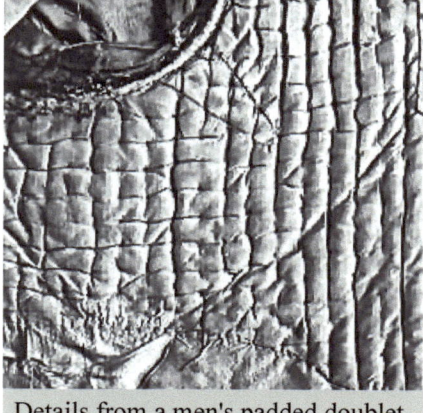

Details from a men's padded doublet (T&D.183-1900), .© V&A

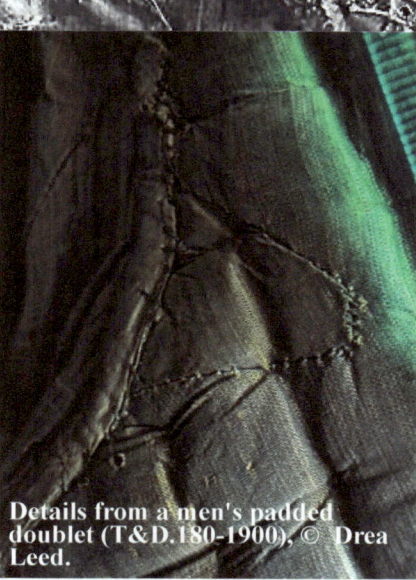

Details from a men's padded doublet (T&D.180-1900), © Drea Leed.

Photos by Courtesy of the Victoria and Albert Museum, London and ©Drea Leed

THE GUSSET

These photographs show the presence of extra fabric added into the armhole for shaping. In the first photo (top left), you can see the structured shape at the front of the armhole quite clearly. The lower two photos are from different garments from different decades, which show a gusset put into the lining to open the armhole and give the shaping. In our lining, we added the gusset to the canvas rather than the lining and simply cut the lining differently to accommodate the added armhole circumference.

In contrast, the doublet above doesn't show the gusset as it's covered by padding. What it does show is a small cut in the wool that has been spread open slightly. This cut is a clear indicator that the gusset is indeed present. When the cut is spread, it creates a disturbance in the flat plane of the fabric that is then rotated into the armhole to give the wool fullness where the gusset was inserted. In our process, we've simply stretched the wool padding to the right shape; if you're using a padding fabric that isn't as stretchable, however, this little slash would serve the same function as the stretching we used in our process. Once you've seen this, you'll notice it in many extant garments.

In some surviving garments, there is no gusset inserted but the armhole has still been stretched. The gusset gives more structure, but is not always necessary if the fabrics are heavy.

Detail from a men's padded doublet (T&D.180-1900), © Mark Goodman.

Detail of a man's brown wool doublet, 1625-1635 (T.29-1938), © Mark Goodman.

Photos by Courtesy of the Victoria and Albert Museum, London

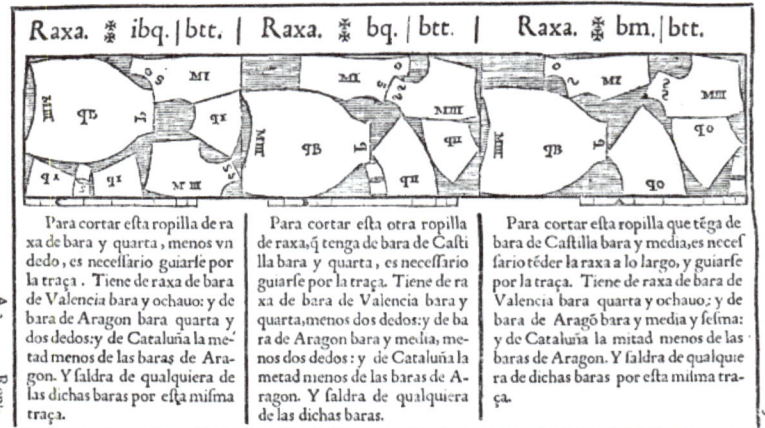

Raxa. ⚹ ibq. ǀbtt. ǀ	Raxa. ⚹ bq. ǀ btt. ǀ	Raxa. ⚹ bm. ǀbtt. ǀ

Para cortar esta ropilla de raxa de bara y quarta, menos vn dedo, es necessario guiarse por la traça. Tiene de raxa de bara de Valencia bara y ochauo: y de bara de Aragon bara quarta y dos dedos: y de Cataluña la mitad menos de las baras de Aragon. Y faldra de qualquiera de las dichas baras por esta misma traça.

Para cortar esta otra ropilla de raxa, q̃ tenga de bara de Castilla bara y quarta, es necessario guiarse por la traça. Tiene de raxa de bara de Valencia bara y quarta, menos dos dedos: y de bara de Aragon bara y media, menos dos dedos: y de Cataluña la mitad menos de las baras de Aragon. Y faldra de qualquiera de las dichas baras.

Para cortar esta ropilla que tẽga de bara de Castilla bara y media, es necessario tẽder la raxa a lo largo, y guiarse por la traça. Tiene de raxa de bara de Valencia bara quarta y ochauo: y de bara de Aragõ bara y media y sesma: y de Cataluña la mitad menos de las baras de Aragon. Y faldra de qualquiera de dichas baras por esta misma traça.

THE BACK SHOULDER

Easing of the back shoulder is such a common technique that most pattern-making books remark on it only in passing, assuming that everyone is familiar with it. These photos show a variety of seam treatments, but the easing of the back shoulder is still present. There are two different examples shown: the lower left image shows the back shoulder stitched down on top of the front, with a stay tape as well. The upper left photo shows the front shoulder sewn on top of the back, yet the back shoulder is still eased in to fit the front.

The pattern draft above, from a tailor's manual of 1618 by Francisco de La Rocha Burguen, is evidence of the difference in the front and back shoulder lengths. As the center layout has the front and back shoulders touching each other, you can clearly see the back shoulder is longer than the front.

In the other photographs, you can also see the size of the stitches that were used and just how large they were. When the front shoulder is lightly stretched and the back shoulder slightly eased, the shoulder seam curves toward the front of the wearer in a way that mimics the natural anatomy of the human body. A hollow is created in the back shoulder for the trapezius muscle, which is slightly rounded in most figures. The stretching of the front shoulder creates a slight hollow over the clavicle bone and smooths the fabric for a clean fit.

Detail from a boy's pink taffeta doublet and breeches, c. 1640 (T.4-1922), © Drea Leed.

Men's quilted satin doublet and breeches (347&A-1905).

Detail from a men's padded doublet (T&D.180-1900), © Mark Goodman. London.

Detail from a man's brown wool doublet, 1625-1635 (T.29-1938), © Mark Goodman.

Photos by Courtesy of the Victoria and Albert Museum, London

In these photos, we show a variety of buttons used on men's pieces of the era. Buttons of the 16th and 17th centuries appear to belong to one of three types:

1. Braided/interlaced

2. Wrapped/knotted

3. Solid/metal

Buttons are worked in thread over a solid core of wood, or more rarely over tightly packed fabric. Buttonmaking was a skill of the silk-workers, a group of people who devoted their time to making woven and passementerie trims of silk. They also made buttons, although this work was frequently farmed out to widows, orphans, and poorhouses.

The few examples of buttons shown here are only a small sampling of the wide variety of styles present in the era. Some buttons were so ornate that they were considered jewelry.

8
Construction Details

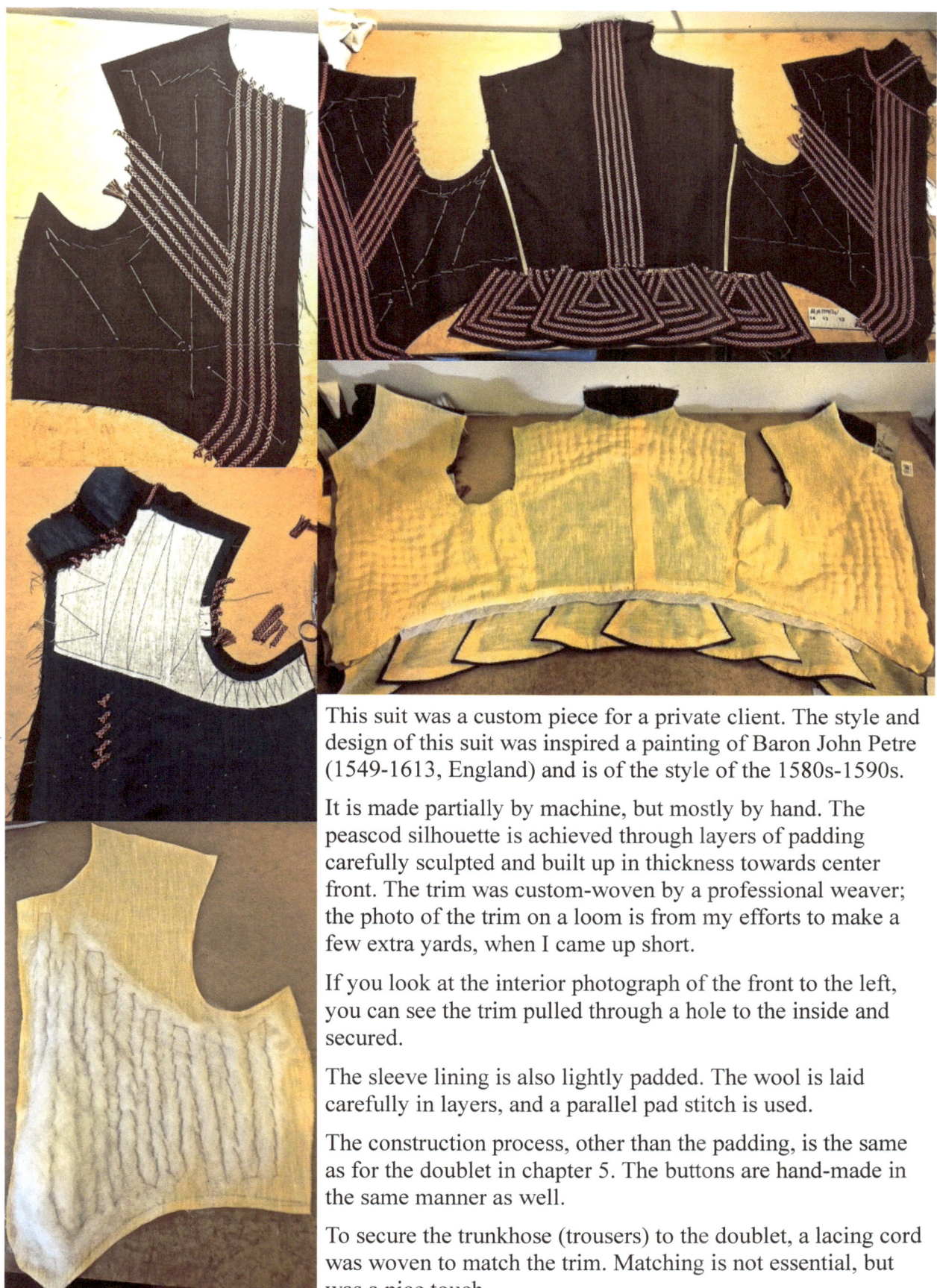

This suit was a custom piece for a private client. The style and design of this suit was inspired a painting of Baron John Petre (1549-1613, England) and is of the style of the 1580s-1590s.

It is made partially by machine, but mostly by hand. The peascod silhouette is achieved through layers of padding carefully sculpted and built up in thickness towards center front. The trim was custom-woven by a professional weaver; the photo of the trim on a loom is from my efforts to make a few extra yards, when I came up short.

If you look at the interior photograph of the front to the left, you can see the trim pulled through a hole to the inside and secured.

The sleeve lining is also lightly padded. The wool is laid carefully in layers, and a parallel pad stitch is used.

The construction process, other than the padding, is the same as for the doublet in chapter 5. The buttons are hand-made in the same manner as well.

To secure the trunkhose (trousers) to the doublet, a lacing cord was woven to match the trim. Matching is not essential, but was a nice touch.

As you can see from the photographs, the lacing holding the top and bottom together is separate from the more cosmetic silk bows on the doublet skirts, though these can be used to keep a belt in place, or for carrying a sword or pouch.

The trunkhose have pockets capable of containing a good deal without distorting the silhouette of the suit.

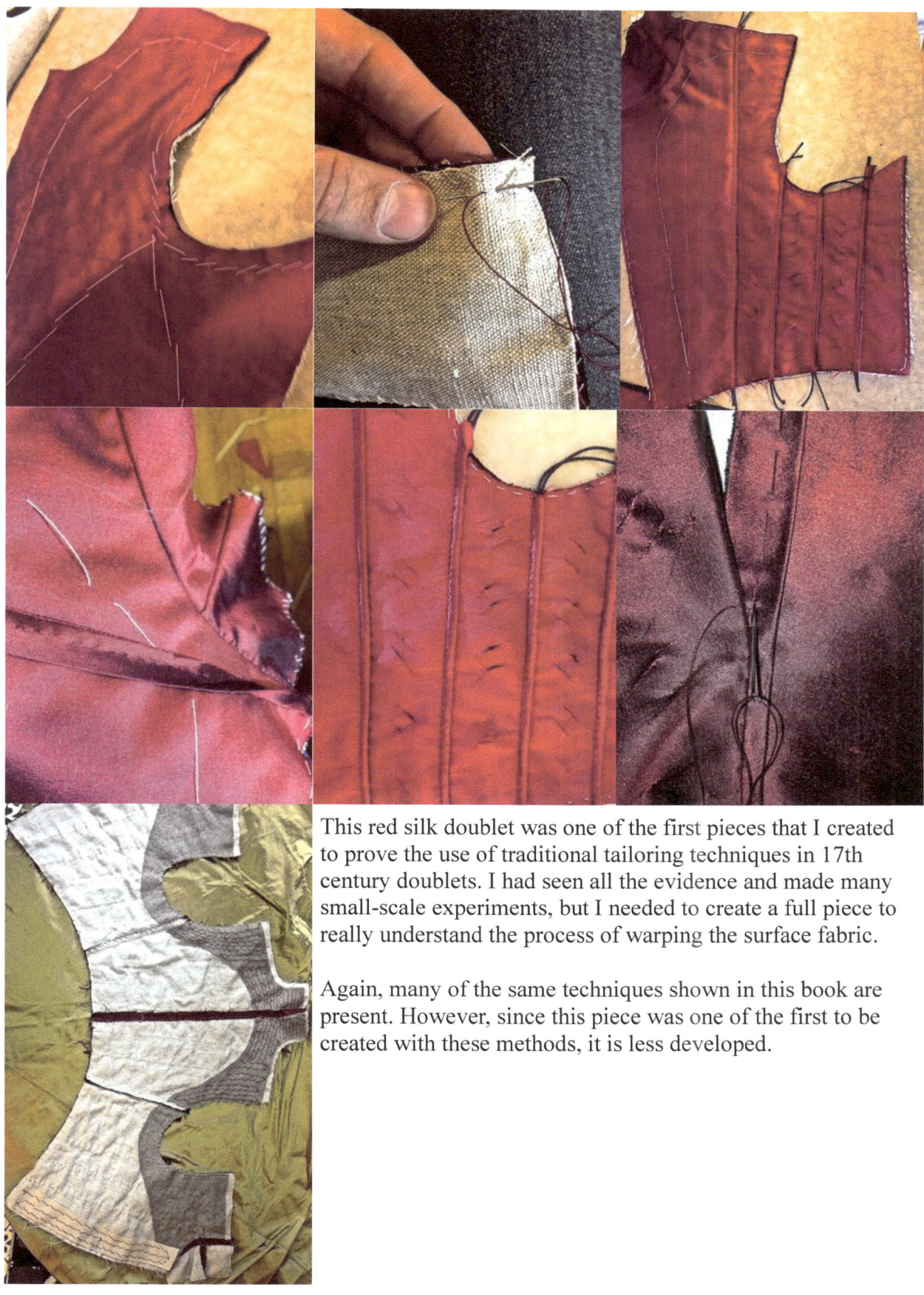

This red silk doublet was one of the first pieces that I created to prove the use of traditional tailoring techniques in 17th century doublets. I had seen all the evidence and made many small-scale experiments, but I needed to create a full piece to really understand the process of warping the surface fabric.

Again, many of the same techniques shown in this book are present. However, since this piece was one of the first to be created with these methods, it is less developed.

This pinked silk doublet was created to be extremely minimal and lightweight. It is based upon an extant summer doublet in the Kunsthistoriches museum in Munich that is nothing more than one layer of silk and one layer of fine linen. Although there is no interior structuring, it has been stretched and sculpted with a steam iron to have the same fit as a doublet with extensive internal shaping. It is remarkably light and cool.

This green silk slashed doublet is entirely machine made except for the buttonholes. The shaping and padding is carefully basted in place and then machine quilted in evenly spaced lines. The cut is based on an extant example which belonged to Moritz of Saxony. It has side seams that are placed at the true side rather than side back, as the majority of extant doublets are made. The true side seam appears more frequently in doublets of Germanic origin.

The sleeves of this version have a taller sleeve cap, which limits movement slightly more than the shallower sleeve cap presented in the pattern making chapter. As styles changed through the following centuries, sleeve caps continued to become taller.

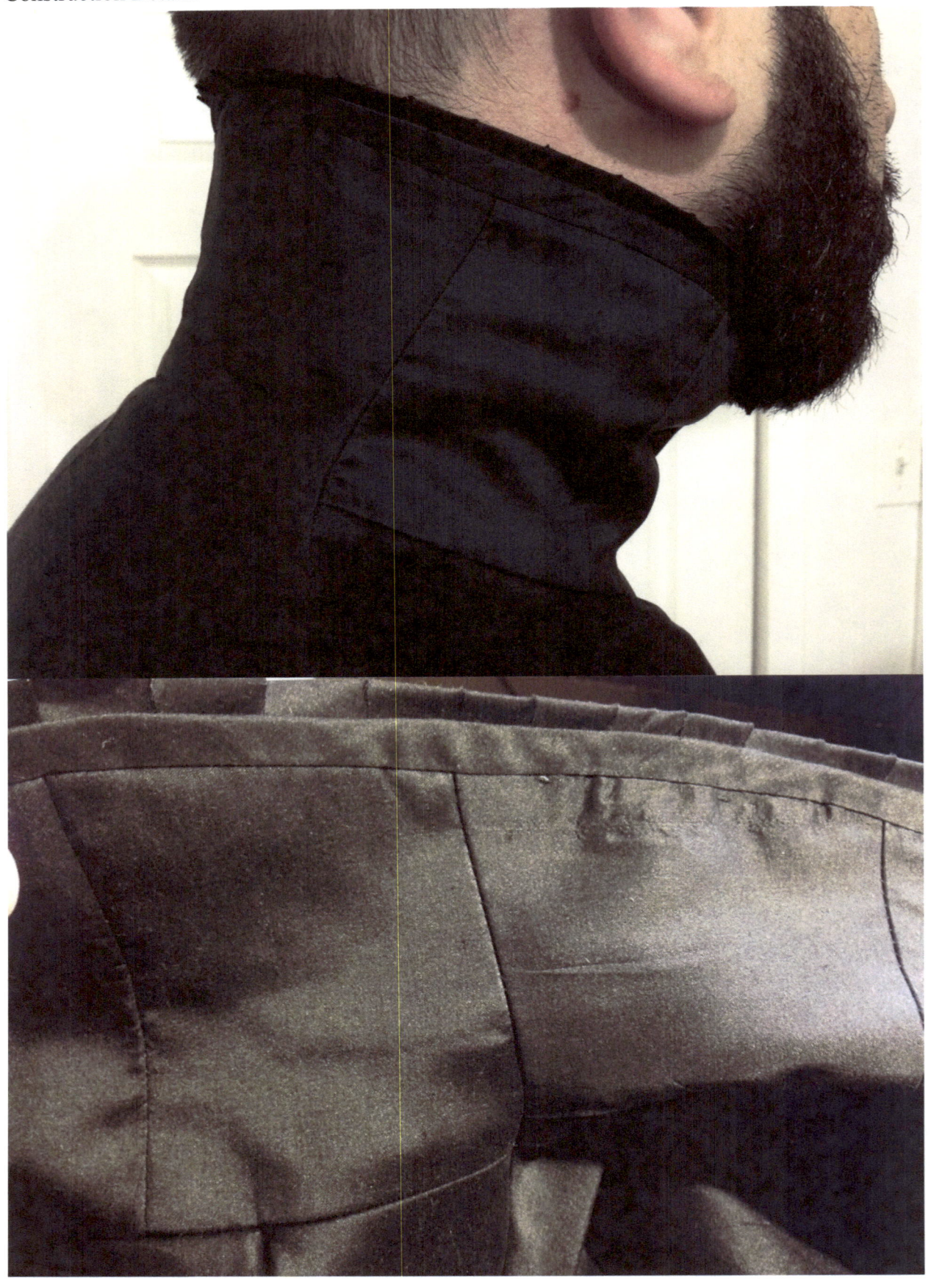

Acknowledgments

I would like to say a personal thank you to my better half, Joey Armon, for listening to countless hours of my stream-of-consciousness mind-work while I puzzled through the process of creating this book.

To Leslie Hodgin, for always being there to say what needed saying and to keep the wind beneath my wings and not blowing at my face.

To my editing and review team. Christina Cato, Drea Leed, Erika Hepler, Truly Carmichael, Marion McNealy, Marlo Whitfield Peck, Donna Green-Tye, Daniel Rosen, Carlos Restrepo, Margo Anderson, Kasia Wasilewski Corbo, Catherine Kinsey, Noel Gieleghem, Maria Dedvukaj, Nola Yergen, Paul Cook-Giles, Susan Taksa O'Dee, Sunny Briscoe, Kathryn Iacampo, Josh Wallwork, Elizabeth McMahon, Daniel Pitrucha....and the many others who participated in workshops and used what I taught you so I could see it in someone else's hands.

Thank you to the backers from the Kickstarter campaign for funding this project.

A special thank you to Mark Goodman who took many of the detailed, amazing photos of surviving garments.

Thank you to the Victoria and Albert museum for graciously allowing the use of the numerous photos of 17th century items from their collection

And most especially thank you to Marcia Schlemm and Sharon Arndt, Bob Trump, Carol Gray, and countless others who met me as a young man and fostered my passions without reserve. Thinking of the years of incredible inspirational energy you all put into my life brings me to tears.

And thank you to the members of the Elizabethan Costume Facebook Group. Never in my life have I met so many people who are as passionate about these clothes as I am.

THANK YOU!!!

Suggested Reading

16th century

de Alcega, Juan. *Tailor's Pattern Book 1589.* London: Quite Specific Media Group, 1999. Facsimile with translation by Jean Pain and Cecelia Bainton.

17th century

de la Rocha Burguen, Francisco. *Geometrica y traça pertinencientes al oficio de James sastres.* Valencia, 1618

de Anduxar, Martin. *Geometria y trazas pertinencientes al oficio de sastres.* Madrid, 1640

Digital copies of these books may be found online free of charge from the following links

Burguen: *http://bdh.bne.es/bnesearch/detalle/bdh0000052415*

Anduxar: *http://books.google.com/books/reader?id=EVBZAAAAcAAJ*

General

Arnold, Janet. *Patterns of Fashion: The Cut and Construction of Clothes for Men and Women 1560-1620.* London: Drama Publishers, 1985

Barrett, Gina. *Buttons: A Passementerie Workshop Manual.* London: Windy House Publishing, 2013

Davis, R. I. *Men's Garments 1830-1900: A Guide to Pattern Cutting and Tailoring.* London: Players Press, 1989

Howarth, Stephen. *Henry Poole: Founders of Savile Row: The Making of a Legend.* Honiton: Bene Factum, 2003

Mikhaila, Ninya and Malcolm-Davies, Jane. *The Tudor Tailor: reconstructing sixteenth century dress.* London: B.T. Batsford, 2006

Seligman, Kevin. *Cutting for All! The Sartorial Arts, Related Crafts, and the Commercial Paper Pattern: A Bibliographic Reference Guide for Designers, Technicians, and Historians.* Illinois: Southern Illinois University Press, 1996

Walker, Richard. *Savile Row: An Illustrated History.* New York: Rizzoli, 1989

Waugh, Nora. *The Cut of Men's Clothes: 1600-1914.* New York: Routledge, 1987

Suppliers

Linens and Plain Silks

Gray Lines Linen NYC
260 W. 39th Street #4 NY, NY 10018-4401
http://www.graylinelinen.com/
(212) 391-4130

Weights used:
Canvas: Warsa Weight
Exterior: Judy Weight
Linings: Handkerchief Weight
Silks: Heavy weight only

Prices range from $8.00 to $18.00 per yard depending on textiles and order quantity. Get a group together and buy in bulk. They do not ship small yardage. It is best if someone in your group has a tax ID. There is a price break after 50 yards.

Silk and Wool

Mood Fabrics NYC
225 W 37th St 3rd Floor
New York, NY 10018
http://www.moodfabrics.com/
(201) 933-7565

They will send small orders. Their silks run anywhere from $18-$40 per yard. Their wools are quite variable but high quality. Request swatches.

Threads and Notions

Atlanta Thread Supply
http://www.wawak.com/atlantathread/

All types of sewing thread, amazing service. They have large and small spools of thread and all kinds of notions. They have needles, machines, pressing boards etc. They are a full-function sewing supply company.

You can request color cards from them.

Costume and Tailoring Books

The DRAMA BOOK SHOP, Inc.
250 West 40th Street
New York, NY 10018
Phone:(212) 944-0595, Toll Free US & Canada: (800) 322-0595, Fax: (212) 730-8739
http://www.dramabookshop.com/

About the Author

Mathew Gnagy was born in St. Joseph, Missouri to Steve and Norma Gnagy. He is the grandson of renowned television artist, Jon Gnagy, and was taught creativity and crafts from a very young age. He filled his youthful summers learning weaving, knitting, sewing, and many other crafts.

At the age of 17 he entered the tailoring trade as an apprentice in a suit shop. His interest in historical clothing led him to study tailoring of the past. By the age of 25 he had designed stage productions, numerous individual costumes for private clients and started his own costume business.

In 2007, he moved to New York City and started working in the professional costume industry as well as fashion. He quickly found his way to Broadway, TV and fashion runways.

His first title, *Knitting Off the Axis*, was released in 2011 by Interweave press. *The Modern Maker* is his second book.

He currently resides with his partner Joey Armon in New York City, where he works regularly as a tailor for both screen and stage and teaches fashion at Parsons University of Fashion Design.

This book is just the beginning.

www.ingramcontent.com/pod-product-compliance
Lightning Source LLC
Chambersburg PA
CBHW060812270326
41929CB00002B/17